BE SMART, ACT FAST, GET RICH

Your Game Plan for Getting It Right in the Stock Market

CHARLES V. PAYNE

John Wiley & Sons, Inc.

Published by John Wiley & Sons, Inc., Hoboken, New Jersey.
Published simultaneously in Canada.

Wiley Bicentennial Logo: Richard J. Pacifico

For general information on our other products and services or for technical support,
please contact our Customer Care Department within the United States at (800) 762-2974,
outside the United States at (317) 572-3993 or fax (317) 572-4002.

Wiley also publishes its books in a variety of electronic formats. Some content that appears
in print may not be available in electronic books. For more information about Wiley
products, visit our web site at www.wiley.com.

Library of Congress Cataloging-in-Publication Data:

Payne, Charles V.
   Be smart, act fast, get rich : your game plan for getting it right in the stock market /
Charles V. Payne.
      p.   cm.
   Includes index.
   ISBN 978-0-470-07501-2 (cloth)
      1. Investments—United States—Handbooks, manuals, etc.   2. Stocks—United
States—Handbooks, manuals, etc.   3. Stock exchanges—United States—Handbooks,
manuals, etc.   I. Title.
HG4921.P39   2007
332.63'220973—dc22

                                                                    2006039467

Printed in the United States of America.

10   9   8   7   6   5   4   3   2   1

My thanks and love can't be quantified for:

Cherie,
my daughter and the reason I fought through those early days of zero commissions and zero paychecks. Cherie, you were and always will be my ultimate inspiration.

Charles,
my son, the light of my life, and my heart. Charles I just adore being in your presence. I could never thank God enough.

Yvonne,
my wife, who has made me into the man I always could have been and should have been. I love you and I love your strength. You are a tower of power and you keep me strong.

Ruth,
my mother. No matter how tough things got, no matter how dark some days looked, I never felt deprived, I never felt poor, and I never felt hopeless. When I told the world I wanted to work on Wall Street, you were the only one who made me believe I could.

CONTENTS

FOREWORD

Being Rich Is Good, Enriching People Is Better, Recognizing the Difference Is What Makes Charles Payne the Best

There is something very refreshing about my friend Charles Payne. As a kid, he just wanted to be rich. I guess it was because he wasn't. As he told me many times, and eloquently puts forth in this book, Charles wasn't only from the wrong side of the tracks, he was from the wrong side of life! But experiences that might have made others bitter made Charles stronger. He didn't take it out on his country. He served his country.

Now I'm not here to extol Charles's four years in the Air Force, or the myriad of odd, low-paying jobs he had before that. Nor am I here to recount how rough it was for him in those days. Life was and is rough for lots of folks. The world is full of such rags-to-riches stories. If that's all there was to Charles, I'd say save the money on this book.

But that's not all there is to Charles, or to this book. There is something much deeper, more meaningful, more thoughtful. This isn't about a man who says you should be rich like him. He shows you how—clearly, lucidly, even humorously.

That's what Charles is all about. He wants to give something back—not with silly platitudes about buying low and selling high, but by discussing *how* to buy low and *when* to sell high. He wants you to learn from his mistakes and pick up on insights real money pros rarely share. Most hot-shot investors speak vaguely. It's as if they're protecting the Temple. Charles opens that Temple. And like Dorothy visiting the Wizard of Oz, you come to realize there's just a man behind the curtain—playing games and keeping secrets.

Charles is pulling back that curtain on Wall Street, stopping the games, stopping the secrets, stopping the Wall Street doublespeak, stopping the ridiculous condescension, the we-know-and-you-don't elitism, and stopping the nonsense, period.

But what makes this book so wonderful is he's telling you that the secret to success really isn't a secret at all. It's hard work and dedication. It's day-in and day-out—sticking to principles and strategies that don't go out of fashion. To be a pro, Charles reminds us, you have to act like a pro, dedicated to the craft and studious as to the world and the markets that reflect it. Great stocks just don't happen. Many have been bubbling for years. Charles is the guy who sees them bubbling when most of the experts don't see them at all.

Charles knows a mutual fund won't get you rich, but a keen investment insight will. A momentarily hot stock won't retire you to Tahiti, while a winning combination just might. He knows that, and let me tell you something: The real pros know that, too. They won't say it. Charles will. So many Americans spend their lives dreaming about making money, hoping that the dough they have in their house or that retirement plan will set them on easy street. They put their faith in averages that aren't average and government programs that aren't guaranteed. They depend on others to provide answers without ever asking so much as a single question themselves.

The reason why Charles has grown to become my favorite commentator on these matters is he lives these matters. He doesn't separate them. Pursuing financial security is as much a mission as it is a goal. He readily admits he works way too many hours and misses far too many vacations. I can't imagine the dinners he's canceled or cocktail parties for which he's had to send his regrets! I've heard the same said of giants like Bill Gates and Warren Buffett, who put in the time because they're having the time of their lives.

In all my years covering this business, I don't think I've ever run across anyone else quite like Charles Payne. Whatever the story I want to share, Charles has read it. Whatever the rumor I want to pursue, Charles has heard it. Whomever the Wall Street whispers have cited, Charles has called. In panel shows, debate shows, all shows, Charles is the guy in the know whom others want to know more. Wall Street legends stop and listen. High-and-mighty politicos stop and write.

I think it's because Charles doesn't parrot the consensus line. Shortly after 9/11, when all the experts were talking deep, lasting recession, he was the guy who promised a quick economic turnaround. He was right. When the media said Enron and Tyco were the tip of a financial iceberg that would send corporate America reeling, Charles pointed out they were the exception, not the rule. Touché again. To a world and media that seem to endlessly trash us, Charles sticks up for us—oftentimes by sticking it to them!

Charles defies conventional wisdom the way he defies tired and lazy reporting and analysis. If everyone's saying it, Charles once told me, it's distinctly possible, even likely, everyone's wrong.

What's more, Charles gets the things that matter. At the height of the Internet stock boom, he was the one guy who reminded us all that profits do matter; all the promises in the world do not. If he doesn't understand a company, he doesn't buy that company's stock, and if he falls in love with a concept, he doesn't fall in love with no return.

He gets the big things right—like the war on terror. It's more than our financial fortunes at stake, he once told me; it's our very lives! In an age when so many put so much trust in government to solve the problem, Charles takes great risks saying maybe *we* are the problem. He's warned me about social programs we can't afford and a clueless naïveté about terror we can't allow.

You see, Charles is a patriot. What's more, Charles is a good man, who sees nothing wrong with being rich but everything wrong with acting rich. I remember joking with him once that there are rich jerks and there are poor jerks. I said on-air once that "jerkery knows no pedigree." It's not money that corrupts the wallet, but indifference and dismissiveness that corrupts the soul.

There's a soul to my friend Charles—a very real earthiness that few I've ever encountered in this world come close to sharing. Charles is the real deal—a guy's guy, who loves boxing, loves playing cards, and loves staying in touch with childhood chums.

He's the same guy he was then, only richer, and with this book, a lot more enriching. To read this is like talking to Charles. To hear the funny mistakes and wicked lessons along the way . . . well, that's like being Charles. And you can't do much better than that.

Invest with my friend. But more, learn what it's like to be a friend—a friend who helps democratize Wall Street and embodies all the simple, decent values of Main Street. He's the kid from Harlem who hasn't forgotten his roots, his friends, or his priorities. Charles is that friend. And this . . . is that book.

NEIL CAVUTO
Anchor and Senior Vice President,
Fox News

When I was 14 years old I decided I wanted to work on Wall Street. My high school at the time, Art & Design, was located across the street from a Rolls-Royce dealer and a Ferrari dealer. When I cut school my friends would go in one direction and I'd head over to the car dealerships. The guys who worked there were cool and let me sit in the cars and fantasize about owning one. Back then I was focused on commercial art, but I knew in my heart I didn't want to go somewhere and cut and paste other people's artwork until my big break came along. I wanted to be rich!

I guess we all equate wealth to the stock market at a very early age, and somewhere in my bones I knew Wall Street was the way to go. I began reading the *Wall Street Journal*; sometimes I'd pay for it, sometimes I swipe it. I didn't have any money and nobody ever expects anyone to swipe a *Wall Street Journal*. I taught myself how to read the tables in the paper and interpret other bits of information. I told everyone I knew I would work on Wall Street one day.

I bought my first mutual fund when I was 17 years old; my mother had to cosign. I earned the money from working a variety of low-budget jobs nonstop since I was 13 years old. I finally landed on the Street after a four-year stint in the air force; I worked in the analytical department of EF Hutton. It was a dream come true, but there was no money in the job so I switched. When I finally became a stock broker I had a rude awakening: These guys were more salespeople than folks digging around for great investment ideas and strategies.

After a few years as a broker I was able to take my passion for the analytical aspects of Wall Street and couple them with the realities of the brokerage world. I began Wall Street Strategies out of a one-bedroom apartment in Harlem with a couple of thousand dollars. It's been a long and wonderful journey to where I am now and why I felt the need to write this book. It seems there was a window from 1995 to 2000 when everyone was part of the stock market. If Joe Kennedy was bewildered to hear a shoeshine kid talk about the stock market, imagine how he would have felt when everyone from cab drivers to the unemployed jumped into the market with dreams of retiring at the age of 40.

The stock market crash was a reality check of sorts and pushed Main Street farther away from the stock market than the years just before the so-called New Paradigm was ushered in on the wings of Internet trading and discount brokerage firms. Now so many people hate the stock market, their disdain leads them to ignore or even question the relevance of the Dow reaching all-time highs. Indifference has them checking off any mutual fund in the company's 401(k) plan. "Who cares?" is the popular assessment of the stock market.

This is incredibly alarming, as now is the time to become an active self-directed investor. Valuations are cheap to reasonable and it is so easy for investors to gain the information they need to outperform the stock market and all those mutual fund managers.

The biggest problem is that the only folks coming back to the stock market are coming back with all the same bad habits that drove their portfolios into the ground the last time around. These brave souls want to look at charts and think they can make money over a sustained basis. Expectations are off base, strategies are nonexistent, and folks just simply are doing it all wrong. I want to help those people who are letting the best way to become rich remain some other world that they've decided was beyond their reach or scope of understanding. I want to help those people who have come back to the market and are doing it the same way. I watch firsthand everyday how they are doing it all wrong.

This book will touch your hot buttons. It will feel like I wrote it just for you, because I know all the mistakes you've made or in some cases continue to make. I was a poor kid from Harlem who dreamed of enjoying a good life because of the stock market, and I'm here. Everyone should be here—it is not hard. But it takes belief and some work.

You aren't going to get rich by simply putting money into a 401(k) and watching it return 7 percent a year. You shop at stores whose shares go up twice as fast or even three or four times as much. You aren't taking advantage of the best money-making machine in the world if you are simply putting money into a bunch of mutual funds that rarely even keep pace with the gains in the broad stock market. If you're diligent, then by all means play funds; but make sure your fund manager delivers results. All too often people park money in funds and let them ride into weak returns.

I demystify the market in a way that will allow everyone to understand how the dots connect and how we are all intertwined in the stock market. Not owning stocks is the same as working for free, denying yourself the fruits of your very existence. There are no shortcuts—no magic elixir for playing the market, no black boxes that spit out winner after winner—but by the same token, it really isn't rocket science, either. Really.

I'm going to teach you how to use fundamental analysis along with technical analysis to discover undervalued stocks and assemble portfolios that are positioned to outperform the market, positioned to make you rich. I'm going to give you the knowledge and tools to stop emotionally sabotaging your stock market investing efforts. I'm going to teach you how to be an investor and not a trader simply flipping stocks for pennies rather than owning them for the kind of gain that buys you real comfort and peace of mind.

Summary of Contents

Chapter 1 welcomes you to the stock market. You are already in the game, so stop making others rich. When you own stocks you become an owner, and the owners are the fat cats. Join the club.

Chapter 2 is about putting fun into the process. You don't have to be an economic genius to find out how well a company is doing and to understand its value and how it relates to future potential. So many investors have no idea if the companies in their portfolio are growing the business, taking market share, or expanding their profit margins, and simply whether these investments are worth the risk.

Chapter 3 shows you how to take the temperature of the companies in your portfolio. There are ways to make sure the stock you own deserves to stay in your portfolio. I don't want anyone glued to a computer screen, but you can't become rich buying mutual funds or holding stocks that aren't moving in the right direction.

Chapter 4 will help you avoid the Captain Ahab syndrome. Emotional baggage killed the myopic sea captain going after a white whale, as it kills investors who cling to bad habits, bad stocks, and flawed logic. This is a chapter you'll want to read over and over again.

Chapter 5, "Pretty as a Picture," is all about charts. The basics are outlined and explained. Somehow charting has been put on a pedestal right up there with forensic science. It's not.

Chapter 6 teaches you that charts are simply your road map. Total reliance on charts is a huge mistake and leads to excessive trading, which in turns mean you won't own the stock for the real big payoff—and believe me, you aren't going to capture a series of wins and trade around each nuance of movement of the stock.

Chapter 7 is about chasing stocks. Investors grapple so much with the eternal question of whether they are too late, whether they've missed the move. Too many people play the stock market as if it had a game clock. I want you to buy stocks that are undervalued, and I don't want you to be afraid to chase on occasion even if you are buying to put it away or buying to make fast money. Eighty percent of your portfolio will be focused on buying and holding, but there should be monies set aside to generate cash in the account, too.

Chapter 8 deals with rules and a level playing field. There has been an effort to make the market fairer to ordinary investors, but I think it hasn't worked. Certainly the new rules haven't drawn folks to the stock market beyond passively handing money over to managers. The key isn't the rules. The key is to use all the information at your fingertips to make smart decisions. Nonetheless, it is important to understand where the boundaries are, because those who know the rules play this game best.

Chapter 9 shows you how to watch the tape and benefit from market manipulation. Let's face it: News is leaked, people know stuff, and you will never be in their inner circle. So what! You can watch the tape and get in on the action. I'm going to teach you how to read the tape to make money and not be a pigeon.

Chapter 10 is about staying in the game. You have to stay informed. You must read what the pros read and learn how to read between the lines. There is so much information out there that you'll need to whittle down your sources to maximize time.

Chapter 11 makes it clear that emotional intelligence is crucial. Some of the smartest people I know have lost the most money in the stock market and I blame one thing: runaway emotions. You can temper those emotions by knowing more about the market and finding comfort in your knowledge. Moreover, you can get to a point where you'll make money off the emotional letdowns of the masses.

Chapter 12 covers the care and feeding of your portfolio. You have to build a portfolio and let it work for you. The portfolio can't be unbalanced or structurally unsound. You don't want one cannonball fired into your portfolio to knock all the walls down. Your portfolio will become your cash register.

ACKNOWLEDGMENTS

I want to thank those who blazed the trail for me on Wall Street, including Russell Goings, Reginald Lewis, and Travers Bell. I know that I work for more than just my family and myself, and I'm proud to carry the baton.

I owe everything to my clients who push me each day and expect me to be great all the time. I'm trying. I've been fortunate enough to meet so many great people and to learn how to get it done.

I want to say thanks to the folks at Fox News Network—there isn't a place with more passionate and caring professionals, all working for the public trust. It's been an honor to be involved. I also want to say thanks to Robyn Walensky for her input and out-of-the box observations and thinking.

There are so many people to thank, so many people who have touched my life. I stand on the shoulders of my ancestors and carry the strength of my grandparents. Along the way many teachers gave me that special push, including Ms. Flood (sixth grade) and Mr. Austin (eighth grade). I have to thank my brothers, Clarence and Cecil, who were and still are the smartest ones in the family, and I also want to thank my father. And there is a special thanks to my loyal and dedicated staff at Wall Street Strategies: This book is your triumph, too.

ABOUT THE AUTHOR

Charles V. Payne is the founder and CEO of Wall Street Strategies. He started his career in 1985 at EF Hutton. In 1989 he switched gears and landed a position with a small research firm, where he first saw a niche for independent and timely equity advice. In 1991, with less than $10,000 in start-up capital and working from his apartment, he struck out on his own and launched Wall Street Strategies, Inc., where he started serving up his unique brand of stock market advice. His stock selections soon began to reap sizable profits for his subscribers and the firm developed a national reputation as a provider of timely and effective equity analysis.

Mr. Payne is in demand as a guest on several well-respected finance-oriented radio programs and is a contributor to the Fox News Channel, and he is widely recognized in the media as a leader among the analyst community. He is routinely sought after for his market opinions by several prestigious news organizations and speaks around the world to a variety of investors, from individuals to institutions.

PART ONE

BE SMART

Welcome to the World You Already Live In— The Stock Market

I cringe when I hear people say they know nothing about the stock market.

You say you aren't interested in the market for a variety of reasons. You're afraid of losing your money. You're skeptical of the system. You think it is rigged for insiders. You have a preconceived notion that the big boys on Wall Street have an inside track on information that you don't have access to.

My main goal in this chapter is to make you aware of how you are already involved in the stock market, whether you are an active investor or not.

For example, if you buy an iPod, you are generating profit for Apple Computer. If you like the product, why not buy some shares of Apple Computer? If you are driving corporate profits, why not be part of the corporation? Outside of your retirement plan, you may think you are not in the stock market. The fact of the matter is you don't already realize that you are already in the market. Simply put, the people are the stock market and the stock market is the people.

The stock market is a measuring stick of the goods and services that are in demand. It is an indicator of companies that are gaining ground and growing and ones that are waning. For example, demand for hybrid cars has driven the price of Toyota shares through the roof, while decreasing interest in gas-guzzlers has driven the share price of Ford Motor right off the road. The company's stock is at a 10-year low and management is selling valuable assets just to stay alive.

Every conceivable type of business has stock that trades on the New York Stock Exchange (NYSE), NASDAQ, and the American Stock Exchange (AMEX). All these entities together represent the economy. The combined buying and selling of these companies indicate where the economy is and where the economy is going. However, the day-to-day fluctuations can be based completely on emotion. For example, a terrorist attack in Indonesia could send our stock market spiraling sharply lower, affecting shares of companies that do absolutely no business in Indonesia whatsoever. But an earthquake in Indonesia that creates significantly more damage and takes more lives would not even register in the U.S. stock market. On the other hand, the capture of a top terrorist could send the market significantly higher based on a general feeling of optimism.

Some of you are like the masses of folks who were driven out of the market (as self-directed investors) and sort of want to jump in, but can't get off the sidelines. You've been watching from afar like a kid peering into the window of your favorite store, longing for the day you can go inside and buy anything you want. Some of you are doing the exact opposite; you are actively engaged in buying and selling, or you day-trade. You are the investor who has been badly burned by your own greed in your search for magic bullets, stocks that will make you instantly rich.

If you have been sitting on the sidelines out of fear, I will give you the confidence and understanding to avoid the pitfalls of investing. Your daily activities are making other people rich, so why not get in on the action? You are wearing clothes, heating your home, paying an electric bill. You're eating at least three times a day, so you're shopping at a supermarket like Whole Foods or eating out at a restaurant like the Olive Garden. People are profiting off of your purchasing power. Why not profit too? I will give you a sound strategy to develop a solid portfolio.

Many people tell me, "Charles, I just don't have the money." I say you don't have to already be rich to become rich in the stock market. Even if you have $100 a month to invest, you are on your way to profiting off of the very corporations that have been profiting off of you for all these years.

For you folks who are day-trading, turning your stock market experience into a losing adventure to an Atlantic City casino, my goal is to get you to stop the bleeding. You need to abandon your notion that an investment is a winner or a loser in less than 24 hours. Short-term trading is not a bad thing, but it needs to be based less on emotion and more on fundamentals. Realistic holding times, realistic profit goals, and the discipline to avoid knee-jerk reactions and emotional mistakes are the keys to being a short-term trader. I look at this kind of approach to the stock market as a way to generate income from the market, but it should never be your primary approach to investing in the stock market.

I'll talk more about the different terms out there, such as *investor*, *trader*, *play*, and *dabble*, as these descriptions have been mangled so much that it actually has added to poor decision-making, unwise behavior, and poor judgment in the stock market. Often, self-imposed labels like *trader*, *investor*, *bull*, or *bear* have made achieving success in the stock market harder. People who label themselves bears miss great rallies, and people who label themselves bulls fail to get out even when there are giant neon signs screaming to get out.

The Hottest Shoes in Town

Recently I was in an elevator in Las Vegas and overheard three women chatting away excitedly. I figured they'd just gotten into town and were gearing up to hit the slots (it is rare that folks have that same level of enthusiasm when they're on the verge of leaving town, as they've either lost too much money or have had great fun but realize they haven't even scratched the surface of what the gambling Mecca has to offer). But as I listened and looked around, I saw that the topic of their glee was right in the elevator. One of the women was showing off her new shoes, which the salesperson called *crocs*. Hmm . . . I know that name, although I'd never had the pleasure of seeing a pair. The company, Crocs Inc., was a new initial public offering, a hot IPO that I was familiar with. The wearer told her friends that the shoes would be the hottest in the market in six months, and they began to inquire as to where they could purchase a pair.

That's when I sprang into action. I asked them, did you guys know that the company that makes those shoes is public? There was a collective "no." Yes, it is public, and if the shoes are going to be the hottest in the market in the next six months, it is probably a great investment *now*. I could hear the wheels turning; they were seriously entertaining the thought of picking up the stock. Unfortunately, these women didn't ask me key questions like how much was the stock currently trading for, what was the stock symbol, or what exchange was it trading on. Of course if they were really active in the market, they may have asked what was the price/earnings ratio and stuff like that. My gut feeling is those fun ladies had a great time with the slot machines, caught the act of an aging lounge singer or an up-and-coming illusionist, walked around so much that no shoe felt comfortable, and forgot all about buying shares of Crocs.

I'm sure those ladies are in the stock market via a 401(k) program that is scattered across a bunch of mutual funds that are probably underperforming the broad market. People put more time into looking for the right pair of shoes or the most comfortable camping gear but virtually no time into assessing the market so they can get out of nonperforming mutual funds and buy the winners that are right in front of their faces. The time and effort put into finding the right shoe is even more ridiculous.

I'm not 100 percent sure where any stock will be in the next six months, but I'm certain that the stock will be worth more than the shoes I saw on the elevator that day in Las Vegas. As fun-looking and comfortable as a pair of rubber shoes might be, common sense says they would soon depreciate in value significantly. I think the shoes are ugly, but it wouldn't be the first time I've seen an unattractive shoe product set the world on fire and become a mind-boggling investment to boot (pun intended).

Having a 21-year-old daughter and a hip wife, I've always been exposed to the latest styles. In fact, I was spending time at the flagship Steve Madden shoe store in the Soho section of Manhattan (one of the coolest neighborhoods in New York, south of Houston Street has always been an arbiter of hip and ahead of the curve). The first time I went to the store was sometime in 1999, and all I could remember thinking was how exciting the buzz was and how ugly the shoes were. These shoes where clunky, big, bold, and in your face. I thought that was okay for my daughter but my wife dug the shoes, too. There were women there from every nationality and age bracket! At the time I didn't even know the company was public, and neither did anyone else in that beehive. Not long after my first visit to the store, the news hit that founder Steve Madden was arrested for stock fraud. The company's share price proceeded to plunge and soon lost more than half its value.

I went to the store soon thereafter and it was busy as ever. As my daughter looked around, I jokingly asked the cashier if they were having a "bail sale" and got only a puzzled look in return. She was completely in the dark about the fact that Steve Madden had even been arrested. I tried my joke on a few more employees and some customers, and each time it bombed. It looked like the security guy was about to ask me to leave the place, but then my daughter walked up with an armful of shoeboxes. After the stock hit rock bottom, it was clear that the arrest wouldn't harm sales, and the experts said the only problem would be a guilty verdict. (See Figure 1.1.)

Steve Madden stock began to climb out of the ashes and within nine months was back at the level at which it had changed hands before the arrest. Then it happened. Steve Madden, a guy on the fast track who would be the last person, one would imagine, to commit fraud, admitted his guilt and was sentenced to 41 months

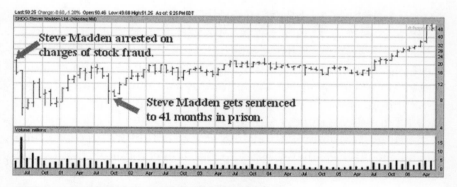

FIGURE 1.1   The Rise, Fall, and Rise of Steven Madden
Chart courtesy of Prophet Financial Systems (www.prophet.net).

of prison time. Once again the share price of the company's stock plunged. I figured the game was over and at the very least the company had lost its creative soul and would move sideways to lower for some time. I took my eye off the stock until a few years later, after I went on a weekend jaunt to the company's flagship store and their other Soho location across the street. I wondered what had become of the stock. The stock was trading at $28 at the time and it hasn't looked back since.

There are a couple of morals to this story, but the key is that all of those people who worked at Madden and all those customers were part of the stock market.

And more important, these people were part of the story of one of the best stock investments, thus far, of the new millennium.

The interesting irony of the market is that those folks knee-deep into each session, watching charts, and being extremely active often miss out on the huge gains than less sophisticated investors could achieve by simply paying attention to the immediate world around them. Although big companies dominate business and mainstream headlines, it is the small company that is at the heart of American capitalism. Small companies provide more jobs than those behemoths. Most important, though, small companies represent ground-floor opportunities for investors. The risk is that small companies never live up to their potential and the stock flames out. Nevertheless, it is still possible to make money on companies that come out of the gate fast, only to fizzle later.

Roller Coaster of Love

Small publicly traded companies are listed on the NASDAQ. This is the go-go exchange that encompasses the Horatio Alger spirit of the U.S. economy. There are many companies on this exchange that don't have earnings; some don't have sales and others don't have products, but they all have a ton of hope. And sometimes they have a ton of hype, too.

Investors who jumped into the stock market for the first time during the last decade probably focused on companies that traded on the NASDAQ. This is where the action has been. While there are some big companies on NASDAQ that are pillars of our economic foundation, people are drawn to that exchange for the lesser-known company that has developed a better mousetrap in a garage, or the one that has ignored the politics of bureaucracy-challenged big drug companies and has decided to focus on cures for cancer, AIDS, and other ailments in a more entrepreneurial setting.

The various exchanges appeal to specific areas of our psychological makeup.

The blue chip stocks that change hands on the New York Stock Exchange *provide the warmth and comfort of an old blanket* or knowing we can always move back in with mom and dad if the days after college prove more difficult than we thought. (Even if those days after college are really years after college.)

The stocks on the S&P 500 index are middle of the road, not too hot and not too cold; these are *established companies that provide a dash of safety and a dash of risk*. On Wall Street the professionals typically refer to the S&P when they want to know what the *market* is doing.

The NASDAQ composite, while it does contain large companies such as Microsoft and Intel, stimulates that same part of our brain that thinks bungee jumping might be fun or says, "What the heck, I will go on that blind date, after all." This isn't to say that there isn't incredible opportunity on the NASDAQ. Besides, most people I know who have bungee jumped say it is exhilarating, and many have met the person of their dreams through blind dates—okay, not many, but some have. The reality is that there is generally more risk with companies listed on the NASDAQ and that the established names were once risky names, too, that made it big. Therein lies the reason so many investors are drawn to the index: It is possible to buy stocks that will double, triple, or increase in value even more in a relatively short period of time.

Of course, where there are mind-boggling reward possibilities, there are also incredible risks.

Many NASDAQ stocks simply aren't for the faint of heart. Yet investors with the most tenuous risk profiles not only tend to buy these stocks but they load up on them.

These stocks are capable of bouncing around like a pinball, pushed violently up and down. One day you're rolling in the dough and the next you're afraid to get a quote. The action in these stocks is known as *high beta*. According to the *Dictionary of*

Finance and Investment Terms, beta is the covariance of a stock in relationship to the rest of the stock market. Any stock with a beta reading above 1.0 is consider high beta, which means the stock will tend to be more volatile than the S&P 500. Saying that stocks with high beta readings tend to be more volatile is an understatement; many of these high flyers are capable of double-digit percentage moves in a single session. Who needs a roller coaster when there are high beta stocks? Of course, this book is about making money and keeping that money, and therein lies the challenge of owning the high beta stocks that dominate the NASDAQ.

The key industries in the NASDAQ include technology, especially semiconductor companies (semiconductors are the computer chips that run everything from personal computers to the brains in electric toothbrushes), and biotechnology companies. Biotech companies find cures for health ailments by focusing on natural sources—hence the name—whereas drug companies work to create synthetic (chemical) compounds to proved cures and treatments.

A look at the NASDAQ since 1995 explains the joy and pain it has evoked and why it is the place where investors looking for fast money and fantastic returns generally focus their investing and trading. In the mid-1990s the stock market became so exciting that it was truly the national pastime. Bars replaced sports television with financial television, cab drivers doubled as stock pickers, and everyone was going to retire within a matter of years. It wasn't the Dow driving this wild excitement—it was the NASDAQ. With Silicon Valley as the epicenter of new ideas that would revolutionize the way we learned, worked, and played, there was a never-ending supply of companies in business niches with funky names and acronyms like Push technology, local area networks (LANs), Voice over Internet Protocol (VoIP), nanotechnology, and countless others.

Each new acronym would replace one that was hot just months before, and we all wanted in. College dropouts got more respect than grad school luminaries and were able to raise money from business plans written on napkins. I had clients from foreign countries using our service and the only word of English they knew was "NASDAQ." NASDAQ, or the National Association of Securities Dealers Automated Quotation system, is owned and operated by the National Association of Securities Dealers (NASD). It is a computerized system that provides price quotes for stocks that trade on the system as well as for many NYSE-listed securities. In the 1990s NASDAQ *was* the stock market. It was the first electronic stock market, in which over 500 market makers provide more than 60,000 competing bids to buy, offer, and sell NASDAQ stocks. An initial listing with the NASDAQ Stock Market required:

- Shareholder equity of $5 million, market value of listed securities at $50 million, or net income from continued operations (in the latest fiscal year or in two of the last three years) equal to $750,000.

- One million publicly held shares.

- A minimum share price bid of $4.00.

- An operating history of 1 year or $50 million.

Figure 1.2 tracks the NASDAQ Composite from mid-1996 to early 2006.

There is also a NASDAQ Small Cap exchange, which has less stringent listing requirements; and the over-the-counter market, also known as the OTC market, which is run by NASDAQ Inc. but isn't really a NASDAQ exchange—its listing and legal requirements have lower thresholds than NASDAQ exchanges.

The dominant aspect of the NASDAQ is that there are so many different types of businesses represented that it can be quite con-

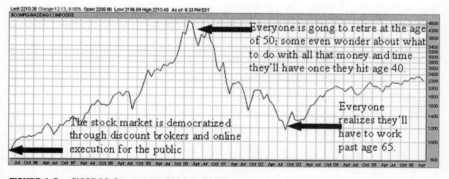

FIGURE 1.2   NASDAQ Composite (1996–2006)
Chart courtesy of Prophet Financial Systems (www.prophet.net).

fusing. Many times investors find themselves buying stocks in companies that sell products they've never heard of. In fact, outside of the worries of losing all their money, playing in a system that is rigged against them (it's actually rigged against their behavior), and feeling they don't have enough money, investors fret that the stock market is too complicated. Yet we all come in contact with growing trends that could be fantastic investment opportunities—we just have to be more in tune with the world around us to notice them. If the shipping department is ordering more boxes than ever before, maybe business is good, and maybe the stock will begin to reflect the increase.

Discussing indexes as a top-down (macro) view is important, but my goal is to make everyone truly understand that they are part of the market and therefore should attempt to reap the rewards. To understand the stock market and your role in it, which you may or may not even realize exists, requires that you pay closer attention and connect the dots.

At the end of the day the market is the sum of its parts. Those parts are the individual companies listed on the various exchanges, and how well management runs those companies to generate profits for shareholders. This seems like highbrow stuff, but you don't have to work in the executive suites to know what's happening at the company you work for or within the industry that your company happens to be part of. Everyone at Spacely Sprockets knew when Cogswell Cogs was eating their lunch, and vice versa. Just about every day, we walk past a game in our children's bedroom, see vans loading in the company parking lot, notice stores that seem to be popping up everywhere, engage in water cooler talk, and interact with our network of friends, all of which could be linked to great investment opportunities.

We are annoyed by the massive increase of those big tractor trailer trucks on the road; we are frustrated by the sticker shock we get every time we go for gas; and it seems like it was just yesterday when the airlines last raised their prices, but they're going up again. Yeah, it's going to cost more to go see grandma this Thanksgiving than it did over the summer. Many times our first reaction to growing trends is to see how they are victimizing our world and us. But if you owned shares in Exxon Mobil, the sticker shock would be replaced by the notion that you are making money from higher gasoline—you're in the game and not a victim of the game. There is nothing stopping you from getting in bed with the big boys.

Sometimes we even have insider information and just don't realize it.

The da Vinci Code

I'm a big boxing fan, and on most big fight nights the whole gang comes over to my house. We have a great time and find ways to enjoy ourselves in addition to the fight, or maybe because the majority of the fights tend to be duds. One of our favorite pastimes is to play cards, particularly a card game known as bid whist. A forerunner to contract bridge, it's a game of communication, luck, and guile. It involves a fair amount of bluffing, and reliance on your partner is critical. It seems like the best players are from the Bronx (I'm not sure why this is, or if it's true—I'm sure not only will players from the four other boroughs of New York and the surrounding area disagree but so will Southerners, where the game has a rich history and tradition), and a number of them are always at the house on fight night.

A lot of folks from the Bronx aren't actively invested in the stock market, although they all dream of bettering their lives. Most are intrigued and many watch financial television, read the business section of the daily newspapers, and have even snooped around online to get the lay of the land. Yet there is this barrier to pulling the trigger, to actually purchasing stock and getting in the game on the winning side of the equation. Obviously fear is the biggest reason for the trepidation and hesitation, but there is a mental element beyond fear that also stops people from doing more than opening an account but never going any further.

The market just seems so mystifying. Don't those downtown bigwigs have degrees from Harvard and Yale and still routinely get it wrong? How the heck could you get it right? Don't you have to be a science major or an expert at crunching numbers to be successful in the stock market? Isn't it true that the real players have the inside track and aren't going to lose money, and I'm at their mercy, so how can I compete? Many people simply put money into their 401(k) and watch it do the equivalent of the Bataan

Death March, where allied prisoners of war were forced by their Japanese captures to walk 90 miles in six days in the Bataan peninsula in the Philippines during WWII.

The march saw numerous lost lives as these POWs were in pretty bad shape to begin with and were denied water and generally mistreated along the way. Many investors view their company-sponsored 401(k) plans as a barbaric attempt at exposure to the stock market with very limited positive results. So that leads me back to one night when the topic of the stock market came up again. My whist partner, who works at one of the largest hospitals in New York City, mentioned he had seen me early in the day on television. During the show I had recommended a stock called Intuitive Surgical (ticker symbol ISGR—see Figure 1.3).

Asked to elaborate, I mentioned the innovative things the company was doing, and it reminded my partner of a hot new device his hospital had purchased several months earlier. It turns out that this device was called the da Vinci machine—a robotic machine designed to assist surgeons and provide minimally invasive surgery. My partner, a very intelligent and gregarious fellow, raved about the machine, its price tag, and the fact that several other departments within the hospital were always vying for the machine.

I just about fell out of my chair when he said the name of this hot device. It was the product that was driving the excitement in Intuitive Surgical and driving its share price. Of course, my playing partner *did* fall out of his chair when I not only revealed that

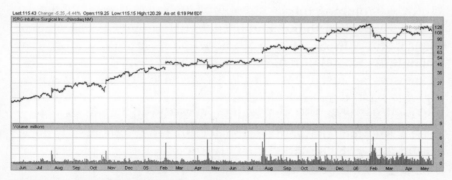

FIGURE 1.3   Intuitive Surgical (ISRG)
Chart courtesy of Prophet Financial Systems (www.prophet.net).

the da Vinci was the key product in the company I had recommended that morning but also told him how much the stock was up since the time his hospital got their first device. Moreover, I told him how much the stock was up in the past year, which meant that if he had bought it when the purchase order was submitted, his investment would have been up 100 percent. But even after witnessing the demand for the device once it arrived at his hospital, an investment in the company's stock would have yielded a 50 percent return.

We lost the next couple of hands of bid whist and eventually the game. My partner seemed preoccupied. I'm sure it had to do with his realization that he had been sitting on a gold mine of information and hadn't acted on it because the stock market always seemed out of his range, above his head—simply too mysterious to fathom.

My buddy and card-playing pal had knowledge of something that would otherwise be mysterious to most of us, but there are usually numerous situations in each of our daily lives that could translate into individual gold mines for each of us. That takes me back to the question, what is the stock market? The stock market is a place where people buy and sell the equity in so-called public companies. Businesses raise money to grow their operations and do so through the public market to avoid owning debt.

In addition, a business may decide to go public in order to create liquidity for shareholders. By now everyone knows of the wave of corporate malfeasance that swept through Wall Street and corporate America in the late 1990s and the early part of the new millennium. The common theme in most of the most highly publicized cases was an effort to inflate the stock price so insiders (corporate officials and company bankers) could sell their shares to the general public.

The Collective, the Borg, the Stock Market

What *is* the stock market? The stock market is every aspect of our lives and we are all a part of this collective that is something like the Borg in *Star Trek*, except the components of the collective dictate the outcome and not vice versa, although the market attempts to speak to us all the time, too, which adds to the mystique and difficulty of investing. In the updated version of the great Gene Roddenberry creation, *Star Trek*, there is a villainous race known as the Borg. The Borg are a race of cyborgs, or cybernetic creatures, from the future. The goal of the Borg is to seek out any race that may have a technology or know-how that would be an asset to the collective. Once the Borg have chosen a victim, they assimilate the victim and take away any sense of individuality the victim once had, and from that point on the victim thinks as one with the collective. The Borg amalgam has been likened to a beehive and the collective thinking is referred to as "hive mind." Having captured trillions of drones over the years, the Borg are a considerable force, whose mantra is "Resistance is futile."

The stock market is like the Borg but it doesn't moderate behavior; rather, it *interprets* behavior, past, current, and mostly future. The market is the collective input of all its parts, which represent virtually every industry known to mankind (along with a lot of industries that aren't really in existence, and even industries that will never come into being). The share prices of the companies in these industries react to buying and selling. Simply put, if there are more buyers than sellers then a stock's price goes higher, and if there are more sellers than buyers a stock goes down.

I didn't make this up, by the way; it's been said so much that I almost don't believe it. Nonetheless, at the end of the day, how people feel about the future of a company dictates the action in the stock. Therefore, on a grander scale, whatever people think about the future of the stock market is also reflected in the movement of the broad exchanges, indexes, and averages.

Each exchange (see Table 1.1) has its own identity and acts as an individual Borg, if you will, sometimes moving up and down in value at the expense of one of the others. For instance, it isn't uncommon for a hot market to see a majority of new money pour into NASDAQ stocks. After all, the stocks on this exchange tend to trade fast (read: higher) when there is excitement in the air. On the other hand, when there is angst over the market, no matter the source, the fast money crowd typically heads for the hills and more conservative investors rotate into NYSE stocks; hence the Dow and/or S&P 500 will perform better than the NASDAQ. Understanding the nuances of the various exchanges and the ever-multiplying funds and alternative investment vehicles is a very

TABLE 1.1   Comparing the NYSE, Dow Jones, and S&P 500

Exchanges and Indexes	Description
New York Stock Exchange (NYSE)	Also known as the Exchange and the Big Board. The members who own the 1,366 seats maintain an orderly market for the securities traded for themselves and on behalf of the public.
Dow Jones Industrial Average (DJIA)	A price-weighted average of 30 so-called blue chip stocks that represent the industrial, service, and technology niches of the U.S. economy. The components of the average represent between 15 and 20 percent of the total market value of the NYSE.
S&P 500	A broad-based composite index of 500 widely held companies designed to measure and reflect the health of the stock market. The index is updated and maintained by the Standard and Poor's corporation.

important key to being able to achieve success and build wealth through the stock market.

These exchanges, indexes, and averages to which I refer are designed to represent certain portions of the market or the entire stock market itself. The one that is most commonly known is the Dow Jones Industrial Average (DJIA), usually referred to simply as "the Dow." Just about everyone has heard of the index, which was created by Charles Dow, Charles Bergstresser, and Edward Jones to reflect the status of the broader industrial portion of the economy. The index has been knocked as being underrepresentative of the economy and broad stock market because only 30 companies make up its components. Moreover, these companies are typically lumbering giants that don't reflect the go-go portion of the economy, the part that adds oomph and underscores the American dream of rags to riches.

The index has worked well over the years. Initially a part of the *Customer's Afternoon Letter* published by the three founders beginning in 1884, the original Dow Jones Transportation Average encompassed nine railroad stocks and two industrial stocks. The first version of the Dow Jones Industrial Average included 12 stocks, which accompanies in cotton, oil, sugar, tobacco, gas, cattle feed, lead, coal and rubber, along with today's lone survivor from the original bunch, General Electric.

The folks who are the gatekeepers of these indexes periodically change the makeup of them to add a little pizzazz. But the truth of the matter is that the Dow and, to a lesser extent, the Standard and Poor's 500 (otherwise known as the S&P 500 or just the S&P) comprise mostly stodgier companies that are well established and produce billions of dollars of profits each quarter as they are the foundation of the nation's economy. In fact, the companies on the Dow are also known as blue chip companies, those that produce the largest of profits in corporate America. The companies in the DJIA used to be known as widow and orphan plays because of their deep financial roots in particular industries, which meant the downside would be minimal while the companies were sure to always generate a lot of cash. Over the years, alas, there have been disasters even on the DJIA, and the notion of widow's and orphan's stocks isn't as prevalent as it was in the past.

In 1999 the powers in charge made changes to the DJIA that included the removal of four companies: Chevron, Goodyear Tire, Sears, and Union Carbide. The timing was pretty good, considering that Goodyear Tire saw its share price peak at $26 in 2002 only to tumble to $4 in 2003. The new names in the index were Intel, Microsoft, Home Depot, and SBC Communications. The inclusion of NASDAQ stalwarts and tech giants was an attempt to keep the index relevant and exciting. Initially the ploy worked, as both of the tech bellwether stocks rose nicely, but for the last couple of years both have been hovering at 50 percent of their highest values since being selected for the index. By the way, the experts always caution against so-called market timing but everyone does it, from the most seasoned of investors to the folks who manage index exchange-traded funds and other conservative investment vehicles.

Exchange-traded funds (ETFs) are open-ended, actively managed funds that serve as a proxy for a niche of the market (e.g., biotechnology companies) or individual markets (such as the Japanese market). They are like stocks in the sense that they can be traded at any time during normal market hours, traded short, or used as hedges in more elaborate investment schemes. Perhaps the most famous ETF is the "SPY," also known as "spyders," which represents the S&P 500 index and trades an average of 72 million shares each session.

Mutual funds can also be open-ended funds that are actively managed. Essentially, an investment company owns a lot of different stocks with money pooled together by various investors. These funds have specific goals and instructions on where monies will be invested.

Despite the slightly tarnished imagine of the DJIA, the fact of the matter is that companies in this index represent solid investments as they are giants in their particular industries and have the wherewithal and financial muscle to stay ahead of the competition. For many investors the DJIA seems too boring. The old-school names were good investments for their grandparents, but the lure of safety isn't enough for the person looking to make an overnight killing. This is endemic of the many poor assumptions made by investors who are in the market looking for 1990s-style movers. Of course, after the stock market plummeted in 2000 and 2001, the Dow has been able to return to and surpass its previous highs.

Let's face it, it could be several years before the NASDAQ composite will be able to reach its former pinnacle. The richest investors in the world, including Warren Buffett, have made their fortunes with blue chip stocks, so there is a place for them in your portfolio, especially if you want not only to get rich but also to stay rich. My philosophy on investing, however, isn't to try to invest exactly like the super rich. The average investor has to be more nimble. Remember, the super rich have as a priority the need to preserve wealth.

Who Knew? You Knew

Did any shoppers of A&P supermarkets (stock symbol GAP) notice major changes in the stores in recent years—bright lights, better displays, better selections, and so on? Obviously those changes made a difference, as shoppers took note and the company's fortunes turned for the better. In fact, to say the company's fortunes turned for the better could be an understatement.

From November 2004 to March 2006, the share price of A&P's parent company, the Great Atlantic and Pacific Tea Company, rose by 600 percent. There is no way to know for sure, but I'm certain very few frequent shoppers of the supermarket bought shares, even as they saw marked improvements and probably recommended the store to friends and neighbors.

For years people have complained about the cars that were coming out of Detroit, the employee layoffs, the recalls, the lost market share. We all knew things were bad (and still not too great at this very moment), yet how many of us bought stock in the main beneficiary of Detroit's ailments? When I mention this to people, many think they had to have taken advantage of the change in fortunes of domestic carmakers 10 years ago; but it may not be too late.

From June 2003 to April 2006 the share price of Toyota Motors (stock symbol SLB) soared by 280 percent, propelled even faster as crude oil prices climbed and the focus of consumers shifted to hybrid cars, an area in which Toyota excels.

Speaking of higher crude oil prices, it really shouldn't be any surprise that gasoline and energy have become important national topics of debate. Whether you subscribe to the theory that there is a lot of oil in the ground or that an energy crisis is right around the corner, the fact of the matter is they aren't making any more of the stuff.

There are many companies that serve as proxies for the oil industry, but I typically recommend oil drillers and service companies because what good is $100-a-barrel crude oil if the oil companies don't have any to sell? From November 2003 to April 2006 the share price of Schlumberger (stock symbol: SLB) increased by more than 300 percent. While it is true that this company isn't a household name, the price of gasoline and home heating is always a topic in every household. You can curse at the pump, an inanimate object with no feelings, or you could get in on the game, too.

High technology is a difficult area to invest in because it is always in flux, with one technology usurping another that just seemed to make its debut only a couple of years earlier. However, it became clear that one tech company had really gotten its act together when it created the hottest consumer product of the new millennium.

Is there a household anywhere in America without an iPod? I think we have six in our home even though I don't own one. (Remember the 21-year-old and the hip wife? Well, there is also a 23-year-old high-tech aficionado and a 9-year-old who is on the cutting edge of anything electronic.) From March 2004 to January 2006 the share price of Apple Computer (stock symbol AAPL) surged more than 700 percent!

I always find it interesting when investors take fliers on tech plays in which they have no idea about how the products work or the potential size of the market. Sure, there are a lot of sexy stories, but even in technology the most compelling stories could be right in front of our faces.

I think the first step in becoming a successful self-directed investor (a person who takes active control of his investments in the stock market rather than blindly handing funds over to a money manager or investment adviser) is to understand the world around you. Of course we are always worried that that shoe we think will be the hippest in six months has already been the hottest on the planet and we buy the stock too late. That is why we work the numbers, read the income statement, look at the charts, make comparisons to rival companies in the same space, and try to understand the overall direction of the industry that the company is a part of. These are things I will elaborate on later in the book, but for now the idea is to demystify the market enough for you to stop kicking the tires and to become actively involved.

At the end of the day I urge folks to understand, when they see all those fat cats in the stock market being driven around town in limos and riding private jets, that the general public put them there. *We* are the general public, we make the fat cats rich, but we aren't barred from getting in on the action, too. There is nothing wrong with people becoming ultrarich, but there is something wrong with individuals who are generating such riches not taking advantage of the system as well.

- Do you smoke cigarettes?

- Do you go to the movies?

- Do you stay at home and watch television all day?

- Do you drive to grandma's house each summer?

- Do you play the lottery from time to time?

- Do you like to own the hottest shoes and get them six months before your friends have even heard of them?

- Have you tried to lose weight?

- Do you have more handbags than you need?

- Do you have more golf clubs than you need?

These aren't rhetorical questions. I'm trying to stress the fact that we all spend money on things that we don't necessarily have to, in the process fueling the stock market and making others rich. Perhaps you noticed the question about staying at home and watching television. Surly that doesn't cost any money, right? Well, aside from whether one is watching cable or satellite television, the correct answer is yes, you're not spending money. But sitting at home and just watching television or listening to the radio or reading the newspaper is still making others rich. Just our mere presence as a number on someone's viewing log is putting money into the pockets of those media outlets. Once again, you are part of the system, a vital part, and yet you aren't being rewarded.

The first superstar stock of the new millennium is Google, the famously popular search engine that has recaptured the imagination of investors, many of whom had written off the stock market but now dream of owning a stock that could one day be worth $1,000 a share. The interesting thing about the Google story is that the company's main product is free (the company is busy developing other services that will be paid for through subscriptions or other fee structures). We type the web address into our computer, and then the site, which isn't very sexy, pops up and we begin to look stuff up.

Every time you use their search engine, you are enhancing the wealth of the shareholders of Google. So, if that indeed is the case, why weren't you a shareholder of the company's stock coming out of the gate? The question of whether it's too late now is explored later in the book, as we learn about fundamental, technical, and behavioral analyses, but the main point here is that you have to be in the market with your money because you're in the market with your wallet, your eyeballs, your ears, and your mere presence.

Open Kimono—Going Public

The stock market—not just NYSE but any part of the system where people can buy and sell equity in publicly traded companies—is a metaphysical world. Your home computer is the stock market. The pay phone you use to call in an order to be executed by a stockbroker is the stock market, too. In the stock market, corporations raise money by selling a piece of the action. That action is opened up for all to participate in, just about every weekday of the year, from 9:30 A.M. EST to 4:00 P.M. EST—and that's just in America. At any given time on just about any given weekday, there is a stock market operating at full tilt, people buying and selling shares of stocks from their respective countries and other countries. You can buy shares of International Business Machines (IBM) in London while most people in the United States are asleep.

Companies that go public come under numerous sets of laws and regulations to protect investors. The Securities and Exchange Commission (SEC), the NASD, and the NYSE administer these laws and regulations, and in more recent times even state attorneys general have gotten into the act. Going public means opening the kimono wide for all to see. Warts, blemishes, and other faults are supposed to be transparent so that the buyer (or investor) knows what they are getting. Of course this doesn't always happen, but to insure that full disclosure is available and constant, publicly traded companies in America must report their earnings every 90 days in what is known as their quarterly earnings report. These reports are filed with the SEC initially as an 8K filing, which is a special update of any material corporate event. Typically, after the 8K has been filed, an even more detailed accounting of the events of the quarter is provided in the 10Q filing. The fourth quarter is included with the full-year results in a 10K filing.

Going public isn't necessarily an easy decision. I took my company, Wall Street Strategies, public in 1999, and while I made most of the mistakes in the book and there were disastrous elements to my decision, the net effect was exactly what the market is intended to be for a small company looking to expedite growth. I was able to raise several million dollars to build the operation, and I also gained new members of the management team through outside members on the board of directors—many of whom didn't share my vision for the company. While philosophical differences between me and the new investors slowed progress in implementing the business model, so too did the stock become a speed bump for progress. The share price of our stock became an enormous distraction. Our stock began trading around $2 a share, dipped to $1, and then zoomed to more than $28 a share, all within a matter of months.

All day long, employees would burn out the circuits in their calculators figuring out how much they were worth. (If there were such a thing as carpal tunnel for the index finger, everyone at Wall Street Strategies would have been walking around with a cast on their index fingers, including me.) Work didn't get done; tempers flared from those who didn't receive any shares and those who thought they should have received more shares than they did. At one point on paper my shares were worth $280 million. It was a heady time, but by the time a full 52 weeks had gone by the stock had swooned to less than $1 a share, the overall stock market was imploding, and visions of riches had vanished, replaced by pangs of anger among the workforce. Nonetheless, I would do it over again as it was the American dream. We raised money to expand our business, but it was too late in the business cycle—we expanded at the wrong time. If we had gone public just one year earlier I'd be writing this book from the Hearst Castle or on my own personal island in the Caribbean.

I share this story because there are thousands like it, each with an individual twist on the tale, but all cautionary. Ironically, one could look at my story and say it is a perfect example of why they don't buy stocks, but the very fact that our stock climbed so high is precisely why people play the stock market. Legally the employees of the company had to wait one year before they could sell their shares, but a lot of people made a lot of money on the stock on the way up, and many lost on the way down, too. The stock was overvalued at $28, plain and simple, and it was inevitable that the share price would retreat, although I don't think it would have bit the dust if the entire market hadn't fallen apart. The stock market is where companies go to chase the dream, to gain the funds to build a better mousetrap, and all corporations have to do is share the dream (and future profits) with others. So with all the overarching rules and regulations and all the second-guessing, and dealing with the ups and downs of the stock price, being able to go public can be a dream come true for any business.

Sure, some companies rue the day they went public. Smaller companies have to spend inordinate amounts of their funds today in compliance with all the rules and regulations. After the wave of scandals in the 1990s, Congress enacted the Sarbanes-Oxley Act, which calls for intense accounting of company records and mandates other guidelines that are prohibitively expense for small companies to adhere to. These rules are draconian and tough to follow even for deep-pocketed companies with billions of dollars in sales. For companies with only millions in sales and little to no profit, the expense of adhering to Sarbanes-Oxley has become ultra-prohibitive.

Moreover, some companies become vulnerable to being taken over by other companies or being ambushed by corporate raiders, sometimes known as *greenmailers*, who buy a large stake (for most public companies the ownership of 5 percent of the float is considered a large position) and make demands of management. More often than not, these raiders walk away with a ransom and pat themselves on the back for doing a public service for other shareholders. As a result, in recent years a lot of companies have gone private.

When a company is public, its day-to-day value is decided upon by investors. It is not uncommon for many companies and, indeed, many industries to feel that the public simply doesn't see the value of their businesses. These companies often decide to go private. They buy back all the stock in the public's hands. I would say one industry where we could see several companies go private is the homebuilders. After the best four-year period in the history of housing, homebuilders have seen the value of their companies plummet to all-time low valuation ratios. They are a screaming buy for anyone willing to hold and anyone who believes at the core of American wealth there is a limit to the downside.

Another reason that many companies go public is for an exit strategy, otherwise known on Wall Street as *liquidity*. Simply put, when a company is private it is hard to extract wealth other than salaries and, perhaps, dividends. Even the mightiest of companies have decided to go public in order to create liquidity. The story of the infighting at Goldman Sachs is an example of the mixed emotions that come with taking a sound company public. A company that doesn't really need operating capital but is sitting on a paper fortune has to grin and bear it as it allows infidels into its sacred organizations in order to be able to ring the register by selling stock and monetizing its holdings.

Of course, liquidity is a legitimate reason for going public, and many insiders, founders of great companies that decide to go public, find a way to have their cake and eat it, too. It is possible for the founders and officers of publicly held companies to retain control of the company and generate a lot of cash for it. Some insiders even have special shares. The descendants of Henry Ford own super shares in Ford Motor that give them exponential voting power. While the general rule of thumb is one share, one vote, there are a lot of public companies where the founders and other executives enjoy super voting privileges. These people are able to sell shares into the public market, reap billions of dollars in real money, and still maintain a fair amount of control. It's legal and not uncommon.

Once a company is public, the average man or woman on the street has an opportunity to become an owner. Of course, when you own 100 shares in a company that has floated 100 million shares you are a small voice in the wilderness, but you are a voice, nonetheless. But the reality is most people don't become shareholders of publicly traded companies to become vocal; instead, most people are looking to make money. In fact, the simple purchase of a stock is a vote of confidence, to a certain degree, for current management, the business plan, and also the industry in general. Most investors aren't looking to make waves; they're looking to ride the waves. We know that, by their very nature, waves go up and they go down, just like the stock market. When the waves are going up our confidence is like a giant surfboard, but during those swoons lower, our confidence and faith become Styrofoam boogie boards crashing against the Great Barrier Reef.

The Never-Ending Tug o' War

When you sell a stock, usually someone is either buying or looking to buy that stock on weakness. Every time you think something is a buy, someone else believes it is a sell. This is what makes the stock market unique. In any other kind of market both the buyer and seller think the product has value (or at least that would be the case in a perfect world). There are great platforms for all to espouse their feelings about a stock, whether they are bullish or bearish. It is easy to be swayed by these sentiments when a stock is moving in a particular direction. It is easy to abandon your thinking when a stock isn't working out the way you thought it would. It is important to understand the other side of the argument on stocks, but be very careful not to change your mind or dismiss your own work if a stock isn't acting the way you'd hoped. Know all points of view, cut through the self-serving clutter of the bulls and bears to formulate a well-rounded opinion, but don't be manipulated by either side.

There are no public odds, but the concept is like betting on the Super Bowl. There is a ton of information about the stock available for all, and yet once the information is consumed, there could be more than one conclusion. At the end of each session it boils down to whether the buyers bought more shares than the sellers sold to determine if a stock closed in the plus or minus column. If you're buying and the stock is falling, then it means you are betting on the underdog. Betting on the underdog, particularly when that wasn't your goal, could be very unnerving. Most people like to bet with the crowd. We cheer the underdogs but rarely do we bet on them, which is why odds makers have to make it more appealing to wager on an outcome that we simply don't believe in.

Sometimes we deliberately bet on the underdog, thinking the rest of the world got it wrong. Sort of like the theme behind most fairy tales and fables, the ugly duckling is going to turn into a beautiful swan. This is known as *contrarian* investing or going counter to the crowd. I explore this kind of investing in greater detail later in this book, as I advocate a philosophy of being where the crowd will eventually come. This is easier said than done, especially when the market is up big and you own a couple of stocks that are just meandering. Yet, at the end of the day, if you only focus on chasing performance, sooner or later you will be the last person in and the consequences could be horrendous. You see, stocks tend to come down a lot harder and faster than they go up.

Sometimes we know why stocks are coming down but sometimes we don't, or at least the reason isn't readily available. But the fact of the matter is there are more sellers than buyers, and those sellers are determined to cut bait at any price. The share price of a stock could go up in a similar scenario, too, but we don't ask a lot of questions when we own stocks whose share price is moving substantially higher on no news. We usually accept a word or single sentence to sate our limited curiosity:

"The stock is up—I think there is going to be news out of the FDA, about their new cancer drug."

"The stock is up—I think some brokerage firm placed a buy rating on the stock."

"It must be a takeover candidate."

"The earnings are good or going to be good."

Of course, it's equally as important to thoroughly understand the news while a stock is moving higher as it is when a stock is moving lower.

The bottom line is that day-to-day action of the stock market represents a giant game of tug-of-war, with sellers looking for dupes in the form of buyers and buyers trying to take advantage of shortsighted sellers. There is also a feeling that individual investors are being manipulated by an invisible hand, the greater powers that be, sitting in their ivory towers overlooking the canyons of Wall Street. I do believe the big boys manipulate the emotions of individual investors. I do believe there are times when the little guy and gal are shaken out of the game, as the big boys know the average investor has limited conviction and will bail out.

The main reason for this limited conviction is the limited homework that has gone into the investment selection in the first place. I think charts and technical analysis are great tools, but when they are your only tools it is easy to get whipsawed out of great investments. When we don't know the news and the stock is moving down, that is the emotional part of the stock market, the part that creates wild gyrations like a tsunami from an underwater earthquake. Sometimes the stocks we think have the greatest fundamental stories crater with the broad market. It takes serious conviction to hold these positions while they're crumbling, and if that conviction is based on a hunch or chart pattern only, then holding them could be disastrous (although it doesn't have to be since charts do reflect pass successes as well as past hype).

By the same token, if you don't hold, and you take a loss on a stock that was cheap from a fundamental point of view rather than the numerical share price, then you are allowing the big boys to manipulate you and your portfolio. Better put, I think most stocks over $100 a share are undervalued while most stocks under $10 a share are overvalued. So bailing on the $100 stock and holding the $10 stock in a down market is more often than not a huge mistake. I go into greater detail on this later in the book.

If the American embassy in some far-flung nation is the target of a terrorist attack, it is likely the stock market will react by dropping, no matter what other economic news and developments are pertinent at the time. This is the part of the stock market that is purely emotion, yet it is real and relevant as it carries an amazing amount of influence. Of course sometimes there is news that eventually justifies the share price move, but it takes time to connect the dots. Then there are times when we connect the dots in the most arcane manner, making a mountain out of a molehill.

Let's face it: Would war, for instance, really have a negative impact on the sale of athletic gear? Probably not, but it is almost certain that if war were declared today between the United States and any nation on the planet (the exception might be Grenada) the share price of Nike would be down along with 95 percent of the rest of the stock market. While life can be the game that ties everything together like six degrees of Kevin Bacon, the reality is that short-term moves in the stock market exaggerate the impact of events and the realities of future bottom lines.

It's one thing to connect the dots, but overly emotional response to things that won't alter the fundamentals (current and future) of the stock market happens more frequently than ever. I blame this on the fact that there are a lot more players in the market, many unseasoned and without sufficient knowledge of the market or even the stocks they are holding. I also blame fast money, a legacy of the 1990s where a ton of paper gains was created and it seemed like there would be no end to stocks making double-digit gains on a daily basis. A lot of people still want incredible returns in a very short period of time. These expectations are extremely unrealistic. To a lesser degree I also think the media plays a role, too.

There used to be a time when it was fine to say the market was up or down because there were more buyers than sellers or more sellers than buyers. Now we have to psychoanalyze each session, combing over it with a fine-tooth comb. Ironically, at the end of the day it seems like most of the media that covers the market comes up with a universal answer. The next day the headlines all blare the same message: "Stocks Down on Inflation Worries" or "Stocks Up on Earnings Results." I think the coverage of the market is great, and in my role on Fox News I try to go beyond the conventional answer. Though there are times when I drink the Kool-Aid, I always suspect there is an answer that isn't so readily available.

Fast and Furiously

I don't want to put all the blame for unrealistic expectations and excessive trading solely on the novice investors. The competition among money managers to outperform has become so intense that they are willing to try anything and to take chances their profession would have never dreamed of in the past. The biggest culprits are so-called hedge fund managers.

Hedge funds have been around for decades but only recently have gained the clout to move markets. Initially these funds were hedged—that is, they developed strategies that acted like insurance policies and that could deliver profits under any market condition. A simple hedge fund approach is being both long (owning stocks) and short (selling stocks in the hopes of buying them back later at a cheaper price) at the same time. Now it's a little different. Hedge funds can and do try any approach to beat the stock market.

Hedge funds:

- Go long.

- Go short.

- Use stock options (contracts to buy or sell specific stocks at a specific price on or before a specific date).

- Borrow money.

- Employ arbitrage.

- Use derivatives (investments where the performance of an asset over time determines value) such as swaps and futures.

These days, hedge funds compete with private equity funds and buy entire companies. If the stock market were an ocean hedge fund, managers would be great white sharks. These guys operate fast and furiously.

The hedge fund manager is expected to wildly outperform the broad market and make clients money under any kind of market condition. For this reason the majority of hedge funds have incorporated or devised extremely sophisticated methods (some would call them ridiculously complicated). I once heard a hedge fund manager say that because overall performance by hedge funds in general was declining rapidly, because all the hedge funds were using the same strategies, his firm would have to come up with more complicated strategies. It isn't good enough for these people to find good investments and hold them; they must have protection for these investments and even insurance on the protection of these investments. Hedge funds have a Plan A, Plan B, and Plan X working at the same time. Their constant quest for immediate profits gives them license to dream up and try any technique imaginable.

Besides complicated formulas and strategies that are held together on a string of intelligent guesses, these funds are so *over-leveraged* (have purchasing power that can be many times the actual amount in the fund—for instance, a fund with $1 billion may be able to borrow funds that give it $5 billion in purchasing power) that losses could mount at breakneck speed. In fact, the entire financial structure of the United States, maybe the entire world, was threatened by the faulty strategy of a hedge fund in 1998.

Founded by John Meriwether, the legendary head of bond trading at Salomon Brothers, Long Term Capital Management (LTCM) boasted a team of principal that was the financial world equivalent of Doc Holliday and the Earp brothers, including Wyatt. The fund's who's who included Robert Merton and Myron Scholes, Nobel Prize winners for their work (along with Fischer Black) on a model to value derivatives. When LTCM went up in smoke, a Federal Reserve governor urged major banks to come to the rescue.

The firm primarily invested in fixed income arbitrage, betting on government debt of the United States, European nations, and Japan. It took four months for it all to unravel. Trouble began in May 1998 and by July the fund was done! These guys had some nerve—when trouble began, the financial assets were as follows:

- $4.72 billion under management

- $124.5 billion in borrowed funds

- $129.0 billion in assets

- $1.25 trillion in off-balance sheetderivatives

Needless to say, hedge funds are risky ventures, but investors continue to fork over their dough and are willing to pay out 20 to 25 percent of profits as a service fee.

Outside of the stock market, paying such an exorbitant sum is called usury and outlawed in the 50 states. The Mafia couldn't have come up with a better business model. By the way, LTCM tried to make a comeback, even offering investors a chance to put in more money at a lower fee. Did I say these guys had nerve?

The Stock Market as a Casino

In addition to the increased volatility and volume in the stock market, the growth of hedge funds serves as a proxy for the gambling mentality that so many folks associate with the stock market. In this sense the stock market is what you make it. If you buy a stock and in your mind it "has to" make a major move the next day or within a matter of days, then you've turned the stock market into a casino. This is one reason I avoid asking people if they "play" the market. This short-term strategy rarely works. Unfortunately the mentality that a stock has to make money instantly is one of the major reasons why investors continue to lose in the stock market. It is the legacy of the easy money of the 1990s. Not only was ignorance bliss but it was very profitable, too.

Who didn't feel like a genius when stocks they owned were going up $10 a day? The crazy thing is you didn't have to know what the company did, whether it was profitable, or if it even had a product to begin with. We were all laughing our way to the bank and early retirement. It's nuts, but people who were burned severely by that line of thinking are coming back to the market and looking for stocks to pop immediately, and when that doesn't happen they are bailing.

Some of you don't believe you have a lot of money to invest. You think that you have to turn whatever you do have into something profitable quickly. Every time you take on a new position, it's like you're playing a hand of blackjack. The stock you buy dips, moving down let's say 5 percent, and you think it's time to bail and deal the next hand. Or the stock isn't sharply down but you've held it—or as one of my clients once told me, "carried it"—for a week, and other stocks were scoring blackjacks in the meantime, so you bail. This constant folding of hands, closing out positions that don't immediately go up or take too long to go up, is where the stock market becomes a casino.

This "buy and bail" mentality can be traced back to the high-flying 1990s when dips in share prices were reversed sometimes in an instant, and it became conventional wisdom that the market would always bail you out. In fact, taking profits became excruciatingly painful for you when the stock you sold was up big the next day.

So some of you simply stopped selling stocks. You didn't take mind-boggling profits while the stocks were zooming because they were only going to move higher anyway, right? When this same position began to slide like the snowball that rolls down the hill and becomes a boulder, you still didn't flinch. You had the confidence to handle significant paper losses, as the market would surely bail you out—after all, that was the modus operandi of the market at the time. But eventually the stock market stopped bailing out investors and significant losses became unfathomable losses. We saw the earth-shattering evaporation of trillions of dollars in equity losses by the end of 2002. The lesson most of you took away was never to be caught flat-footed in stocks again.

However, comparing then to now is an entirely different ball of wax. The problem back then was you were holding shares of companies that had no fundamental justification for their valuations—ever! These were pipe dreams, and when the goals of these companies weren't achieved, the dreams went poof! Thinking that you must bail on United Technologies (symbol UTX) because you once took a big hit on a dot-com stock is misguided thinking. You are once again victimizing yourself or being victimized by the past.

Now, one of my missions is to convince you that a 100-year-old railroad or a company with billions in sales isn't the same as a dot-com company with an operating history of just a couple of months. Sure, there were large-cap scandals that have also scared investors. Nobody born before 1980 will ever forget the names Enron or WorldCom. These were unique houses of cards deliberately manipulated to artificially inflate value.

The wreckage created by Ken Lay, CEO of (former) Enron, and Bernie Ebbers, CEO of (former) WorldCom, will live in the psyche of investors for years to come, probably decades. Now investors believe that no matter how large the company, it could come crumbling down. I don't think this is going to be the case in 99.99 percent of the cases. Even when there were waves of corporate malfeasance, the percentage of wrongdoers was a drop in the bucket compared to all the companies that followed and played by the rules.

These days the casino mentality also has a negative effect in the sense that investors are selling too soon, and once this becomes obvious the level of disgust for the stock market increases. I'm sure everyone reading this book has sold at least one stock too soon. While the pain isn't quite as severe as losing all your money, it is tough to watch a stock you took a loss on come roaring back, even if it's months or years after you took the hit. Bottom line, you feel burned. Protecting profits is important—in fact, preservation of capital is paramount and second only to our goal of making money. However, sound investments in the stock market move down in value from time to time, and there is simply nothing we can do about it, but we don't have to fold the hand if there is evidence that it could still become a winner.

The market doesn't have to be a casino. It doesn't have to be an endeavor that works out every day. The stock market won't work out every day. The stock market isn't a day trip to Las Vegas or Atlantic City. The optimum concept to remember is that you should be an investor for the long haul, and that requires time and patience. Not blindly believing, but believing in quality research.

Play-by-Play Announcers

We live in a world of instant analysis. Even though we know the guy with number three on his uniform missed the shot, we still need the folks calling the game to explain why one team won and one team lost. If something bothers us physically, we see a doctor and we're filling prescriptions by the end of the day. We need immediate explanations for everything, including the stock market. Of course when the market is going up we may skip the market wrap show, just as we don't see the doctor at all when we're feeling great. But when the stock market is going down, somebody better have an explanation, now!

The chore of explaining the stock market every day is one of the problems with the demand for intense media coverage. Every twist and turn of the market has to be explained as it happens, like play-by-play announcers explaining every step of a football game. While earnings and fulfillment of potential will ultimately dictate where a stock lands long term, the reality is that in the short term, the stock market is emotionally driven. Behind the often-tumultuous roller coaster ride is pure emotion, hype, or unrealistic expectations.

In the meantime the media will run with a dozen reasons why stocks are down, and it seems like every day by the time the closing bell rings there will be a consensus rationale.

The market was off today because corporate earnings were too strong.

The market was up today on strong corporate earnings.

The market fell after investors were spooked by economic data.

The market was off today on concerns of a weak economy.

The market was off today on concerns that the economy is too strong.

Higher oil prices help stocks to a big day.

Higher oil prices depress the stock market.

Stocks rally with rising gold and commodity prices.

Stocks crumble as commodity prices continue to soar.

The market stumbles after comments from a Federal Reserve member.

The market climbs higher after comments from a Federal Reserve official.

I think you get the message. Sometimes a strong economy moves the market higher and at other times it is considered the reason the market is moving lower. At the end of the day we are often left wondering what the heck is going on, as it could take weeks, even months, to understand the true message of the market. Unfortunately the media has daily deadlines, and we are often forced to accept an answer that is mostly boilerplate stuff and sometimes completely off the mark.

The Great Oracle

It's one thing when the market reacts emotionally to obvious events, but when the market begins to swirl, bounce, and sway and there isn't any obvious news, then the market is assuming its vital role as the great oracle of our society. The action in the stock market can be an indicator of things to come. Just as a nagging ailment could be the warning sign of a much more serious medical condition, sometimes the stock market predicts serious ailments in the economy. In the end, however, I stress the importance of knowing how well the companies in your portfolio are doing. The best way to do this is to monitor the financial health of a company through its quarterly financials, periodic industry news, and the progress of its main rivals.

I've outlined how everyone has profitable knowledge around him or her and how we all play a part in the stock market at all times. Often investors believe they're onto something but just don't know for sure. This brings us to the first step in understanding our investments in the stock market: fundamental analysis.

Judging a company through this method can be very intimidating. There are so many different ways to check under the hood. The big brokerage firms send teams to actually visit companies. They look at management and use an array of sophisticated tools to determine the fundamental worth of a company. Most investors realize they don't have the ability, money, or time for this kind of approach. Because it seems so intimidating, many investors just skip the fundamental analysis and rely solely on the charts, newsletters, or talking heads on television and radio. Some opt to just go with their gut.

One night in June 2005, I left my office on Broadway, just a couple of blocks from the New York Stock Exchange. As I walked down the street a guy from the phone company stopped me. He was a technician, working with a yellow tent and night lights. He recognized me from Fox News Channel and wanted to chat me up about the stock market. We talked and he was very knowledgeable, but what captured my attention were his comments on Corning Works. Corning is a 100-year-old company that at one time was known more for its decorative glassware than its telecommunications products. That all changed in the 1990s when the company began pumping out fiber optic equipment and became a darling of the fast money crowd.

In September 1998 the stock was trading just north of $7 a share, and by September 2000 the shares had peaked at $110 a share. Then the implosion began and the stock tumbled hard and fast, skidding all the way to $1.25 by October 2002. By the end of November, the shares were trading at $4.50. This is important to know because the worst quarter in the last five years for the company, at least with respect to total revenue, was the fourth quarter of 2002. By the time my new friend from the telephone company stopped me, Corning had reeled off 10 consecutive quarters of sequential revenue gains, beginning with the first quarter of 2003. Each month was better than the last. This was good stuff; this was a fundamental story that couldn't be ignored.

I already had clients in Corning. But after talking with the tech on Broadway I was weighing whether we should consider taking a profit. After all, the company's share price had exploded to \$16 from \$8 just months earlier. The key to this decision wasn't just about total revenue gains (also known as *top-line results*) but had more to do with earnings per share or bottom-line results. The telecommunications glut was massive by 2000 and it's still being worked off to this day. The result was incredible quarterly losses and historic write-offs by the stalwarts in the industry, Nortel and Lucent. Corning suffered through huge quarterly losses; in 2002 the company lost \$1.29 a share and in 2003 the company lost \$0.19 a share.

Earnings began to smooth out in 2005 and it was apparent management was gaining control of expenses; therefore they were able to bring more to the bottom line. I still have clients in Corning stock today. Table 1.2 shows the revenue history for Corning.

I knew Corning was a good stock that had paid a heavy price for being overvalued and suffered mightily from the glut in telecommunications equipment. At times many of you will come upon compelling situations and consider the investment opportunities therein. When this guy from the telephone company began telling me of all the money being spent, again, on certain telecommunications equipment, I had to take a closer look at the financials. This is what you're going to have to learn to do. Whether you passively invest through a 401(k) or you're an active trader, you must learn to evaluate the fundamentals to see if the greater story is already totally reflected in the share price. The fundamentals also serve as a scorecard on management's abilities, which isn't always reflected in the day-to-day movement of the price of the underlying stock.

TABLE 1.2   Corning (GLW) Revenue History

Revenue (in millions of dollars)	2002	2003	2004	2005
First quarter	\$839.0	746.0	844.0	1,050.0
Second quarter	762.0	752.0	971.0	1,141.0
Third quarter	752.0	772.0	1,006.0	1,188.0
Fourth quarter	736.0	820.0	1,033.0	1,200.0

Charts are great tools, but at the end of the day, one has to be able to quantify the potential of a company and the ability of management to reach that potential, by examining past results and making comparisons to the industry and to rivals in that industry, too.

Takeaways

The most important takeaways from this chapter are:

- You *are* the market, so get in the game and stop getting played.

- Pay attention to the world around you. You have special insights at work and at play—use them.

- There is always someone who thinks differently than you—sellers think buyers are stupid, and vice versa. At least try to understand the opposite position.

- The market is volatile, and stocks come down faster than they go up, so be ready to be shaken up but not necessarily shaken out.

- The game is rigged to take advantage of your emotions. To mitigate these emotions, you have to understand fundamentals.

Looking under the Hood

You Have to Know the Fundamentals

Contemplating the potential of a company doesn't have to be as difficult as solving a black belt Sudoku puzzle. The key is to look under the hood of a company and not just at the glitzy interior. Looking under the hood is known as *fundamental analysis* on Wall Street.

I spent my teenage years riding the subway system of New York to get around, so by the time I learned to drive a car and finally purchased one, I was too intimidated to look under the hood. I've been driving for over two decades now. I know how to check the oil and add windshield wiper fluid, but I'm still in the dark about engines, drive trains, and exhaust systems. Over those last two decades I bet I could have saved thousands of dollars if I'd known more about what's under the hood. Instead I have been victimized by repairmen and sales guys—I knew it, but there was nothing I could do about it.

Investors have a lot more at stake than the price of a used car and yet they continue to put themselves into a position to be victimized by the stock market. I'm not talking about unscrupulous operators touting shaky stock picks, or waiting for slow-moving Wall Street analysts to lead you down the right path (which is all too often too little too late). Most individual investors aren't making the money they should in the stock market because they're afraid to look under the hood.

Unfortunately, many individual investors don't use or understand fundamental research. They rely on charts, scuttlebutt from chat rooms, convictions based on fuzzy information like a positive article in a newspaper or magazine, or a good yarn from their drinking buddies. They *should* be looking at the *facts*—the trends and the abilities of management of the companies in their portfolio. By evaluating income statements, cash flow statements, and balance sheets you can better understand a company's ability to generate cash and profits (the ultimate goal of any business) and to compete with rivals to either take market share or protect it. At the end of the day, the success of the stock will depend on management's skill set in various economic conditions to deliver on promise. These elements are the underpinnings of fundamental analysis, and they can't be determined by looking at chart patterns.

Don't get me wrong—there is a place for technical analysis, the analyzing of charts to assist in investment decisions, but too many investors rely solely on charts. I see online brokerage firms touting their interactive charts as "research tools," and far too many investors believe that simply reading charts is doing research. Folks, you have to look under the hood of a company to understand its true value. The share price means nothing and the chart pattern will tell you more about the near-term parameters and possible ways the stock could break. As a self-directed investor, however, you must know the fundamentals.

I think fundamental work is fun: You learn so much about industries, the economy, and neat things about the future. Consider this: Trends in trucking tell us about spending habits at home and abroad. If steel companies are making money it's a reflection that the overall economy is doing very well, and it could have implications, good or bad (after all, if steel prices are higher, wouldn't that have an adverse effect on companies that make products that use a lot of steel?), for your portfolio.

Through fundamental analysis we can connect the dots and form an opinion on the broad economy and even micro niches of the economy. I know about movies, toys, and hip new products long before they come out, and sharing that information with my kids gives me a ton of cool points—not to mention this information gives me confidence to be an investor. In fact, one of the main goals of the book is to make you more of an investor, a person willing to hold a stock for more than 48 hours or through a down period for the share price. Knowing the fundamentals helps me see through the hype and avoid emotional mistakes.

The system I want to share with you in this book is how to do fundamental analysis to the point that you have a great handle on the business background of the stock you own. There are some forms of fundamental analysis that are extremely complicated. In fact, the trend on Wall Street is to make fundamental analysis more complex than it needs to be. For me, fundamental analysis tells me *what* to buy and technical analysis tells me *when* to buy. However, if you only use the charts to signal when you should be a buyer or seller, then you will take unnecessary losses in good companies and make the stock market a merry-go-round without cute horses and joyful smiles. There will always be angst when your portfolio is heading in the wrong direction, but in the long run few things feel worse than taking a hit on a stock that comes back, and then some.

After two decades of hand-holding, it is my mission to make sure investors (defined as people who plan to be engaged in the stock market for the rest of their lives) stop panicking so much that they take large losses on stocks that come back in short order. I'm not just talking about stocks roaring back days after you've taken a big hit, but hanging on to stocks that will rebound weeks and months after you could have taken a big financial hit. There are times to toss in the towel and there are times to hang on because the fundamentals are still intact and the company has the ability, and management the skills, to do wonderful things that will eventually be reflected into the share price.

The Importance of Fundamental Analysis

There was a surge of Americans into the stock market in the early 1990s. Throughout that decade, initially drawn by cheap commissions of discount brokers and later by the hope of making a lot of money in a short period of time, individual investors took the bull by the horns and changed the rules. In the late 1990s there was talk of a shift to a new paradigm. The shift covered almost every aspect of business life, from business models and growth strategies to investing techniques and investor expectations. Historically, a company would grow from a regional base and develop a set of expertise that could be employed throughout the country, or even throughout the world. This history became the basis for qualifying for listing on a public exchange. This long-term history also formed the fundamental foundation that continued when a company began trading.

With fundamental analysis you have a clear way of judging whether companies are overvalued or undervalued, based on absolute factors such as execution of the business model, how well they compete, and whether they make money. While there is no guarantee with any system of analysis in the stock market, knowing how well a company has done in the past and understanding how well it could do in the future is vitally important in a stock market that moves up and down, which is normal behavior.

The biggest and most persistent challenge to investors is knowing when to take a loss. All too often investors are willing to bail out of the market with large losses, simply because they have no conviction in their holdings. Your lack of conviction is mostly the result of the fact that you don't know the facts about the companies in your portfolio. Sure, you know what the company does, and you know the industry, but you don't know if their top-line growth is ahead of the industry average or below. You're not quite sure if their margins are growing. You're not sure if their margins are growing through organic means or through acquisitions.

I believe there is a place for charts in your investment decision-making process, but nothing beats understanding where a company stands from a business point of view. In my 20 years of helping investors on Wall Street, nothing burns me up more than when investors are victimized by the dips in stock prices when they should actually either be buyers or at the very least stay cool and let the dust settle and watch the stock rebound. The most commonly known Wall Street axiom is "Buy low and sell high," but these days too many folks head for the hills when the market begins to swoon.

The absolutely most difficult message I've ever tried to get across is to get folks to buy when the market is slumping. I understand the reason for fear. I know people are afraid to lose all their money. But these same people race to their local malls every time there is a sale. People see value in buying a sweater for $50 that only days earlier retailed for $100, but they shudder at the thought of buying a stock of a Fortune 500 company that is off by 50 percent.

Part of the fundamental story is the numbers. The numbers tell a tale, paint a picture of skill sets at a company. Charts, on the other hand, paint a picture of supply and demand for the stock at certain price points. The charts tell you very little about the company, but they can reflect investor fear and desire. Understanding fear and desire, or the emotional parameters, illustrated in charts is very important, because you'll understand the crowd but also be able to avoid the mistakes they make over and over again.

The Importance of Financial Releases

Recent insider trading scandals, poor and biased Wall Street research, and other negative events in corporate America have resulted in extremely emotional reactions to earnings releases. All publicly traded companies must file certain forms with the SEC in conjunction with various events. The 8K filing was for years just for general changes at the company, but now that form is the de facto earnings report. Officially the SEC form 10Q is designed specifically for quarterly earnings. (The fourth-quarter financial results are lumped in with the full-year results in the SEC form 10K.) While there is more detail in the 10Q, it is typically released weeks after the 8K and by that time the damage is done.

To get a company's financials, it is best to go through their web site. I often get to the home page or investor relations by going through Reuters (www.reuters.com) or Yahoo! Finance (http://finance.yahoo.com). Once you're on the company's web site, you will be able to see financial results as a news item or as part of the SEC filings previously mentioned. Keep in mind, when you are reading the financial results as part of a news release, there will be a lot of hype or soothing verbiage to mitigate disappointments and shortcomings. Investors may look at the same data and not come up with the share management's assessment. However, although companies can spin press releases, companies cannot spin the filings they submit to the SEC.

Most companies have a link to the SEC under their "investor" drop-down menu. There you will find a long list of filings, so make sure to go straight to "quarter results," or if you are looking for the 8K, look for the largest filing; otherwise you could spend a lot of time opening filings that you don't have time to read. I don't want you to be dissuaded from looking under the hood because you feel like you're wasting your time.

We will look at all the aspects of fundamental analysis and regularly scheduled financial releases, beginning with analyzing the income statement. Also known as the profit and loss statement (P&L), this report sums up the revenue, costs, expenses, and earnings for a company within a specific time period, normally a quarter (three months).

There are usually two versions of the income statement or one version with a lot of footnotes to denote the GAAP and non-GAAP aspects of the report. "GAAP" stands for generally accepted accounting principles. This term is used for financial reports that give investors all the data from events that occurred in a specific time frame (again, you want to be on top of your portfolio so you will always review the 8K and 10Q and 10K). These accounting principles are determined by the Financial Accounting Standards Board (FASB—I know, it seems like alphabet soup), an independent organization formed in 1973 to establish private sector standards for accounting. The SEC could actually establish its own standards but it recognizes the work of FASB instead. (By the way, when you're talking to an investment professional or trying to impress your friends in your investment club, FASB is pronounced "fas-bee.")

Although GAAP numbers are as close to an open kimono as we can come to seeing what occurred financially during a time period, most analysts eschew it for non-GAAP numbers. In fact, I do all of my earnings estimates in non-GAAP form. I know this seems odd in an era when full disclosure and a desire to turn over each rock is what everyone is after. However, GAAP results include nonrecurring events like charges associated with mergers, legal fees, and other one-time events that shouldn't happen again and probably didn't happen in the preceding quarter or the previous year (the most often used comparable period for assessing progress or lack thereof). Measuring comparable quarters is the best way to gauge the health of the business and management's ability to navigate and execute. Year-ago quarterly periods provide benchmarks, tests, and additional parameters that serve as the backdrop to assessing success or failure.

Although I prefer the non-GAAP numbers, this doesn't mean you shouldn't be vigilantly looking for frequently occurring, nonrecurring events and expenses. When you are comparing one quarter against another quarter (mostly year over year) you want to compare apples to apples, so one-time hiccups that are supposed to be anomalies are dismissed. But if the company has a lot of these anomalies, then maybe these events shouldn't be dismissed.

Let's Look at the Income (or P&L) Statement

The income statement illustrates the numeric changes in a company's business, beginning with sales and ending with profit or loss. It doesn't take into account intangible things like how much a company brand is worth or the value of that product in the lab that could be the best mousetrap ever invented and send the shares into a new orbit. But for my money the income statement is the first place to look and learn about the ability of the company to make money on a consistent basis. The income statement is all about how much money the company is making or losing, hence the name "profit and loss." For the purposes of this discussion, let's stick with quarterly periods.

Income statements come in many forms but essentially are one of two types:

- *Single-step income statements* simply subtract expenses from revenues to come up with a net income. See Table 2.1 for an example of this type of income statement.

- *Multiple-step income statements* provide a clearer view of operational success and failure, breaking out input from nonoperating activities. Table 2.2 shows an example of a multiple-step income statement.

It's not unusual for a company to have a unit that has been discounted but still continues to generate revenue. The same is true of certain investments and joint ventures in which the management

TABLE 2.1   Financial Results for Wyeth, Second Quarter of Fiscal Year 2006

In Thousands except Per Share Amount	March 2006	March 2005
Net sales	$4,837,937	$4,578,998
Cost of sales	1,337,118	1,349,457
Gross profits	3,500,819	3,229,541
Selling, general, and administrative expenses	1,464,596	1,452,681
Interest expense	5,513	29,999
Other income (expense)	(114,575)	(234,562)
Operating income	1,460,615	1,373,466
Provision for taxes	341,032	295,295
Net income	1,119,583	1,078,171
Diluted earnings per share	$0.82	$0.80
Average number of shares outstanding	1,372,567	1,357,143

plays no role in the decision-making process. While the revenue and expenses associated with such investments are part of the income statement, they aren't a part of the operational picture. Companies that employ multiple-step income statements do investors a big favor, especially when the information isn't flattering.

Net Sales or Total Revenue (Also Known as the Top Line)

Changes in net sales are driven by four factors. I've outlined them in order of importance:

1. Pricing power
2. Volume changes
3. Currency changes
4. Acquired sales versus organic sales

Pricing power should carry the most weight when considering a company's sales. A company's ability to raise prices speaks volumes for the company's products or services and also has the greatest impact on the bottom line. Don't ever forget that all we

TABLE 2.2   Financial Results for John Deere & Company, Second Quarter of Fiscal Year 2006

In Millions of Dollars except Per Share Amount	March 2006	March 2005
Net Sales and Revenue		
Net sales	$6,029.0	$6,019.2
Financial and interest income	416.9	341.9
Other income	115.6	79.7
Total revenue	6,561.5	6,440.8
Cost of sales	187.8	170.4
Gross profits	6,373.7	6,270.4
Selling, general, and administrative expenses	613.8	563.1
Interest expense	250.4	180.1
Other income (expense)	181.6	94.1
Operating income (income of consolidation group before income taxes)	785.2	887.4
Provision for taxes	269.9	294.4
Income of consolidated group	515.3	593.0
Credit	.2	.1
Other	1.5	6.2
Total	1.7	6.3
Income from continuing operations	517.0	599.3
*Income from discontinued operations	227.6	4.7
Net income	744.6	604.0
Diluted Per Share Data		
Continued operations	2.17	2.41
**Discounted operations	.96	.02
Net EPS	3.13	2.43

*On December 6, 2005, Deere sold its managed care subsidiary to United Health Care for $500 billion or a net gain of $350 million pretax and $225 million after tax. The deal closed on April 1, 2006, which is why the results were included.

**I find it interesting that the company sold its John Deere Health Care business unit, considering the $0.96 in earnings (the year-ago period doesn't include the same business unit) and the fact that earnings from continued operations actually declined to $2.17 from $2.41.

are looking for in the stock market are companies that are able to generate profits, preferably improving profits. If you invest $1,000 in a local pizzeria, your biggest question each month will be "How were the profits?" If there isn't anything unique about a product, there will not be any pricing power. This is why even the greatest companies must continue to come up with innovative new products. This is why every time you go to the supermarket, there is some 100-year-old product with a new and improved formula, or souped up with new fresh ingredients. The makers of these products can ask for and get higher prices.

Let's face it: How many blades in a single cartridge is Gillette going to foist on the public? Eventually they'll run out of room for more blades (I guess?), and then you can look forward to the debut of a straight razor that's the biggest thing since . . . well, the straight razor. As for shampoos, I'm looking for the one that has vitamins A, B, and C, vanilla extract, aloe, coconut oil, conditioning cream, and dandruff-fighting nanobots. Oh, and it has to be hypoallergenic. Once that product debuts, the next great leap will be shampoo made up of just soap—and we'll pay a premium for it.

Even that pizzeria is expected to see higher profits through price increases and, yes, through innovation. One day the pizzeria gets a license to put tables on the sidewalk, then it gets a new espresso machine, and later it offers delivery service. The bottom line *is* the bottom line, and the best way to get it growing is to be able to ask for and get higher prices.

Volume changes help to mitigate the lack of pricing power (of course when a company has both, it's Shangri-la). Volume is simply how much stuff was sold to meet demand. Often volume changes occur as a result of lower prices, which trigger greater demand. Say that pizza shop is selling pies at $5.00 each and typically selling 100 each day for a net profit of $1.00 for each pie. At the end of each day there is $100 in profits. Then management decides to sell the same pizzas for $4.50, reducing the profit on each to $0.50 (assuming ingredients, overhead, and other costs stay the same), but daily sales increase to 140 pies. At the end of the day there will be only $70 in profits. Sales volume would be higher by 40 percent, but profits would be down by 30 percent.

As you can see, volume changes are very important. However,

there will be times when the increased volume doesn't result in increased sales. When this happens it is obviously a red flag development. When evaluating income statements you have to be mindful of the type of business the company is in. Retail stores, gasoline stations, and restaurants are always opening new stores, so if you simply take net sales for the current period and measuring it against a prior period, the numbers will be skewed. Every year will see year-over-year increases in sales, and that is very misleading. In such cases it is important to measure same-store sales of stores or branches that were in place in the comparable period. To gauge the success of new stores, you'll have to see how much they were generating in sales in the past.

There comes a point in every great company where volume sales alone will dictate changes in net sales. The prices for computers, flat-screen televisions, and cell phones continue to drift lower, and that leaves the companies that manufacture them more vulnerable to changes in *cost of goods sold* (COGS).

Currency changes impact so-called multinational companies the most. Companies that sell their products and services around the world are impacted by the fluctuation of the U.S. dollar and other currencies. In its fiscal year 2005, which ended on May 31, 2006, FedEx generated $22.1 billion in revenue in the United States and $7.2 billion internationally. Both sources of revenue grew at 19 percent year over year, but it is more likely that in the near future the rate of revenue growth will be greater from international business than domestic for the Tennessee-headquartered courier. You can be sure there are a lot of people working for the company whose job is strictly to watch the changes in the foreign currency market (known as the FX market and significantly richer in value than the U.S. stock market). Some even trade currency to mitigate the wild swings in relationships between other currencies and the U.S. dollar.

This stuff is critical because it affects the top line. Here's how it works. FedEx makes a sale in Europe and the customer pays in euros. Those euros are eventually exchanged for dollars. If the dollar is weaker than the euro, then FedEx will actually get more dollars and bolster total revenues.

When you are doing your fundamental homework, always be sure to measure revenue in what is known as *constant currency*.

This is an apples-to-apples comparison of foreign revenue, assuming that currency exchange rates haven't changed. Every business would love to be able to sell its products and services around the world; as an investor, however, you must make sure that top-line growth reflects a real demand in those products and services and not a quirk in the currency market.

Acquired growth is different from *organic growth*. Just as it is obvious that total revenues will grow for businesses that open more outlets or branches over the course of time, so too will total revenues grow for companies that make acquisitions. Acquired growth refers to business acquired during the previous 12 months. Growth through takeovers can expedite a company's long-term business game plan, but all things being equal, you want to focus on organic growth when examining one quarter's results versus a past quarter's result.

Obviously you are going to take into account the impact of acquisitions as they pertain to future potential, both problems and profitability. If you've ever bought a used car, you have experienced the problems of dealing with someone else's headaches. Of course it's more complicated than that in the corporate world. When one company takes over another, it must tackle the following issues and more.

CLASH OF CULTURES Usually the company that's acquired will have a lot of unhappy employees; a lot of their friends will be fired, and they'll lose status in the new organizational chart. Additionally, every company has its own quirky and unique culture that is often the soul that makes it successful. When that soul is erased, the deal loses its value. The interesting thing about culture is it can't be measured or quantified.

There was a serious culture clash when Daimler-Benz took over Chrysler. Only after the deal was complete did a German executive remark to a reporter that the deal wasn't a merger (of equals), a suggestion that must have been a rude awakening for many Chrysler executives.

Another major boondoggle was the takeover of Time Warner by America Online (AOL). Not only was AOL a smaller company in terms of market value, but its true assets were in cyberspace while Time Warner was a brick-and-mortar behemoth that had been around for decades. To this day there is a bitter taste in the mouths of Time Warner employees, who watched their hard work given away for nothing. Jack of "Jack and the Beanstalk" fame got a better deal.

CREATING VALUE Many deals are done simply to increase production of products and services using economies of scale, but this is a lot easier said than done. I've never been a big fan of deals made simply to save money. They call it synergy on Wall Street—putting two pieces together with the outcome of lower costs and greater value. In some ways one would assume that these deals would take two companies and morph them into a larger, more streamlined company. The reality is that too many deals end up being like two guys chained together, like Tony Curtis and Sidney Poitier in *The Defiant Ones*, where two men with total disdain for one another escape from a chain gang, shackled together, their common interest propelling them toward a unified goal but their mutual hatred holding them back at the same time.

When you're assessing acquisitions, don't be distracted by large numbers. So what if the company earned $1 billion more in the most recent quarter versus the year-ago period, if the net margin decreased to 9 percent from 12 percent.

How to Read the Top Line

Ever own a stock and the company reports what look like blowout total revenue numbers? That's because the numbers mean nothing in absolute terms. The key is the *quality* of the number. Following are some guidelines for putting these numbers in context:

- Companies with pricing power rule. These companies command higher valuation multiples. Quality revenue numbers begin with the ability to raise prices and not negatively impact demand.

- Rapid organic growth will be rewarded, while acquired growth can bog a company down and more often than not put the company in a position of having to prove itself to the Street. The prevailing wisdom is that the company being acquired couldn't cut it alone, or that the company making the purchase has an

Achilles' heel (or two) that management couldn't fix without an expensive patch.

- Volume growth is fine, but if it's the result of lower prices and not end-user demand, then the results will get a cold shoulder from Wall Street. Sure, every business wants to increase volume—just make sure of the reason for any increase.

- Don't be fooled by results skewed by fluctuations in currency. Know how large a company's global footprint is and take that into account when evaluating the top line. Remember: The weak dollar actually helps multinationals while a strong dollar hurts them.

Costs of Sales

After we get the total revenue number we look at costs of sales. Cost of goods (also know as cost of goods sold, or COGS) refers to the amounts spent to generate products and services, including raw materials, labor, energy, inventory, and in some cases amounts paid to suppliers of products sold. Costs of goods sold reflect macroeconomic trends such as the increase or decrease in commodities that go into the production of steel, packaging (paper and plastic), and other materials that go into making the finished goods that are the source of revenues. While it is incumbent upon management to be able to contain costs, there is often little that can be done to effectively combat rising commodities costs. There are ways to hedge fuel costs through futures contracts, and there are ways to get suppliers to share the burden of rising prices, but in the end companies have to be able to increase volume and pricing at a faster rate then the increase of COGS.

I've said this before (and throughout the book I'll say it again), but the goal of every company is to produce *improving* profits. Being able to hold down COGS is the best way to create profit momentum for the rest of the income statement.

Gross Income

Gross income is the amount of revenue remaining from sales minus COGS. From the gross profit we gleam gross margin. You get the gross margin by dividing gross profits into net sales. The gross margin should be higher year over year and, unless the company in question is affected by seasonal shifts in demand, it is desirable that gross margin also increase quarter over quarter.

Expenses

Now we're getting into the nitty-gritty. This is where management gets to show its stuff. Being blessed with riches is one thing; sometimes it could be just a matter of being in the right place at the right time. How many stories have we read about the lottery winner who eventually lost it all, and then some? How many formerly hot companies can't seem to get it together now? (Hint: Take out one of your brokerage statements from January 2000; I'm sure it's littered with a bunch of companies that were in the right place at the right time and are now stuck in the mud or in some cases slowly sinking in quicksand.) Potential is great, but turning it into something long-lasting and special takes skill.

How companies handle expenses says a lot about the foresight of management and their collective courage. When we see how a company handles its operating expenses, we either gain confidence or lose confidence in the broader vision.

Summary of expenses:

- Selling, general, and administrative (SGA) expenses get to the heart of the matter: Are white-collar workers making too much money? Does it cost more to get would-be buyers of a company's product in the door? And how creative is management when it comes to finding less expensive ways to communicate in general? Ideally this line should show year-over-year improvement all the time. There is a relative factor, too, where macro forces make lower SGA costs impossible. At such times it's important to see that the company is still doing better than its peers at containing these costs.

- Research and development (R&D) spending should remain strong at all times. When it begins to fade, it means management is too concerned about making a quarterly earnings estimate rather than putting pieces into place for long-term growth. I love higher R&D spending, but also be mindful of the company that wasted a lot of time, lost market share in the process, and only then began to spend more to create new products, medical cures, and therapies.

- Depreciation and amortization mark the natural decline of equipment (bought for use of one year or longer) experienced by all businesses as well as consumers (your toaster loses a fraction of value every day).

SELLING, GENERAL, AND ADMINISTRATIVE EXPENSES There are numerous lines in the expense portion of the income statement. Some are industry-specific, like fuel costs for transportation companies, but all contain selling, general, and administrative outlays.

SGA costs include all direct and indirect expenses such as advertising, rent, heat, electricity, telephone, and postal. This line also includes salaries of nonsales personnel. This is the first place a company looks to cut costs. This is also the first place to see if companies are spending too much money on salaries and other executive compensation. There is no way the SGA line should grow faster than the total revenue.

RESEARCH AND DEVELOPMENT (R&D) In business, it's all about innovation. The new thing is vital to the growth of any business. Remember that pizzeria at the beginning of the chapter? It has to come up with new products and new ways to make existing products more attractive. There are certain industries where the clock begins to tick on the profitability shelf life of a product the day it's created. The pharmaceutical industry lives and dies by its pipeline of new products. Once a drug is developed, the patent lasts for a certain number of years, and then anyone in the game can make the same drug—and of course, they do, for a lot less money (and a lot lower profit margin). Hence, the generic drug industry is a billion-dollar business, but even the most successful generic drug players are now creating proprietary drugs—their own in-house cures and treatments. Technology is another area where research and development are paramount.

Sadly, U.S. companies have cut back tremendously on R&D in the past six years. I mentioned courage, and this is an area where it really shows up. The circus mentality associated with making the consensus earnings estimate has forced many managers into tepid distribution of funds for capital projects and R&D. A company that makes the consensus number but does so by cutting R&D should be judged suspect.

DEPRECIATION AND AMORTIZATION   In accounting terms, depreciation and amortization are a way to assign the periodic cost of long-term investments (mostly equipment that is designed to last longer than a year and is known as fixed assets). Businesses are expected to make large investments to facilitate their ability to create products. Instead of having the entire amount of the fixed asset investment weigh on a single quarterly time period, businesses are allowed to spread the costs over a longer period of time.

Depreciation of fixed assets involves a fair amount of guesswork as to how long the equipment will last, so this line comes under scrutiny from investment purists from time to time. Once values and timetables have been established, however, there shouldn't be major changes and this line should be easy to use in making assumptions for future earnings outcomes.

OTHER EXPENSES AND INTEREST   There are a myriad of additional expenses that don't fit neatly under SGA or R&D. These expenses are often temporary, and one must try to be clear on how long they will be prevalent, which could be done through reading the notes in the filing, listening to the conference call (more on that later), or even contacting the company (you should be on the mailing list of all the companies whose stocks are in your portfolio). The main things to look for with any expense are that it's moving lower and is less than the industry average.

Operating Income

Operating income, in a nutshell, is the gross margin minus operating expenses. This is the single most important line in the income statement. In my mind this is the most important information in the entire financial statement. While the earnings per share gets all the ink and occasionally total revenue gets a share of the spotlight, too, the greatest financial correlation to direction of a company's share price is the direction of operating margin, which is operating income dividend into total revenue.

PROVISION FOR TAXES You may think the effective tax rate is a foregone conclusion and there is nothing there to help assess the skill set of management, but you'd be very wrong. Tax rates change from community to community and even within a specific community. According to an article in the May 18, 2004, *Washington Post*, corporate taxes, as a percentage of all federal taxes paid in 2003, were only 7.4 percent, versus 32 percent back in 1952. In fact, for that year corporate taxes were just 1.2 percent of the gross domestic product (GDP), down sharply from 6 percent in the 1950s.

While the U.S. tax code may be the most complicated set of standards about anything, anywhere, there are so many loopholes that it is almost a sin when corporations can't figure out how to take advantage. In addition to the loopholes there has been an array of tax breaks that saved corporations billions of dollars a year. Politically sensitive industries like industrial and farm equipment makers have received incredibly large tax breaks over the years. Without a doubt, tax breaks are the area in which lobbyists have proven most successful, as industries like military, telecom, transportation, and aerospace have extracted huge tax breaks.

Large corporations are increasingly moving their operations and profit centers to nations that are extremely tax friendly. Those nations include:

- The Netherlands
- Ireland
- Bermuda
- Luxembourg

Of course there is an unpatriotic aspect to a U.S. company moving jobs and financial opportunity offshore just to lower taxes. There was a great backlash against companies that engaged in this practice in 2003 and 2004. Now the ruckus has faded, but the anger from the general public will not go away because there is a feeling that companies trying to do the right thing (keep jobs in America) are getting shafted. On the other hand, shareholders typically care about the bottom line and want to see companies lower their effective tax rates. It is a sad reality that frequently Wall Street applauds and rewards things that are repulsive to Main Street. So outsourcing is here to stay.

From a fundamental point of view, companies that are able to lower their tax rates will be rewarded.

Net Income

Net income is the amount left after subtracting expenses and taxes from total revenue. This is the proverbial bottom line. This is where the buck stops! Ideally the year-over-year change in net income should be greater than the year-over-year change in total revenue, gross profits, and operating profits. *Net income is more important than earnings per share* because the amount of shares outstanding fluctuates from period to period.

Table 2.3 shows three companies that reported earnings around the same date for the same quarter, which ended on March 31, 2006. Only one company in the table saw earnings per share improve at a better rate year over year than net income. Of course that company was McDonald's. Care to guess which of these stocks opened lower and continued moving south?

- Weatherford was up 4 percent 24 hours after reporting its financial results.

- Nutrisystems' stock climbed to $68 from $50 the day after its earnings were released, an increase of 36 percent.

- McDonald's shares closed down 2 percent.

TABLE 2.3   Three Kinds of Fundamental Stories

Year-over-Year Change	Weatherford (WFT)	Nutrisystems (NTRI)	McDonald's (MCD)
Revenue	79%	293%	6%
Operating income	145%	552%	2%
Net income	152%	597%	−14%
Earnings per share	111%	500%	−12.3%

I'm sure you've owned shares of a company that posted earnings that on the surface seemed disappointing or fantastic, and yet the reaction in the stock was the exact opposite of what you thought it would be. Keep in mind that once a company has been cast into a certain category, it has a different set of parameters that determine whether a quarter was good or not.

Weatherford was expected to post strong earnings because crude oil prices were higher. The company delivered.

Nutrisystems is a super-hot growth stock and was expected to deliver outsized earnings per share growth. The company delivered and then some.

McDonald's has been around a long time and isn't a growth company anymore, so there aren't high expectations for significant earnings per share growth. Therefore, when the company comes up short of those expectations, the share usually pays a heavy price. Having said that, the stock is rewarded for the kind of growth that would sink a Weatherford or Nutrisystems, and in fact, as the company executed better in 2006, its share price began to take off.

A Closer Look at the Balance Sheet

The balance sheet is designed to give investors a clear idea as to the actual worth of a company. Assets are measured and counted, then liabilities are subtracted, resulting in *net worth* or *shareholder equity*. While the income statement tells you whether the company is a thoroughbred, the balance sheet gives you a look at the actual health of that thoroughbred.

Assets

The first half of the balance sheet lists assets, beginning with actual liquid assets, then hard assets, followed by so-called intangible assets. Figure 2.1 shows an example of the assets part of a balance sheet. The following sections examine each entry. *Total assets* means all assets combined—current, long term, and intangible.

CURRENT ASSETS *Cash and cash equivalents* refer to cash (of course) and assets that can be quickly converted to cash (within three

Assets (in Millions of Dollars)	April 1, 2006	December 31, 2005
Current assets		
Cash and cash equivalents	$204.9	$657.8
Accounts and notes receivable	782.4	609.6
Inventories	548.5	460.7
Other current assets	90.5	84.2
Assets held for sale	3.4	13.3
Total current assets	1,629.7	1,825.6
Property, plant, and equipment	1,536.1	1,297.0
Less accumulated depreciation	1,044.7	829.9
	491.4	467.1
Goodwill	969.0	740.9
Trademarks	296.8	119.2
Customer relationships	166.2	157.6
Other intangible assets	60.3	42.7
Other assets	184.5	192.0
Total assets	**$3,797.9**	**$3,545.1**

FIGURE 2.1   Assessing the Assets

months or less), such as stocks, bonds, Treasury bills, certificates of deposit, money market funds, and funds in checking accounts.

Cash is obviously important, and I prefer to see a company be able to grow its business, invest in research and development, and make capital expenditures, and still grow its cash. The interesting aspect of balance sheets is the varying importance of each line depending on industry. Ideally, the larger the percentage of cash and cash equivalents of total current assets, the stronger the company is financially.

Accounts and notes receivable represents money owed to a company for goods or services provided. Credit sales produce invoices, notes, and statements, which become part of the accounts receivable balance. These are assets, but if an account receivable lingers too long, it ultimately has to be written off as an expense. Following are some rules of thumb:

■ Accounts receivable should grow at a slightly faster pace than total revenue.

- Accounts receivable should grow at a pace faster than inventories.

- Accounts receivable that have been on the books for three quarters or more have to be considered suspect.

- *Days sales outstanding* (DSO) shouldn't be more than 30 days, although this number could vary from industry to industry.

- Accounts receivable that represents more than 15 percent of the total assets should be examined closely for the history of such an occurrence and frequency of payment.

Inventories are goods owned by the company that haven't been sold yet. These goods (merchandise) are considered assets because it is assumed they will be sold in a short period of time.

Some of the risks of inventories are obsolescence and spoilage. In the case of the former, industry innovation could devalue products as they sit in warehouses; and in the case of the latter, certain items are perishable and must be sold fast.

You want inventories to gradually increase as a sign that management expects an increase in demand and wants to be able to meet that demand. Even in this era of just-in-time manufacturing (made popular by Dell Computer and used in every industry), it is important to have products available to immediately meet demand. By the same token, *it is always unnerving and raises a red flag when the growth rate of inventories is rising faster than the growth rate of accounts receivable.*

Inventories are broken down into three components:

1. *Raw materials* include the stuff used to make products such as steel. This is a great way to measure the impact of higher commodities. It should also be noted that when there are uncomfortable levels of inventory buildup because of higher raw materials prices it is less of a sin than if the buildup is the result of a backlog of actual raw materials at similar or lower prices than in the year-ago period.

2. *Work in process* (WIP) denotes the fact that the raw material is in the system and the products are being made. There should be a correlation between percentage changes in WIP and raw materials. If raw materials values decline and WIP doesn't, it could point to problems in the manufacturing process. Con-

versely, WIP that declines even as raw materials are increasing points to better manufacturing efficiency.

3. *Finished goods* are products ready for sale right now. It goes without saying that there mustn't be a buildup of this stuff!

Other current assets are noncash assets such as long-term receivables and prepaid expenses that convert within one year. This category could also include assets from discontinued operations. *Assets held for sale* refers to noncurrent assets that management is committed to selling. The company anticipates that these assets will be sold in less than a year.

We take all of these components, add them together, and come up with *total current assets*.

LONG-TERM ASSETS *Property, plant, and equipment* (PPE), obviously, refers to fixed assets such as buildings, vehicles, fruit-bearing trees, animals, land, and machinery. It also includes certain tools and furniture. Just think of things that will be around longer than one year. We take these items and subtract accumulated depreciation (already accounted for on the income statement) for a total PPE.

By the way, noncash (and cash equivalent) assets all depreciate or lose value over time—except land, which may explain why so many wars in the history of mankind have been fought over it. Most companies use what is known as the *straight-line method* to calculate depreciation. This takes the so-called *residual value* (also known as *salvage value*), which is the value of an item down the road after it's been used, and subtracts it from the cost of the item; the difference is divided into a particular time frame.

INTANGIBLE ASSETS Intangible assets, also known as *soft assets*, can't always be quantified or even seen, but they are there and their value is evident. Over years, a business develops a reputation for quality (or at least they're always telling us so in commercials, such that we finally buy into the notion). That reputation can't be quantified, but it is valuable. This is even more the case for name recognition. Why could McDonald's command so much more than Johnny Rockets as a franchise? Let's face it, McDonald's is well known, and when those doors open for business there won't have to be a lot of coaxing (unless people have seen that documentary about the guy who ate McDonald's exclusively for a month).

Intangible assets include:

- *Goodwill* (for businesses employing the purchase method of accounting) is the excess dollar value the acquiring company pays over the book value of the acquired company. This excess or premium paid is carried on the books as an asset that amortizes over a 40-year period.

- *Trademarks* are names, pictures, logos, or other identifiers of a company that have been seared into our brains. They have entered into our subconscious so firmly that if we fell off a bicycle and forgot the names of our family members, we'd still know the trademark of most Fortune 500 companies. It's an intangible asset for sure, but one that has been bought and paid for, generally through years of marketing and product sales.

- *Customer relationships, other intangible assets,* and *other assets* reflect the value of such things as customer satisfaction, which, at the end of the day, is the ultimate measuring stick of business success.

Liabilities and Shareholder Equity

In general, financial liabilities are obligations and debts that must be paid back within a specific period of time. These debts are owed to creditors, which gives the creditors claims on assets. This is why creditors get paid before shareholders when there is a company bankruptcy or liquidation. Figure 2.2 shows the liabilities for Stanley Works in April 2006.

CURRENT LIABILITIES *Current liabilities* are debts and obligations that a company must pay within a one-year period, including short-term loans; accounts payable; dividends; interest payable; bond payments; and reserves for tax payments, including payroll, interest, and federal taxes. For the most part, current liabilities are the antithesis of current assets.

Short-term borrowing (also known as *notes payable*) is a way for

Liabilities (in Millions of Dollars)*	April 1, 2006	December 31, 2005
Current liabilities		
Short-term borrowing	$300.1	$148.1
Current maturities of long-term debt	100.6	22.1
Accounts payable	411.0	327.7
Accrued expenses	464.5	374.3
Liabilities held for sale	NA	3.1
Total current liabilities	1,276.2	875.3
Long-term debt	821.3	895.3
Other liabilities	373.4	329.6

*Actual filing from Stanley Works.

FIGURE 2.2   Liabilities

companies to raise money to meet working capital challenges or to take advantage of business opportunities—for instance, to build inventory that would allow a company to meet short-term demand for products. If the dollar value of this line is larger than the cash and cash equivalent line on the asset portion of the balance sheet, you should be worried. If the amount is larger than cash and accounts receivable, it is a clear red flag, a reason to head for the hills.

Short-term borrowing is usually billed by way of written notes, which make collection easier and provide legal record keeping. In addition to bank loans, short-term borrowing can be achieved through T-bills and commercial paper.

Current maturities of long-term debt are the current portion of debt that must be paid.

Accounts payable obligations are monies owed by the company for goods or services received from other vendors, who invoice the company for the amounts due. Obviously it is preferable to have lower accounts payable obligations than account receivables.

Accrued expenses are the opposite of prepaid expenses as they accumulate over a period of time and must be paid out in the near future (typically in less than one year). Such payments may include earned wages of employees who haven't yet been paid and the taxes on those wages.

The total *current liabilities* figure is the sum of all current liabilities listed above it and occasionally other entries, too.

Working capital is the net of current assets minus current liabilities. This figure is extremely important in assessing a company's financial health. Suffice it to say that without solid working capital, a company would have to raise money by borrowing, which would be expensive and add debt or be dilutive. But you don't want to see working capital increase—instead, you want to see it gradually working its way lower.

LONG-TERM LIABILITIES *Long-term debt* refers to obligations that must be paid beyond a one-year period. The majority of long-term debt comes from payments on the principal of bonds previously issued by the company, but also includes long-term credit arrangements with financial institutions, private placement, income taxes, and pension obligations. Most of this debt involves interest payments, monies paid for the privilege of borrowing above the principal amount borrowed.

Other liabilities are an assortment of liabilities that are rolled into one component of the balance sheet. These could include sales tax or borrowing between various segments within the same company.

SHAREHOLDER EQUITY Shareholder equity is the amount left over after all creditors and outstanding debts are paid. In effect this is what the shareholders own; it is their collective equity in the company. Figure 2.3 shows the shareholder equity filing for Stanley Works. It includes these elements:

- *Common stock par value* is the dollar each share of common stock would fetch from the company should there be liquidation. These funds are part of the original monies raised when the company initially went public.

- *Retained earnings* are the accumulated profits that haven't been paid out as a dividend or used to repurchase common stock in the open market.

Shareholder Equity (in Millions of Dollars)*	April 1, 2006	December 31, 2005
Common stock par value $2.50 per share	$237.7	$237.7
Retained earnings	1,679.0	1,657.2
Accumulated other comprehensive loss	(81.6)	(91.3)
ESOP	(106.4)	(108.2)
	1,728.7	1,695.4
Less cost of common stock in treasury	401.7	250.5
Total shareholder's equity	1,327.0	1,444.9
Total liabilities and shareholder equity	$3,797.9	$3,545.1

*Actual filing from Stanley Works.

FIGURE 2.3   Shareholder Equity

- *Accumulated other comprehensive loss or gains* come from, among other sources, deferred gains or losses on hedges on cash flow, unrealized gains and losses on available-for-sale securities, and pension liability.

- *Employee stock option programs* allow for the purchase of the company's common stock that has been authorized but is not yet issued.

Total liabilities and shareowners' equity should be a dollar amount equal to total assets—hence the term *balance sheet*.

Cash Flow Statement

This statement measures cash that enters and leaves a company. I'm sure you've heard the old saying, "Follow the money trail." The cash flow statement is the way investors can follow the money trail. Through this document investors get a clear understanding of where cash is coming from and how it's being distributed. There is also an old saying that goes back long before there were cash flow statements or quarter financial reporting: "Cash is king." Ultimately a company's goal is to generate cash.

By the way, the term *cash flow* has been butchered and misused for a long time. Its misuse began with the so-called New Paradigm of the 1990s when companies with zero earnings needed to justify astronomical valuations.

I'm sure you remember when scores of publicly traded companies saw their stock trading at more than $100 a share. Many of those companies had no sales, but what was more shocking was they didn't have a road map to ever achieve earnings. The fact of the matter is companies were discouraged from generating earnings. It was all about raising more money to pursue that dream of a better mousetrap, or software program, or contraption that would revolutionize the world. (We got caught up in that mind-set, too, at Wall Street Strategies, raising money to build a wonderful headquarters across the street from Goldman Sachs. We were trying to raise $10 million when the market imploded. Our fortunes went spiraling down, too, and we struggled over the next four years to survive.)

So the 1990s brought us a new view of cash flow, using *earnings before interest, taxes, depreciation, and amortization* (EBITDA). In other words, EBITDA was cash, and all the other stuff such as working capital, debt payments, and entrenched business obligations, as well as capital spending, didn't matter and weren't calculated. Neither were accounts receivable taken into consideration. Yet this acronym became the de facto cash flow and the key metric in valuing businesses and their potential. I bought into the notion hook, line, and sinker, because I had to. As a result, we were exiting stocks thinking we had made a killing, only to watch them soar higher. We all know Wall Street bought into the game, not so much because they really believed but because the environment was such that business had to continually go to the well to raise more and more money.

There are really two cash flows that count: cash from operations (my favorite) and free cash flow. Cash from operations takes into account elements from the income statement and balance sheet (see Figure 2.4). This portion of the cash flow statement begins with *net income* directly off the income statement—that's where it all starts. Also there is an accounting for *depreciation and amortization*. Remember, these aren't cash items; they are assumptions of value that are subtracted from sales on the income statement, so they are added back on the cash flow statement.

There are also adjustments made for accounts receivable (AR), which affects cash in certain ways. When AR increases, that means the company is actually getting less cash; when AR decreases, there is more cash. Inventory affects cash, too, depending on how it's

Cash from Operating Activities (in Millions of Dollars)*	March 31, 2006	March 31, 2005
Net income	$275.1	$450.1
Depreciation and amortization	261.0	192.0
Changes in operating working capital	(9.1)	(81.4)
Deferred income tax provision	(80.4)	11.1
Net losses on asset dispositions	63.9	3.5
Equity company's earnings in excess of dividends paid	(37.7)	(33.6)
Post-retirement benefits	3.3	29.0
Other	42.8	37.7
Total cash provided by operations	518.9	608.4

*Actual filing from Kimberly-Clark.

FIGURE 2.4 Cash from Operations

paid for. If inventory is paid for with credit, there is more cash available, and vice versa.

When assets are sold, it impacts the cash flow statement; otherwise it isn't factored at all. Since assets begin to depreciate the moment they are purchased (think of your car), they are sold at a loss.

Other lines under "Operating Activities" are self-evident. The tally gives us cash provided (or used) by operations. *When cash from operations declines from one comparable period to the next, it is a serious red flag.*

INVESTMENT ACTIVITIES   Investment activities measure how a company uses its cash to generate future cash (see Figure 2.5). Essentially a company will invest cash into investments designed to generate future sales, or in investments that will generate cash inflows in the form of dividends and note payments.

Capital spending represents larger, long-term investments such as a building or plant from which the company believes it will be able to produce more goods and therefore more sales and profits.

I mentioned free cash flow earlier, and this is where you get to calculate this all-important metric. Cash from operating activities minus capital spending gives you free cash flow. This is the real

Investment Activities (in Millions of Dollars)	March 31, 2006	March 31, 2005
Capital spending	(179.1)	(108.9)
Proceeds from sales of investments	8.5	10.5
Net decrease (increase) in time deposits	32.6	(17.4)
Investments in marketable securities	(7.1)	—
Other	1.4	(12.1)
Total cash used for investing	(143.7)	(127.9)

FIGURE 2.5   Investment Activities

bottom line. We've taken earnings and made adjustments for working capital, taxes, and other investments. Many Wall Street analysts consider the trends in free cash flow to be the holy grail of a company's value. Obviously it's important, but I think cash from operating activities is more important because I think businesses should be rewarded for investing in the business. However, that doesn't discount free cash flow, which doesn't take into account the service payment obligations for debt. I simply think of one measure as "1" and the other as "1A."

Other components of investment activities include proceeds from sales of investments, net decrease (or increase) in time deposits, and investments in marketable securities.

FINANCING ACTIVITIES   This portion of the cash flow statement reflects the flow of monies raised and monies owed to investors. Monies raised are called *cash in* whereas monies paid out in dividends or the repurchase of stock as well as payments of notes are called *cash out*. See Figure 2.6 for an example.

In addition to the income statement, balance sheet, and cash flow statement, financial filings offer details on the sources of revenue, either through various business segments or geographically, or both. Moreover, these filings also include management's discussion and analysis of financial condition and results of operations (MD&A).

MANAGEMENT'S DISCUSSION AND ANALYSIS OF FINANCIAL CONDITION AND RESULTS OF OPERATIONS   Although it only seems like the SEC

Financial Activities	March 31, 2006	March 31, 2005
Cash dividends paid	(208.6)	(194.2)
Net (decrease) increase in short-term debt	(25.7)	301.5
Proceeds from issuance of long-term debt	2.2	—
Repayments of long-term debt	(16.5)	(84.5)
Proceeds from exercise of stock options	63.2	67.0
Acquisitions of common stock for treasury	(152.2)	(321.9)
Other	(15.6)	(3.3)
Total cash used for financing	(353.2)	(235.4)
Effect of exchange rate changes on cash and cash equivalents	3.2	(5.6)
Increase in cash and cash equivalents	25.2	239.5
Cash and cash equivalents, beginning of period	364.0	594.0
Cash and cash equivalents, end of period	$389.2	$833.0

FIGURE 2.6 Financial Activities

has demanded accountability from management in recent years, the MD&A originated in 1968 and was expanded in 1980 and 1989. As the name implies, this is a wide-ranging discussion of financial statements that covers capital, liquidity, cash flow, and sales trends.

Between 2000 and 2004 a ton of companies opted not to give earnings guidance; many cited a lack of so-called visibility. The reality was that most had no clue, and those that did have a clue didn't want to share the dismal news. I'm always concerned when management can't see as far as the current quarter or doesn't have the nerve to toss out a number, even if it's frowned upon by the Street.

I strongly urge you to listen to the conference calls of the companies in your portfolio. Most of the calls follow the same pattern: Management will recite verbatim the press release portion of the earnings release and bring a bunch of people on stage to go over the numbers that are also in the filing. If you are pressed for time or prone to suicide when boredom sets in, one shortcut would be to skip straight to the question-and-answer period. Although Wall Street analysts should do a much better job than they do, these men and women know the industry (and company) better than you do, so piggyback off their questions during the Q&A session, which is the last portion of the call. Make sure you've gone through the filings and the worksheets in the next chapter before listening to the call, to make sure your questions are asked and answered, too.

Summary of Fundamentals

Understanding fundamentals is the first step toward developing a portfolio that allows you to sleep at night. The things that seem to excite the Street alternate from time to time, but the era of companies without any earnings making mind-boggling moves is over for the foreseeable future. These days the stocks that rally the most are from companies that can:

- Grow the top line via organic growth.

- Expand margins, most importantly operating margins (this is the most important line on the income statement and the best way to assess the ability of management to execute).

- Grow earnings.

- Generate cash from operations.

- Generate free cash.

- Collect on accounts and keep inventories lean.

Perhaps the biggest reason to understand the fundamentals is so you know what to buy and, more important, what to hold. For all the bluster about being a trader or using firm stop-losses, your account would be much better off if you had held a lot of the stocks that you sold when the broad market looked vulnerable.

Selling at the wrong time happens more often than not because people don't know the facts of a company. Quick, can you tell me if the companies in your current portfolio are increasing operating margins? Are they taking market share in their particular industry? Is the top line growing organically and is it growing at the same pace it grew at a year ago or two years ago?

Taking a Company's Temperature

Now it's time to take the temperature of your investments in the stock market by assessing quarterly financial reports. My main goal is to get you into the habit of taking down factual data and analyzing it in hopes that you will stop being victimized by the volatility of the market and instead will have the confidence to ride out the wild waves driven by the emotions of the crowds. You cannot become rich in the stock market only by day-trading and selling shares of great companies, because they come under pressure from time to time.

Over the past 10 years the stock market has become too myopic with respect to what is happening quarter to quarter. Brilliant companies may miss the earnings estimate for a particular quarter, and investors bail out by the dozens as if it's the end of the world. I see brokerage firms downgrade companies, not based on the long-term potential of the business but because the stock has moved too high in a short period of time. Sure, the stock may temporarily come down in such a case (pushed lower in fact by the downgrade), but in the overwhelming majority of cases that same stock is going to rebound very quickly.

I don't want you glued to the PC every day, all day, with your long-term holdings, but you have to take the temperature of the companies in your portfolio by checking news, financial filings, and the general trends of the stock itself.

Looking at the Income Statement

Ideally you want the year-over-year (and month-over-month when applicable) percentage gains to be higher as you move down the income statement, beginning with:

- Sales
- Gross margin
- Operating margin
- Net margin
- Earnings per share

There is a chance that net earnings could increase at a higher pace year over year than earnings, as many companies issue more shares to the public during a particular time frame. Although the perfect storm is for the year-over-year improvement to become greater as we move down the income statement, it isn't alarming if shares increased slightly year over year.

When we examine a company's financial filings, we are looking at two sets of developments and trends: absolute and relative. These are covered in the following sections.

Absolute Trends

Absolute trends deal solely with progress made by the company. We measure this progress against historic results and also against parameters previously established by management and by Wall Street.

It is really important to understand the expectations game. Many companies in the public market offer some form of forward-looking guidance, typically for the current quarter and the full year. Mostly this guidance is focused on earnings per share and total revenue. Some businesses have such a great handle on their operations that they offer very in-depth guidance such as assumptions about capital spending, stock repurchases, and even profit margins. Wall Street firms also come up with assumptions about the company that usually cover all aspects of a financial filing. They look at execution trends and listen to conference calls to arrive at these assumptions. *These are things you can do and will begin to do, too.*

In some cases, analysts also speak to company management and to other companies that are in the food chain. By "food chain," I mean businesses that supply raw materials and important parts to that company. The notion is that if a company is ordering more raw materials and key parts than normal, then perhaps business is going better than expected. Conversely, canceling orders or cutting back on raw materials could point to lower demand or product delays, both of which would have a material impact on sales and earnings.

One way for *you* to get a sense of how well the food chain is doing is by placing the stocks of suppliers and customers of certain products together on your chart screen. This way, when a supplier stock declines, it will alert you to look further into the company you're holding.

Here is the rub about expectations. Management of publicly traded companies and the analysts who follow those companies are generally working under a cloud of fear. Simply put, if a company delivers quarterly financial results that differ dramatically

---

Setting Up Your Screens

Every online brokerage firm offers its clients the ability to monitor their holdings as well as other stocks they may have an interest in. Make sure you have the ability to monitor all the companies you feel are necessary. Many systems can be programmed to highlight changes you deem important. The key items that must be monitored and flagged include:

- Current quote

- Average daily volume

- Current volume

- News alerts

- Option activity

from the consensus estimate and previous guidance from the company, its stock will pay a heavy price. As a result, we are in a world where companies that beat the consensus estimate often see their shares beaten down. I'm sure this has happened to you as it's happened to every investor in stocks from time to time. Talk about frustrating—the company beats the estimates and the share price moves lower.

Before the scandal-scarred period of the late 1990s (when the stock market was all about total excesses, fun, and bravado), most companies really tried to set the earnings bar at a level that would underscore genuine achievement. Back then, earnings projections by management weren't a game of sandbagging. Publicly traded companies had to work to make their earnings projections, and more often than not their share price would move higher when those earnings estimates were matched. There was integrity in the system as publicly traded companies and Wall Street tried to get it exactly right instead of building in wiggle room.

This isn't to say that purists were happy with the way some larger companies were able to manipulate their earnings results. For years there was criticism of companies like IBM and General Electric, and how they made the numbers by sharpening their pencils and borrowing from a division or a future quarter. Yet for the most part earnings were still the heart and soul of the stock market.

With the new millennium this has all changed. During the stretch from 1995 to 2001, earnings were an afterthought. They simply didn't matter. When the hottest stocks in the market were from companies that barely even *had* sales, it was only natural that earnings wouldn't matter. Promises and hype replaced execution and earnings. Talk about a free pass. No wonder we all believed we'd retire at 40 years old and travel the world. All a company had to do was hire a rambunctious CEO (chief excitement officer) and it was off to the races.

Then it happened. Earnings, or, better yet, *lack* of earnings, became important. The game was over and the meltdown began. What we got in the immediate months after the Dow peaked in March 2000 was an avalanche of earnings restatements and record-breaking write-offs. Suddenly earnings were important again. There was a problem, however: Most companies had been cutting corners with shoddy accounting and business models that placed little emphasis on execution. Poor business habits were coupled with an economic backdrop that included a short-lived recession. Earnings were such a far-off dream that companies began to simply admit they didn't have "visibility." In other words, they had no clue when they would make a profit other than it wouldn't be any time soon. Although I have misgivings about businesses that cater to the short-term mentality of meeting quarterly earnings projections, any company that says it doesn't have visibility is a screaming sell.

Then came the postrecession era and the recovery of the stock market from 9/11-induced lows, a period of low confidence and little faith. The wave of corporate malfeasance that stained the stock market in the late 1990s was still fresh in the minds of most investors. Real estate began to boom, in large part due to the lowest interest rates in 46 years as well as a lack of faith in Wall Street and its supposed guardians—the brokerage firms investors entrusted with their hard-earned money and the regulatory agencies such as the Securities and Exchange Commission. A lack of interest plus a lack of faith sent the stock market to the nether regions of importance.

Since 2001, corporate America has adopted a new approach to communicating with investors. It would be the antithesis of the hype days when all talk and little action was the order of the day. Now it's all about low-keying promises, including sandbagging on earnings estimates. The poster child of this new move was tech industry giant Cisco (stock symbol CSCO), whose chairman, John Chambers, morphed from vocal optimist into the most unenthusiastic guy on the planet.

Cisco was often a spark during the heyday of the tech rally, and for a couple of years after the bloom was off the rose for the entire space, investors (myself included) still waited with bated breath for some sort of upbeat optimism during the earnings call. Instead the reports seemed ho-hum, but it wasn't the critics downplaying achievements—it was the company's chairman. After declining from a high of $75 in early 2000, Cisco stock drifted lower and lower, then bounced a bit, but has been spinning its wheels, trading at or below $25 since the start of 2004. The company's chart has more or less meandered in a straight line.

So now corporate America has taken the official stance to underpromise and overdeliver, and supposedly we are too dumb to realize this. The worst case of this approach came from the homebuilders, whose stock made fantastic moves during the unprecedented housing boom, only to stumble drastically at the first sign the housing market was returning to normal. This is an example of how sandbagging earnings guidance backfired and lessened the impact of great earnings results. The lost credibility mitigated upside moves when homebuilders were still knocking the cover off the ball, and then homebuilding stocks were completely torpedoed when they finally missed the consensus estimate.

Centex (stock symbol CTX) is one of the nation's largest homebuilders and for a long time a bellwether stock in the group. The company's shares more than doubled in value, climbing to $76 a share by July 2005 from $32 in October 2003. Those gains were generated by incredible earnings growth that confounded the experts, many of whom were predicting an end to the housing boom as early as 2003.

The company reported all-time record results in each quarter of its fiscal year, which began March 1, 2005:

June quarter (1Q06) beat the Street consensus by $0.05.

October quarter (2Q06) beat the Street consensus by $0.40.

December quarter (3Q06) beat the Street consensus estimate by $0.04.

March quarter (4Q06) missed the Street consensus estimate by $0.19.

Despite record results quarter after quarter, including a major eclipsing of the consensus estimate in the second quarter that brought the company's share price back to life, the stock never totally regained its luster from the previous few years. One of the biggest reasons for this inability to recapture traction was the out-of-sync nature of the company's guidance. After a while investors came to expect homebuilders to beat estimates by double digits, and when that didn't happen the underlying share price headed south. When the Street expected a high number and got something substantially less (see the March quarter), the shares of Centex, already under pressure, fell off a cliff. (See Figure 3.1.)

FIGURE 3.1   Centex: Paying the Price for Missing the Earnings Consensus
Chart courtesy of Prophet Financial Systems (www.prophet.net).

The so-called *consensus estimate* is the average estimate of a number of major brokerage firms that cover a particular company. Several organizations offer a consensus number, including Zack's, Bloomberg, and Reuters' First Call. However, when one hears the word *consensus*, more often than not it is referencing the First Call.

The moral of the story is a company must give investors realistic guidance, which brings us back to absolute performance. Sure, you want companies in your portfolio to beat the consensus estimates, both their own and the Street's, but you measure how well the company did in the various areas outlined in the previous chapter.

By the way, Wall Street has been fudging on the numbers, too. Years ago everyone used to talk about the so-called whisper number. This was the real earnings estimate, not the numbers officially put out there by the Street. I'm not sure why there isn't much talk about the whisper number anymore, other than the fact that the Street has lost so much credibility that it doesn't matter. Much like publicly traded companies that lost face, the analytical community of Wall Street has taken a serious hit over the years.

It's all out in the open now: Many firms operated research departments simply to provide positive coverage for corporate clients. The dilemma was clear; commissions from individual investors were shrinking even as individuals piled into the market because of cut-rate commissions. In the meantime, large Wall Street firms made billions managing different kinds of offerings for their large corporate clients. When push comes to shove, it is the individual who gets the shaft. The result was a settlement with the top 12 brokerage firms that totaled more than $1.4 billion. This may sound like a lot of money, but it has largely been a joke, and once again the laugh is on the individual investor. We've won several coverage contracts at Wall Street Strategies as part of the settlement, but I still think the general public was given short shrift again.

The so-called independent research program is a halfhearted attempt to make amends, but in reality, independent research isn't being pushed to the degree that it should be. Instead, it is underplayed by regulatory bodies and, of course, by brokerage firms. The vast majority of contracts for the so-called independent research were farmed out to large players, leaving the small, truly independent firms out in the cold. It is a shame that there is no unified system for judging the research and no accountability for those folks who are actually picking the research.

Now the pendulum has swung from too much hype to too little nerve, and most financial estimates by the major brokerage firms are conservative to say the least. That's why stocks generally take huge hits when companies miss the consensus estimates. Everyone knows both the company and the Street were sandbagging to begin with.

Taking a Company's Temperature Using Total Revenue Line

Most companies lump all revenue from all business segments into a total revenue line, although some separate the various revenue streams. Obviously the latter is a more desirable method, but there are other details in the lumped report and accompanying conference call that can help you unravel revenue streams and costs.

Table 3.1 shows a portion of an income statement from Callaway Golf (stock symbol ELY; March 2006 consolidated condensed statement of operations). This statement gives investors net income and cost of sales, to come up with a gross profit. In this case total revenue (net sales) increased 0.09 percent from the previous year period, while cost of sales rose 2.2 percent. Needless to say, there is

TABLE 3.1   Callaway Golf March 2006 Income Statement Excerpt

Item	March 2006	March 2005
Net sales	$302,445	$299,857
Cost of sales	170,933	167,251
Gross profits	131,512	132,606

an immediate red flag when cost of goods sold grows faster than net sales.

As a result of the rapid increase in cost of sales versus the tepid increase in the top line, Callaway Golf saw its gross margin decrease to 43.48 percent from 44.22 percent. Margins are the key to valuation, plain and simple. The gross margin is extremely important, because negative developments at this point in the income statement will mitigate positives farther down the income statement. The fact of the matter is that operating margins and gross margins have more influence on how a stock acts than do the bottom-line earnings.

In the case of the Callaway Golf financial results for first-quarter 2006, the company actually missed the consensus estimate for revenue but beat the estimate for earnings per share. By missing the top line, the company's gross margin suffered.

What do you think had the greater impact in the share price of the stock of Callaway Golf—the narrower gross margin or the better-than-expected bottom line?

Whenever margins begin to shrink, there is going to be incredible pressure on a stock's price. While people who only employ charts typically use a stop-loss (a price point at which they automatically sell their holding regardless of any other factors), the only time you should sell a stock is when there is evidence the company will no longer be able to improve margins. I go into greater detail about this in Chapter 12. For now, watch for lower margins on a year-over-year basis (e.g., first-quarter 2006 versus first-quarter 2005) and sometimes on a sequential basis (e.g., first-quarter 2006 versus fourth-quarter 2005).

In answer to the earlier question, the decline in gross margin crushed the share price of Callaway Golf (see Figure 3.2).

FIGURE 3.2 Callaway Golf: When Gross Margins Fall, Stocks Fall

Chart courtesy of Prophet Financial Systems (www.prophet.net).

Taking a Company's Temperature Using Itemized Revenue Streams

Some companies are nice enough to itemize their financial results. By breaking out various revenue streams and the individual costs associated with those streams, it's much easier to analyze results and make key investment decisions. Some industries lend themselves to itemized revenue recognition and some don't; in those cases, don't hold prejudice against them.

Itemized income statements often bypass gross numbers and move straight to the operating outcome. Tables 3.2 and 3.3 show portions of an actual income statement from Las Vegas Sands (stock symbol LVS), a casino operator with properties in Las Vegas and Macao.

All business segments for Las Vegas Sands enjoyed year-over-year gains in revenue, but there were three red flags:

1. The business segment with the best operating margins (rooms) also experienced the slowest year-over-year increase in total revenue. (Table 3.2)

2. Expenses at the casino business segment surged to 54.7 percent of revenue from just 49.64 percent in the year-ago comparison. (Table 3.3)

3. Total operating margin slid to 27.5 percent from 31.03 percent—the biggest red flag there could be in an income statement! (Table 3.3)

TABLE 3.2   Las Vegas Sands Revenue

Revenues	Most Recent Quarter	Year-Ago Quarter
Casino	$375,382	$265,786
Rooms	91,138[1]	86,077
Food and beverage	51,816	43,489
Convention, retail, and other	35,005	28,454
Less promotional allowances	(22,977)	(20,012)
Total revenues	**530,364**	**403,794**

TABLE 3.3   Las Vegas Sands Operating Expenses

Operating Expenses	Most Recent Quarter	Year-Ago Quarter
Casino	$205,344[2]	$131,953
Rooms	21,753	21,115
Food and beverage	24,057	20,965
Convention, retail, and other	16,395	14,374
Provisions for doubtful accounts	4,989	3,386
General and administrative	54,812	45,773
Corporate	12,954	10,882
Rental	3,707	3,705
Pre-open	2,219	—
Development	9,168	5,175
Depreciation and amortization	25,005	19,965
Loss on disposal of assets	1,081	1,165
Total operating expenses	381,484	278,458
Operating income	**145,880**[3]	**125,336**

With these flags, including lower operating margins, where would you guess the company's share price went?

The stock moved higher!

That reaction is a great illustration of how expectations and hype can play a greater role in the short-term price action of a stock. This is where it becomes very tough for investors to reconcile fear of the obvious (the margins decreased) and fear of missing out on a company with a lot of irons in the fire. In this case, Macao is going to be a bigger gambling mecca than Vegas; in fact, during the quarter shown in this income statement, the company's revenues soared 63 percent in Macao and only 2.5 percent year-over-year in Las Vegas. Emotions and visions of riches exceed reactions based on realities of actual numbers. Of course, revenue growth in Macao validated excitement about being a major player in the hottest market in the industry.

The moral of this story is that quarterly financial reports, while important, are just a small sliver of time. This is why investors should know the longer-term trends, current trends, and possible future trends, too. Numbers are important and tell a story, but common sense is even more important. When a company misses the consensus estimates or stumbles with respect to execution, the stock could take a hit, sometimes a big hit. Jumping out isn't the automatic reaction. The first thing investors are going to want to know is whether disappointing results are a short-term event (read: just that particular quarter) or the first crack in the armor with more to follow.

The first thing every investor should know is whether the company has missed the Street consensus in the past or if the margins have dipped only recently (over the last four quarters). If a company has missed before in the last year and then performs poorly again, I would sell the stock, as the would-be fundamental story would be fractured beyond my confidence. The story could still be sexy, in which case I would continue to monitor the stock and even consider getting back in, once management proved it had the skill set to make dreams reality.

Use the charts along with fundamental research. Before a company even reports, pull up a two-year chart and look for the gaps (the points where the company's shares opened for trading significantly higher or lower than the previous close). No matter how adept management is, there will be missteps. Managing super growth is difficult, as is managing super expectations.

Absolute Worksheets

When taking the temperature of companies in your portfolio, you have to measure quantifiable changes in fortunes. I suggest using a worksheet. With the absolute worksheet you are looking for trends, but at first blush you want to get a general feel as to whether developments were positive or negative. I call them positive highlights or red flags.

As you accumulate these worksheets, you'll develop a running commentary on the companies in your portfolio that will serve as an easy-to-read checklist and a way to monitor the health of your investment. If you are doing these worksheets for the first time, I suggest you go back a year or longer to see established precedents from which you can compare and glean current developments.

THE INCOME STATEMENT WORKSHEET   Use a worksheet (see Table 3.4) to illustrate execution trends and to help make determinations as to the effectiveness of management over the last 52 weeks. This worksheet will give you signs of the challenges facing the company and whether it has to spend more money to generate profits.

POSITIVE HIGHLIGHT VERSUS A RED FLAG   Table 3.5 shows what you should look for when assessing income statements.

THE CASH FLOW STATEMENT WORKSHEET   I've separated the worksheet in Table 3.4 into three parts to better explain what we're looking for. All three components (Tables 3.6 through 3.8) should be attached once you begin your calculations.

You want the companies in your portfolio to generate cash from operations, which is more important than a company that's earning money but doing so from sales of assets or interest payments. There has to be demand for the company's good and services in order for you to continue to own the stock.

Some companies are adding share-based compensation on the cash flow statement; you should ignore that line. First, many tech companies are only now adopting this maneuver and it's adding money to cash flow that wasn't there in the year-ago period. It bolsters cash flow artificially, in my opinion. Furthermore, we only concern ourselves with non-GAAP numbers in the income statement, which means we have already ignored the impact of share-based compensation and we don't need to make any adjustments.

TABLE 3.4 Absolute Worksheet, Income Statement

	Current Quarter	Previous Quarter	Year over Year	Positive Highlight or Red Flag?
Percent revenue growth (you are concerned with organic growth)				
Cost of goods as percentage of total revenue				
Gross profit margin				
Selling, general, and administrative outlays as percentage of total revenue				
Research and development as percentage of total revenue				
Depreciation and amortization as percentage of total revenue				
Interest as percentage of total revenue				
Company-specific item as percentage of total revenue				
Industry-specific item as percentage of total revenue				
Other as percentage of total revenue				
Total expenses				
Operating profit margin				
Interest expense, nonoperating				
Interest income, nonoperating				
Gain/loss from sale of assets				
Other				
Net income before taxes				
Provision for income taxes				
Income after taxes				
Minority interest				

(Continued)

TABLE 3.4 *(Continued)*

	Current Quarter	Previous Quarter	Year over Year	Positive Highlight or Red Flag?
Equity in affiliates				
Discontinued operations				
Extraordinary items				
Net income				
Diluted weighted average shares				
Diluted earnings per share				

Note: The previous-quarter information may be inconsequential if the company has a seasonal business. Also, I often work off the actual income statement and write my notes and denote the mathematical changes, particularly year over year.

TABLE 3.5 What to Look for When Assessing an Income Statement

Line Item	Key Observations
Percent revenue growth (you are concerned with organic growth)	Make sure that this is an apples-to-apples comparison. During a 52-week period companies will make acquisitions, and these skew year-over-year comparisons. If the data is the same year over over year, it is obvious that an increase is a positive highlight. Lower revenue is a huge red flag and, like Lucille Ball, management will have a lot of explaining to do.
Cost of goods as percentage of total revenue	Obviously we want this number to go down year after year.
Gross profit margin	We want this to move higher, period! If there are acquisitions and this number takes a bump, pay close attention to verbiage in the press release from the company, or during the conference call, that would suggest a better impact (read: synergies) as the deals are digested.
Selling, general, and administrative outlays as percentage of total revenue	This is the line that more often than not makes or breaks the income statement. When businesses have to spend more money to generate sales, it's a red flag and worrisome.

(Continued)

TABLE 3.5 *(Continued)*

Line Item	Key Observations
Research and development as percentage of total revenue	It is a red flag when R&D declines. Companies that cut into this number in order to bolster the bottom line are sacrificing the future.
Other as percentage of total revenue	This is often a so-called GAAP occurrence, an event that is nonrecurring; don't become too concerned about this line unless it continues to occur.
Total expenses	We obviously want this number to move lower, but it has to move lower because management has found legitimate ways to cut cost.
Operating profit margin	For me this is the most important line in the income statement. We want to see the operating margin increasing all the time. I feel this line has a greater correlation to the movement in a company's share price than any other metric in the financial statement, even cash flow and free cash flow.
Provision for income taxes	Lower taxes are important; divide this number into net income before taxes to get the effective tax rate.
Net income	This number is only slightly less important than operating income in my book because of the impact of interest income and expenses as well as other factors that aren't directly related to how well management is running the company.
Diluted earnings per share	Occasionally a company meets or beats the Street by repurchasing enough stock to swing the bottom line. Be sure to pay close attention to how pure the year-over-year earnings-per-share comparisons truly are, and be aware of efforts by management to manipulate the shares outstanding in order to meet the number.

TABLE 3.6   Absolute Worksheet, Cash Flow—Operating Activities

	Current Quarter	Previous Quarter	Year over Year	Positive Highlight or Red Flag?
Operating activity highlights*				
Operating activity highlights*				
Cash provided by operations				

*These boxes are for unusual changes in operating activity. Keep in mind that depreciation is placed back on the cash flow statement, as it's really a noncash charge that negatively impacts the income statements, so pay close attention to this number.

TABLE 3.7   Absolute Worksheet, Cash Flow—Investing Activities

	Current Quarter	Previous Quarter	Year over Year	Positive Highlight or Red Flag?
Investing activity highlights*				
Investing activity highlights*				
Cash used by investing activities				

*Capital spending is the key component of this part of the income statement. Remember that we subtract this number from cash from operating activities to come up with free cash flow. This free cash flow is considered the most important bit of information in the quarterly financials by some of the largest and smartest money managers out there. I continue to think it is wrong to penalize a company for investing in its future, but higher free cash flow lends credence to a higher share price.

TABLE 3.8   Absolute Worksheet, Cash Flow—Financial Activities

	Current Quarter	Previous Quarter	Year over Year	Positive Highlight or Red Flag?
Financial activity highlights*				
Financial activity highlights*				
Cash used/provided by financial activities				

*The cash dividend line should be increasing or the same year over year; it is a red flag when a company has to decrease its dividend. A case of such a dilemma is the U.S. automakers. Ford and General Motors continue to pay out hefty dividends even as there are swirling questions about whether these companies can stay in business without filing for bankruptcy. If a company lowers its dividend payments, it is simply bad news for shareholders in many ways, not the least of which is the actual smaller amount one receives from management. Also pay close attention to acquisition of common stock for the treasury.

There are essentially two ways a company pays back its shareholders from the cash the business is generating:

- Quarterly dividend payment

- Company share repurchases

The notion that buying back stock is a way of paying shareholders may seem wacky to some, but it boils down to the fact that slices of the pie are taken out of the system, which means existing slices increase in size and, hence, value. By the way, when a company is sitting on a lot of cash, let's say $1 billion and higher, and isn't buying back stock or paying a dividend, that is a serious red flag. However, I'm not a big fan of companies only buying back stock. These days too many companies are opting to buy back stock rather than invest in their own business or cut investors a check.

As I alluded to earlier, this tack is used in part to bolster the bottom line, which is supposed to make management look good. The truth is many folks know this trick but it is still used by boards of directors to justify salaries and bonuses. Of course, I like the stock buyback more than just sitting on the cash. I also like stock buybacks more if the insiders aren't selling at the same time the company is buying—there is something inherently wrong with that picture.

Cash Is King—But Too Much Suggests Management Are a Bunch of Jokers

Microsoft was sitting on a lot of cash coming into 2003—more than $40 billion in cash, an astounding figure. For years critics couldn't understand why management was sitting on so much cash. It was if Bill Gates was a Depression-era child, afraid of not having money for a rainy day. In this case it would have to be a monsoon, one that would last for several years before depleting the cash hoard.

Finally in January 2003 the company warned investors and announced lower earnings guidance and knew it had to open the vault, which had been labeled "open in case of emergency." In an effort to offset the disappointment with its lower financial guidance, Microsoft authorized its first-ever dividend and a stock split. Shareholders were paid $0.02 (the company authorized an annual payout of $0.08 to be paid quarterly) in March 2003. In September 2003 the company announced it was doubling its dividend to $0.16 a share. These points are marked with arrows in Figure 3.3.

The news of the dividend payment couldn't mitigate warnings of financial shortfalls, but it may have helped the stock rebound quickly, and when management raised the payout, it added a spark to the share price.

In the end I would rather see companies investing in the business looking toward the future. The focus investments of this book are companies that are looking to expand their turf via geographic growth, market share gains, and innovative product pipelines that will enable them to stay ahead of the competition and raise prices. However, if a company was going to try to directly compensate shareholders, I'd rather take the cash in dividends than see it go toward buying back shares.

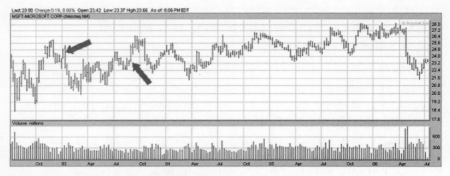

FIGURE 3.3   Bill Gates Shares the Wealth

Chart courtesy of Prophet Financial Systems (www.prophet.net).

THE BALANCE SHEET WORKSHEET   The balance sheet (Table 3.9) gives us a glimpse of the company's ability to collect money as well as an idea of how much of the product is moving out the door. You don't want to own stock in a company that has inventory building up, even if the numbers on the income statement paint a glowing picture.

ABSOLUTE WORKSHEET SUMMARY   Cash and equivalents are taken from the cash flow statement and then from other assets, including accounts receivable and inventories. Look for accounts receivable to rise at a faster pace than inventories. However, it is a red flag if accounts receivable is increasing faster than total revenue growth. If inventories are increasing faster than accounts receivable, this is a red flag, too.

TABLE 3.9   Absolute Worksheet—Balance Sheet

	Current Quarter	Previous Quarter	Year over Year	Positive Highlight or Red Flag?
Cash and cash equivalents				
Accounts receivable				
Inventories				

After you have filled out your worksheets, you'll have a general idea how the company fared. Obviously we want the company to beat the consensus estimate, but we also want to see the following:

- The company had solid top-line growth.

- The company's margins improved.

- The company's cash flow improved.

- The company's working capital expanded.

- Management didn't cut corners to reach its goals or appease the Street.

Relative Trends

A company sees total revenue up 35 percent year over year and comes in with operating margins of 25 percent. Offhand, is this good or bad? You will know from the absolute worksheets whether it was a good quarter with respect to historic precedent, but you still have to know if the results were good versus the performance of the company's rivals.

Business backdrops change all the time and often can make so-so execution look brilliant. Sometimes metals prices are high, and that means higher revenue for mining companies. Sometimes the housing market is hot, and that means higher revenue for the housing market. However, a company could see its absolute performance slip and it could still be viewed as a positive. In the post–bull market period, technology and telecommunications companies saw incredible declines in top-line demands. Companies that stumbled the least saw their share price hold up best (although at a certain point all these companies experienced dramatic decreases in share price).

Businesses play on the same playing field. Gauging how well they performed during a particular period and comparing those performances gives us relative comparisons. There are considerations for size when using relative comparisons; you wouldn't expect Shaquille O'Neal to have the same vertical leap as a point guard on the other team, but you would expect his team to win, and we would expect Shaq to continue to hold his own as a player year after year.

Along with measuring execution among rivals, this section looks at valuation metrics such as price to earnings, price to sales, price to book, and price to cash flow ratios.

Price to Earnings Ratio

The price/earnings (PE) ratio is the market share price divided by the earnings per share. I find it amazing when analysts can determine whether a company is undervalued or overvalued, based solely on the PE ratio. As far as I'm concerned, the PE ratio is *nothing more than a gauge of popularity*. If a company has a high PE ratio, it means it's a popular stock and investors are willing to take the risk of owning it.

Somewhere along the way, all PE ratios will come down as growth begins to slow. After all, it is normally sizzling growth and/or the promise of sizzling growth that makes a stock popular to begin with. Typically stocks with high PE ratios make for good trading vehicles, although in the early stages of a company's growth curve, when it takes off and enjoys a period of uninterrupted growth, the PE ratio will be well above the industry average and the average of the S&P 500.

Certain industries are known for horrific boom and bust periods, and as a result their PE ratio never gets higher than the S&P 500. The homebuilders are a prime example of that. This is why we compare PE and other ratios against industry averages and not against the broad market. I like stocks with high PE ratios for intermediate-term investing. I also like companies with low PE ratios that are exhibiting signs of revenue and margin appreciation, but these investments can take longer to work out.

The curious thing about PE ratios is that the higher the ratio, the more forgiving the market, at least when a company stumbles for the first time. However, when a company that already has a low PE ratio stumbles, its share price takes heavy punishment. This is the case because the company with the low PE ratio has probably already come up short of expectations in the recent past (previous 52 weeks) and there is a stigma in place already.

Remember, the PE ratio is a popularity gauge, and stocks with lower PE ratios have to win back popularity. It takes more than one good quarter to do this.

Price to Sales Ratio

Dividing the current share price by revenue per share for the past 12 months provides the price to sales (PS) ratio. This metric is popular with folks trying to get a handle on valuing businesses with fast top-line growth but limited bottom-line results. In the past this metric has been very important when comparing technology companies.

The idea with this metric is that a company with a low price to sales ratio (generally 1.0 or lower) has the potential to rally should the company get its act together and begin to filter revenue down to the bottom line. This only makes sense. For the most part, like all key valuation metrics, it is believed businesses make mistakes, learn from them, and fix them, and then the valuations of their underlying share price will move toward the industry average.

Price to Book Ratio

The price to book (PB) ratio is another gauge for measuring the value of a company's shares. To get this ratio you divide the current share price by book value per share.

In order to determine the book value per share, take the assets on the balance sheet (from the most recently reported quarter) and subtract the liabilities. Then take that difference and divide it into the number of shares outstanding. The result is the book value per share.

This is one of the more popular gauges of value among purists. If a company has a PB under 1.0, it means the stock is changing hands for less than its intrinsic value. The sum of the parts is more valuable than the company. And this doesn't even take into account intangible assets, which are subtracted out along with liabilities. Of course if a company is trading at a PB lower than 1.0, there is a serious problem with credibility—the Street doesn't believe management will right the ship, and there could also be skepticism about the true value of assets on the balance sheet.

Nonetheless, when a stock with a PB under 1.0 begins to see

improved revenue gains, its share price could come on strong, but it doesn't happen overnight.

Price to Cash Flow

We come up with the price to cash flow (PCF) ratio by taking the current share price and dividing it by cash flow per share. As you already know, cash flow adds back monies taken from the income statement for depreciation and amortization, so this metric is very important for valuing businesses that carry large depreciation costs. Businesses that see their fortunes move up and down as part of the normal backdrop also benefit from the use of this metric.

Valuation

Some pundits believe stocks fall into cracks and somehow their share prices become marginalized because the crowds have moved on and aren't paying attention. I don't believe that's true. Yes, the crowds have moved on because they're chasing performance, but there are so many funds and so many investors out there, stocks don't accidentally begin trading at subpar valuation metrics.

At some point the company made a mistake or two and the Street simply walked away. Our goal is to get back in before the Street rekindles its love for these undervalued stocks. The trick is to understand that the herd moves hard and fast, and changing course doesn't happen easily. So you will have to have patience when you buy stocks with seemingly cheap valuations.

Once the worksheet shown in Table 3.10 is completed, investors have to dissect the results. On the top line, make sure the revenue growth is organic. Of course companies that are growing revenue fastest are going to be rewarded, but also look at total revenue growth, not just the percentage change. It's a lot easier to double your sales from $100 million to $200 million than from $1 billion to $2 billion.

You aren't necessarily looking for the company with the highest margins but with the growing margins. Ideally you want your investment to have expanding margins, but to be trading at a dis-

TABLE 3.10   Relative Worksheet

	Your Company	Rival #1	Rival #2	Rival #3	Rival #4
Percent revenue change					
Total revenue					
Gross margin					
Percent gross margin change					
Operating margin					
Percent operating margin					
Tax rate					
Net profit margin					
Percent net income change					
Working capital					
Industry metrics					
Industry metrics					
Industry metrics					
PE					
PB					
PS					
PCF					

count with respect to the various valuation metrics previously outlined.

I've said it before and want to reiterate it again: Operating margin is the key. Managing cash isn't easy. Avoiding the temptation to goose earnings results isn't easy. Finding innovative ways to save money isn't easy. When management does these things well, the stock will respond.

Let's take a look at how operating margin developments of one company had a direct bearing on that company's share price.

CASE STUDY: STARBUCKS   It's hard to imagine anyone not knowing about Starbucks; with 11,225 locations around the world, the stores are almost as ubiquitous as streetlights. It is even hard to fathom that there are adolescents not familiar with the brand, a fact that the makers of the hit movie *Shrek 2* capitalized on when a bunch of people in a coffeehouse that was unmistakably Starbucks were forced to evacuate and just ran across the street to another Starbucks-like coffeehouse. Here's a quick rundown of Starbucks' history:

1971   Starbucks opens its first location in Seattle's Pike Place Market.

1982   Starbucks hires Howard Schultz as director of retail operations and marketing.

1983   Schultz travels to Italy and is impressed with the popularity of espresso bars in Milan.

1984   Starbucks tests the coffeehouse concept in downtown Seattle.

1985   Schultz founds Il Giornale brewed coffee and espresso beverages made from Starbucks coffee beans.

1987   Il Giornale with local investors acquires the assets of Starbucks, changes the name to Starbucks Corporation, opens locations in Chicago and Vancouver, and finishes the fiscal year with 17 locations.

1989   The company finishes the fiscal year with 55 locations.

1991   The company ends the year with 116 locations.

1992   The company goes public through an initial public offering (IPO).

Unlike many initial public offerings in the 1990s, Starbucks had a product, sales, and experienced management when they went public.

While I was writing this book, a friend asked me, "When should a stock be sold?" These days the answer would be "At the first sign of trouble." The short-term mentality has added to volatility and makes it virtually impossible for people who watch the market closely to really achieve a big payoff. I do believe there are times to sell stocks, but such decisions are mostly based on fundamentals. There have been times over the last 14 years when I felt Starbucks was a sell, mostly when it seemed as if the company's

CEO was becoming too interested with things outside of the core business. But looking at the history of Starbucks since it has gone public, the answer to my friend's question is that some stocks can be held indefinitely (see Figure 3.4).

The stock has split five times over the years. With that in mind, Starbucks (SBUX) began actively trading around $0.65 and has been as high as $40 a share in 2006. An investment of $5,000 in 1992 would have been worth as much as $307,600 at the high point in 2006. I bet you or a friend have consumed $5,000 worth of Starbucks coffee since 1992.

A *stock split* is a mechanism whereby the share price is lowered as additional shares are given to shareholders. Let's say you owned 100 shares of a $50 stock and the management of the company decides to forward split the stock two for one. Your 100 shares would become 200 shares and begin trading at $25 a share. The value of your holding doesn't change. This doesn't change a shareholder's value but the lower share price makes the stock more attractive to investors.

Of course there were bumps in the road. The first major test for the company came in 1998 when it's operating margin began to rapidly decrease. It was during this time that the CEO began to express interest in stuff other than selling coffee. His interest in the Internet and how to weave it into the Starbucks story is well

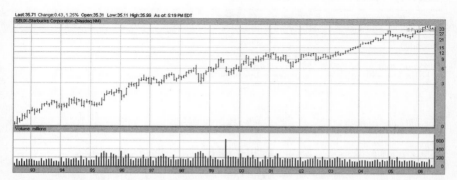

FIGURE 3.4   Starbucks, 1992 to Present
Chart courtesy of Prophet Financial Systems (www.prophet.net).

known. Of course at that time simply adding ".com" to your corporate moniker would add millions if not billions in value to a company faster than one could say "large latte." Later in 1999 the stock hit another major stumbling block, and by this time the Street was convinced Howard Schultz was too concerned about being an Internet café and not taking care of the Xs and Os of running the business. This was when investors abandoned the stock (myself included), and in hindsight this was the time to be a buyer of the stock.

Starbucks operates on a fiscal year that ends in September, and its share price was humming along until it stumbled into an abrupt change in the operating margin. The 1998 fiscal year began nicely with solid results in the first and second quarter, but the third quarter was the humdinger.

In the first quarter, the company's revenue increased 32.5 percent from the year earlier period, but even more impressive was the fact that the company was able to manage its costs of sales and other operating expenses to achieve an increase in the operating margin. (See Table 3.11.) The results were released in January 1999; the stock moved higher and eventually broke out later in the month.

In the second quarter (Table 3.12), the company saw its operating margin decline from the preceding quarter but still improve year over year. Released on April 23, the results didn't spike the

TABLE 3.11   Starbucks, First Quarter 1998

Income Statement	First Quarter 1998	First Quarter 1997
Revenue	$316,952,000	$239,142,000
Operating margin	**10.89%**	9.16%

TABLE 3.12   Starbucks, Second Quarter 1998

Income Statement	Second Quarter 1998	Second Quarter 1997
Revenue	$289,606,000	$214,915,000
Operating margin	**7.74%**	6.51%

stock, but the upside bias remained in place. For us the results would have raised a yellow flag, but the year-over-year increase in operating margin would have been good enough news to hold the stock.

The company posted its third-quarter earnings results on July 24 (Table 3.13). It showed a huge shift in operating margins, which declined sequentially for the second straight quarter and were down considerably year over year. My focus on operating margin growth over total revenue growth is validated with the series of events at Starbucks during fiscal year 1998. While operating margin was steadily declining, total revenue growth was steadily increasing, but in the end the stock responded to the lower operating margin.

There were two distinct trends occurring during fiscal year 1998 (see Table 3.14). Revenues were soaring versus the year-ago period. This isn't uncommon with retail businesses, which typically have significantly more units each year; hence revenues are going to grow exponentially (which is why we value these businesses more on same-store sales). In the meantime the company's operating margin was progressively becoming worse on a sequential basis. Each quarter the operating margin declined, and not by an insignificant amount. Figure 3.5 shows the path the stock's price followed as quarterly results were released. The stock fell apart on the sharp third-quarter decline in the operating margin.

TABLE 3.13 Starbucks, Third Quarter 1998

Income Statement	Third Quarter 1998	Third Quarter 1997
Revenue	$334,429,000	$244,241,000
Operating margin	**5.06%**	9.24%

TABLE 3.14 Starbucks, Fiscal Year 1998 Financial Trends

Quarterly period	Y/Y Change in Total Revenue	Y/Y Change in Operating Margin
First quarter	28.91%	10.89%
Second quarter	34.75%	7.74%
Third quarter	41.20%	5.06%

FIGURE 3.5 **Starbucks Activity, Fiscal Year 1998**
Chart courtesy of Prophet Financial Systems (www.prophet.net).

That was at the height of the Internet boom, which is when the stock fell out of bed just as companies with no fundamentals were underscoring the notion of a new paradigm. Here was a company that captured the imagination of the hot money crowd. Interestingly the stocks didn't stay down for long, which underscores my contention that high-PE stocks can disappoint and rebound faster than low-PE stocks. The momentum from the oversold bounce that began in late September picked up steam when fourth-quarter and full-year results were posted. (See Table 3.15.)

What is really interesting about the fourth quarter is that while the operating margin was slightly lower year over year, it was up more than double the preceding quarter. Again the stock responded to operating margin growth (in this case sequential growth) more so than revenue growth, which actually increased at a slower rate than in the two previous quarters. (See Table 3.16.)

Interestingly, the pace of total revenue growth slows in the fourth quarter to 30.2 percent from 41.2 percent in the preceding quarter, but the real news and the factor that drives the share price is the operating margin, which boomerangs back to above 10 percent.

TABLE 3.15 **Starbucks, Fourth Quarter 1998**

Income Statement	Fourth Quarter 1998	Fourth Quarter 1997
Revenue	$357,705,000	$274,724,000
Operating margin	10.46%	10.66%

TABLE 3.16   Starbucks, Fourth Quarter Fiscal Year 1998 Financial Trends

Quarterly Period	Y/Y Change in Total Revenue	Y/Y Change in Operating Margin
Fourth quarter	30.20%	10.46%

THE TEXTBOOK PLAY   By following the guidance in this book you would have owned SBUX from $4 and bailed out around $6.50 to $6.25 when the stock gapped lower. Sure, you would have missed the absolute top of $7.50. Then you would have bought the stock back at $6.00 or slightly lower. The operating margin remained virtually the same in the first quarter of 1999 but slipped to 7.12 percent in the second quarter of 1999, which was posted on April 22. That should have been the red flag to exit the stock; even though the share price continued to move higher, the stock ultimately gapped lower in July to the tune of a 30 percent decline.

The conference call can be long but it is very important. If you are stuck on timing and have read the press release that accompanies the financial results, then cut to the chase and just listen to the question-and-answer period. You'll be able to piggyback on the questions brought up by analysts who cover the company and the industry for a living. They will come up with questions you haven't though of—and it's informative and educational, as well.

Conclusion

There is a fair amount of work to be done, but it's not as time-consuming as you might think and, more important, it's worth it. The stocks you're holding have to demonstrate the ability to grow the bottom line through strong top-line growth and deft cost controls. Large giants that can't be expected to grow the top line quickly or expand margins beyond small increments should be judged on cash from operating activities. I'm mostly interested in you investing in companies with long-term growth potential. Filling out the worksheets and understanding the business will make the difference when there is an urge to toss out great stocks with nonperformers simply because the broad market is acting poorly.

Strongly consider selling when:

- Year-over-year revenue declines (unless there are mitigating circumstances, such as the selling of a division, especially if that division was a drag on margins).

- Year-over-year operating margins decline (this could be mitigated if margins were higher in the preceding quarter).

- The company issues an earnings warning for the full year.

- The company doesn't have so-called visibility.

Consider selling in the near future when:

- Revenues are up but organic sales are moderating, not growing as fast as they did in the past.

- Year-over-year margin improvements are slowing from historic pace (past 52 weeks).

- The company issues an earnings warning for the current quarter.

- The company's CFO or other member of upper management leaves abruptly.

Avoiding the Madness of Captain Ahab

n January 2006 an investor contacted our firm, Wall Street Strategies, about signing up for our service. His only problem: He was long a stock and waiting for it to come back first. That company was Exabyte, a former hot stock that we actually used to mention from time to time. I had totally forgotten about the stock. I didn't deliberately write it off the way I've written off stocks like Intel and Sun Microsystems (which I could one day change my mind about); I simply forgot the company existed.

I took the phone from one of our representatives, and since I'm always digging to learn more about human behavior, I quickly turned the tables and began asking questions of my own. I asked him why he was holding when shares were changing hands at $0.80 a share. I don't remember the exact answer, although it didn't matter; this guy was going down with the ship. Even the band on the *Titanic* would have jumped ship by then. And yet there he was, waiting for the stock to get back to $4.00 or $5.00. This scenario plays out over and over again on a daily basis: Investors are holding stocks that are major losers. Making a mistake and buying the wrong stock isn't a big deal, but compounding this mistake by holding that same stock and eschewing other possible investments is a blatant example of the Captain Ahab syndrome and its debilitating impact on your financial health. (See Figure 4.1.)

I don't want people to be shaken out of the stock market by each dip or negative reaction to news. It's really hard to be in a major

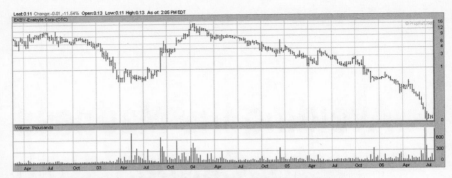

FIGURE 4.1   Biting the Dust Instead of Biting the Bullet with Exabyte

Chart courtesy of Prophet Financial Systems (www.prophet.net).

winner that doesn't see its share price stumble from time to time. I don't want people to be victimized by each twist and turn of general consensus and opinion. I know investors would make more money if they just held on to stocks longer. If you want proof, pull up a chart of the Dow Jones Industrial Average. Take a look at the past year, then the past 3 years, past 10 years, past 20 years, and past 50 years. The farther out you go, the more obvious it becomes that there is some merit to buying and holding.

Yet there is a time when you have to sell. By closely monitoring your investments (I'm not talking about being glued to the screen all day), you should be able to filter out the noise. But there are times when you have to take off the blinders, let in the noise, and call it a day by selling off your stocks.

There is an ocean of opportunity in the stock market. Don't miss out because of an obsession. Captain Ahab destroyed his ship and killed his entire crew save for one person, because he became myopic and too rigid in his belief. As an investor, you don't want to do the same to your portfolio.

The Captain Ahab Syndrome, in a Nutshell

In the classic book *Moby Dick* by Herman Melville, a wide-eyed whaling ship captain loses his mind and gets everyone on his ship killed (save for one survivor) in a single-minded crusade to kill the magical white whale. Captain Ahab passes huge pods of whales just to pursue Moby Dick, missing out on riches and in the end crashing and burning. I see this all the time in the stock market. Investors simply aren't willing to take a loss on a company that is fractured beyond repair, or should I say beyond any near-term possibilities of repair. I call this obsessive inability to jettison certain stocks the *Captain Ahab syndrome.*

The Captain Ahab syndrome is all about self-destruction. Maybe it's part of the human makeup; maybe we can't help it unless we are cognizant that it exists innately. After all, many humans are wired at birth to eventually suffer from an assortment of ailments including cancers, hair loss, and mental illnesses. In fact, the smartest medical research being done these days isn't focused on cures but on how to detect and lessen or even avoid the impact of this inner programming. We are self-destructive.

We destroy ourselves in the stock market for various reasons, including:

- The angst over losing money.

- The hit to the ego at being wrong.

- The unshakable belief that the wrong stocks will eventually become the right stocks.

You aren't stupid; you should not have angst over losing money. You should have a healthy ego, and you have to believe in your investments and the stock market in order to get into the game in the first place. Taking a loss is par for the course in the stock market—at some point we all have to bail out of a stock with a sizable loss. But there is a difference between a big hit, say a loss of 20 percent, and a major hit, say a loss of 50 percent that could have been avoided.

"I can't stand losing money," you say. Welcome to the club. We all hate losing money. But there is absolutely no way you're going to be an investor and *not* lose money. More often than not, the inability to lose money by jumping off one horse, thereby passing up better investment returns from faster horses (those actually heading for the finish line), compounds our anxiety. Still, taking the hit is very tough at times. Just as so-called traders take too many hits, most investors don't take enough hits. I don't want to be cavalier about taking losses, but the sooner you're able to do so without getting emotional, the sooner you'll be on your way to consistently (year over year) making money rather than wasting time pouting, swearing off stocks or a specific stock, and sticking your head in the sand.

"Everybody plays the fool sometimes; there's no exception to the rule . . ." You know the song. The late-1990s stock market meltdown from the crashing of technology and telecommunications companies along with the overall market resulted in incredible losses for the public. There are some reports that the losses exceeded $8 trillion.

I'm not sure if the actual amount has been or could ever be accurately calculated. It is safe to say that just about everyone got waxed, pure and simple. However, losing money in investments isn't new, and usually the massive losses come from those too-good-to-be-true schemes that have the ability to suck us all in.

One of my favorite books is *Extraordinary Popular Delusions and the Madness of Crowds*, by Charles Mackay (New York: Random House Three Rivers Press, 1995). In the book, the author reviews three of the most incredible financial manias of all time, and also examines alchemists, modern prophecies, fortune-telling, the Crusades, and witch mania. The book is a great reminder that schemes and scams have been around from day one and also that everyone can become a victim. When these investment manias blow up, and they always do, small investors like to think they were the intended victim from the very beginning, but the truth is, the emotion of greed knows no economic boundary, and everyone gets wiped out. Case in point: the so-called South Sea Bubble.

The South Sea Company of England was established to make profitable trades with the Spanish colonies of Peru, Chile, and Mexico. The company was formed in 1711 with limited agreements with Spanish officials to conduct trade. This was the time the New World seemed like a marvelous pot of gold—in fact, reports of the gold and other valuables gotten by Spain were irresistible to the citizens of England, and even the English government.

The company, along with the government, was actually able to convince holders of short-term government debt of £10 million to exchange it for shares in the South Sea Company. As the years went on, the company was able to gain more government debt in return for shares and outrageously generous incentives until it held £117 million of government debt, versus £3.4 million held by the Bank of England and £3.2 million held by the Dutch East Indian Company.

The company didn't even make its first voyage until 1717, and it yielded little profit. The fact was that the structure of the company was a one-way ticket for disaster, but the general public overlooked many problems because the hype factor was too good to ignore. There was also the frosty relationship between Spain and England and the actual terms of the deal, which were never clearly articulated to investors.

Still, despite the lack of transparency, folks jumped into the stock, and not just poor, hardworking blacksmiths and shopkeepers and regular people, but also aristocrats and a guy named Sir Isaac Newton. Newton, whose name is still synonymous with intelligence, wrote the most important document of the Scientific Revolution, "Principia Mathematica." There are stories of Newton actually warning the general public about the risks of buying stock in the South Sea Company, but he eventually took the plunge and made money—the first time.

In fact, this guy who discovered the secrets of gravity doubled his money the first time he jumped in and picked up shares of South Sea. Later Newton picked up the stock again, but this time it wasn't as profitable, as his loss was more than twice the amount he came out with the first time around. I don't think he liked those apples. His losses led Newton to say: "I can calculate the motions of heavenly bodies, but not the madness of people." That was a great comment but something of a cop-out, too.

The best deal the South Sea Company ever got from Spain was the right to supply Spain's colonies with slaves for 30 years; in return, once a year the company could bring in one ship and load it with 500 tons of stuff. There were a couple of strings attached even to this portion of the deal. The King of Spain would get 25 percent of profits and there was a 5 percent tax on the remaining proceeds. Newton blames the crowd, but it was simply greed that he couldn't calculate or manage.

Insider Arsenic and Old Lace

The Brewster sisters in *Arsenic and Old Lace* didn't mind killing people for whom they felt sorry. During the brouhaha of the 1990s, many CEOs just didn't mind killing everyone in order to artificially inflate the value of their stock options, but some drank the arsenic as well.

Recently there have been other examples of people drinking the Kool-Aid with eyes wide open. Of course, excitement begets excitement, and anyone could be lured into a hyped-up situation where they chuck common sense in the heat of the moment. The problem is getting out of these situations, especially when the hype factor is working only on you as everyone else has seen the light and is bailing out. Again, I know it's really easy for an outsider to gain a small amount of knowledge and become a full-blown believer. What is really incredible is when people who should know better look beyond their insider status knowledge and still fall victim to the hype as any ordinary investor would.

Bernie Ebbers, a former high school basketball coach who began a small telecommunications company in Mississippi known as LDDS, will go down in the annals of corporate fraud as one of its most notorious perpetrators. Investors lost $180 billion in WorldCom, the company that LDDS eventually became after a series of 60 acquisitions, which became larger and grander along the way.

I remember the hype and excitement when the company took over MFS Communications, at the time a favorite stock of mine,

---

Margin and Margin Calls

In equities accounts, *margin* is the difference between the share price of a stock owned by the investor and the amount of money the brokerage firm lent the investor to make the purchase. Investors borrow money from the brokerage firm in hopes that an ensuing increase in share price will be substantially more than the amount of interest that has to be paid back for the privilege of the loan. It sounds neat but the problem comes when the stock goes down. The brokerage firm, in order to protect its loan, will issue a margin call. Requirements and terms of margin vary from firm to firm, but most are adamant about not letting losses get ahead of the value of the stock in the account.

for $12 billion. Then there was the acquisition of MCI Communications for $40 billion. Through the run-up of WorldCom's stock, Ebbers went on buying sprees and acquired a marina, a hotel, and other assets, as well as loading up on stocks in the market. Once WorldCom's share price began to wane, Ebbers convinced the board of directors to front him loans against his stock in order to meet margin calls.

Those loans ended up being consolidated into one large loan of $408.2 million. Many folks who know Ebbers think the need to prop the value of WorldCom stock price, which would have stopped the margin calls, was the motivating force behind the accounting scam that eventually resulted in a 25-year prison sentence. I bet there isn't a day that goes by when Ebbers doesn't say to himself, "Why didn't I just take my lumps, close the margin account, and ride off into the sunset?"

Here was a guy who knew he was cooking the books, and he must have figured others were cooking the books, too. Yet he got knee-deep into the game, lured by thoughts of taking his one-time net worth of $1.4 billion significantly higher. Here was an insider who nevertheless fell victim to the inability to get out and take a loss. The stock market bust had far-reaching reverberations that could never be quantified. There were suicides, divorces (man, there were a *lot* of divorces), and a loss of self-confidence and faith in one's fellow man. But having to do 25 years in prison is a harsh lesson.

Even the Wisest Can Lose Their Way

Another cautionary tale from a person who should have known better comes from the life story of Warren V. "Pete" Musser, founder and until 2001 chief executive officer of Safeguard Scientific. A local business legend in Pennsylvania, Pete Musser began life in the business world as an engineer and then a stockbroker. He eventually branched out to become a venture capitalist, although that term wasn't around back in 1953 when he started the company that was originally called Lancaster Corporation. Two name changes later, the company when public in 1967 and began trading on the NYSE in 1971.

Safeguard has been a holding company that invests in small

firms. In the past 10 years the company has invested in or acquired 180 businesses and has been involved in 40 mergers and acquisition exits as well as 24 initial public offerings. The company has been an incubator of companies, and it knew the ropes better than any average investor could. Yet Pete Musser began to buy the shares of other high-tech companies in his own account, and with it began to run up his margin account.

Safeguard shares changed hands very quietly for years and only caught fire after the public learned it was an incubator of small companies and could have a series of hot initial public offerings from its pool of holdings. Throughout the initial excitement Musser was a cool customer, but soon the ghost of Sir Isaac Newton took position of his soul and it was off to the races.

At Safeguard's peak in 2000, Pete Musser's 8 million shares were worth close to $700 million. (See Figure 4.2.) I guess any of us would have bought in to the hype, but this is a guy who understood business. He understood how nuts the systems was—or maybe he didn't. There was talk of the "new paradigm," when earnings and even sales really didn't matter. I bought in to it for a while, too.

Safeguard shares began to tumble hard. Even though the stock's descent was almost straight down, terra firma didn't come until late 2002. By this time Pete Musser was in terrible financial shape.

Recently Safeguard Scientific settled a class action lawsuit for loans of $10 million and guarantees of $35 million to Musser to

FIGURE 4.2 Safeguard Scientific: A Sinking Stock Couldn't Drown Unfounded Optimism and Hope
Chart courtesy of Prophet Financial Systems (www.prophet.net).

help him cover margin calls. In addition, Musser sold 7.5 million of his shares. By all accounts Musser is a great guy, a visionary, and a charismatic figure who got caught in the swirl of hype and promises of endless riches. Perhaps he should have known better. Like Bernie Ebbers, whose defense was that he didn't know what was going on, didn't own a computer, and was a victim of poor business execution, he was in the eye of the storm. If there were such a thing as a bird's-eye view, these guys had it.

In the end, it doesn't matter if you are one of the puppet masters or the greatest mind of your generation. *Anyone* is capable of succumbing to the thrill of the game and greed. Even when the jig is up, it's typical for investors to hold on to visions of riches and images of grandeur and take the ride all the way down. In fact, sometimes the smarter the investor, the bigger the financial hit when the wheels comes off an investment.

Call it arrogance or ego, but as a broker and analyst I've seen doctors lose a lot of money in medical and biotechnology stocks over the years. I think it is partly a factor of doctors feeling like they are the supreme authority in their field (much like Alec Baldwin in *Malice*). This leaves them vulnerable to making huge mistakes in the stock market. They hear a story, decide the story is great, buy the stock, and go into autopilot mode. Once they've bought into the potential of a company they're all in, hook, line, and sinker. The same happens to other intellectual professionals, folks whose mental prowess brings home the bacon. If they have it all figured out, it's tough to get them to unfigure the situation even as the underlying share price of their stock tumbles unabatedly.

During the 1990s I had the toughest time trying to get people who made their living in Silicon Valley to sell any tech stocks. I can still hear the echoes of these brainiacs (and I don't say that in mean-spirited way) saying things like "XYZ can't lose, it makes a blah blah blah that allows for fast transfer of information through a unique blah blah blah." Obviously, back in the 1990s, you didn't have to have a degree in computer science to think you knew everything about tech stocks.

I used to work hours trying to keep up. During the troughs of the tech rally, there were corporate fillings and a ton of other material to read. Magazines like *Red Herring* and *Business 2.0* were the size of the Manhattan phone book, and it was impossible to stay completely abreast of the newest thing. Yet I would have folks who didn't even know what a company did tell me with unshakable resolve that their investment was foolproof.

Like the famous song says, "Everybody plays the fool sometime." And if you're in the stock market, you don't begin being foolish until you have totally ignored all the writing on the wall.

Of course, there is always hope and there is always the future, which goes on forever, so in theory any company could "eventually" be a gigantic winner. I've seen a lot of stocks, once left for dead, come back over the past few years, but it still would have been smarter to bite the bullet, rather than waiting for the crash landing.

Swearing Off Stocks

A lot of investors have been bailed out of the negative aspect of sulking this time around because of the unprecedented rally in real estate. However, I think that, just like in the stock market, most people piled into real estate during the eighth and ninth innings of the boom and a large percentage will be hammered. (Although real estate doesn't go "no bid," the probably soft landing was harder than some expected or wanted, especially for those who jumped out of the frying pan of stocks and into the fire of the late-stage real estate rally.)

The point is that while it hasn't received the ink that the housing market has, the equity market was climbing off the canvass, and folks who dumped but bought other stocks that were excessively oversold are doing well and will be doing great over the next couple of years.

Thus far the bounce that began on the eve of the war in Iraq has seen a lot of money being made, but not by a lot of people. If you're saddled with a bunch of nonperformers like Lucent and other former high fliers and are reluctant to buy other stocks until those chestnuts come back, then you've compounded the problem. (My son is long in his college fund— I'm happy he's still young, plus there's always state school.)

If you're holding a stock simply out of ego, and the company's margins are falling apart, revenues are decreasing, the product pipeline is drying up, and there are rapid losses of market share, then sell.

That's one piece of the Captain Ahab puzzle. Another piece of the puzzle is being able to bite the bullet and then get back into the game. Sooner or later you are going to either get back into the stock market or at least seriously consider getting back in. If you pout through the best periods to be a buyer, then you've shooting yourself in the foot for the second time.

Even if you own a stock that climbed off the canvass from $10 to $15 (a 50 percent move), if your cost is $45, you may have wasted a lot of time and opportunity by not investing in other stocks that aren't merely bouncing with the broad market. (If you have such plays and have been able to create additional holdings, then it's not such a big deal.) By failing to jettison the old laggards in your portfolio, you create a series of problems, including:

- The emotional toll of looking at huge loses every time you look at your account.

- The financial limitations of not creating cash to find a better investment.

- Wasting time monitoring yesterday's losers when you could discover tomorrow's winners.

Emotions and Psychology

According to *On Death and Dying* (New York: Scribner, 1997), the book in which Elisabeth Kübler-Ross introduced the idea of five stages of grief a terminally ill person goes through, there is a range of emotions. They include:

1. Denial

2. Anger

3. Bargaining

4. Depression

5. Acceptance

The progression is similar when an investor holds a stock that only goes lower and lower. Except for disciplined day traders, the first reaction when a stock moves against us in a major way is denial. Of course, the rest of us should take a moment to consider the situation, do our fundamental work, and make an assessment on how likely it is the stock will come back. For sure the stock is unlikely to bounce back fast. An investor understands this fact and doesn't panic, but once the stock begins to move lower it turns up the emotional heat. You will question yourself and the wisdom of holding a stock when you could simply sell it and buy it back later.

The problem is that people rarely buy back stocks at the levels at which they sold them unless the bottom has totally fallen out of the stock, which would mean the new purchase is a major crapshoot.

The anger part I know all too well. As a provider of independent stock market research, our phones never stop ringing, as more than likely one of our ideas will be against us at any given point. I've seen people hold the worst pieces of garbage for years, but when one of my ideas dips, for even less than a point of a small fractional decline, they go off the deep end. It is easier to be angry at others than at yourself, but if you could turn that same anger against your own thinking, it could minimize a lot of future angst and potential monetary losses.

I've heard so many investors blame their broker, blame the fund manager, blame distractions, and blame the system for their losses. While there are varying degrees of truth to each of the notions that others caused your losses, in the end most investors who lost a lot of money share some of the blame. They were up at some point during the frenzy and wanted more. On any given night you could troll the bus depot at Atlantic City and find people with barely enough money to make it back home. I know—I've been there, and the common denominator for many of these poor souls is that they were up at one point; they were winning, but couldn't walk away from the tables or the slot machines.

We all bargain on the inside on what we'd like to do and how we plan on taking our lumps . . . at a higher price. You probably have been in a situation where you've said yes, this investment is a dud and I know it and I'll close it out once the stock gets back to a certain price—as if it's preordained that the stock will make such a move. Plus, if the stock does, many people renege on that bargain and change the terms.

Depression in the stock market is a commonplace emotion since March 2000 and it could continue to be for the foreseeable future. Although I think that as each year goes on, there will be greater traction, eventually the market will break out to a point where there are fewer pitfalls and fewer disasters because investors are fleet-footed and abandon ship so often. Depression is a serious enemy of investors; it paralyzes them and leads to any number of mistakes, as people will stick their heads in the sand and wallow in grief.

The fifth step, acceptance, is a key to recovery and moving on. Nonacceptance of a loss means the stock will sit in your portfolio forever, always reminding you of your mistakes and always making you hesitant to get back into the game.

Nobody Likes Being a Chump

And in the end, we were all chumps during the roaring bull market of the 1990s. There is a special psychological element to losses that people took during the tech rally. There was a wave of corporate malfeasance, false accounting schemes, and complicity from those who were supposed to know better. The entire system broke down. I'm not going against what I wrote earlier—everyone got too greedy and we all lost a little (or a lot) of our religion during the height of the boom period. Most investors could have walked away with fortunes but they didn't. Sure, the fact that many of the stocks we invested in were nothing more than houses of cards is particularly painful.

Psychologists have a list of all the emotions and angst people go through when they've lost money through fraud. This list is similar to the five stages of grief but significantly longer (list from www.yorkcounty.gov):

- Guilt

- Self-blame (often extremely high)

- Shame

- Disbelief

- Anger

- Depression

- Sense of betrayal

- Sense of violation

- Isolation ("suffering in silence")

- Social indifference

- Social stigma ("victim-blaming")

- Loss of faith in the world and in the system that was supposed to protect them

- Financial problems (due to actual monetary losses, lost work, and/or identity theft)

- Health problems (related to stress)

Ken Lay and many others in the system—from corporate chieftains to agencies in charge—either let us down or downright betrayed us. The pain may have been greater from letdown by our would-be guardians, those agencies and powers that looked the other way and in many ways encouraged the malicious behavior of publicly traded companies. The SEC, NASD, and NYSE were supposed to be protecting us.

Eliot Spitzer, the newly elected governor of New York, rode in like the cavalry to save the day and boost his political stock. Many of the fines and rulings and laws put in place since the height of the scandalous period have been insulting, toothless, and in some cases too extreme (complying with some rules has driven a bunch of smaller companies to delist as the costs have been prohibitive).

We were betrayed by the media, which became a wild cheerleader and as caught up in the moment as all of us. Sure, there were articles and publications that worked to warn of the hazards and craziness of the moment. But to this day, CNBC should have accepted more culpability about the massive madness and its part as enablers of misguided greed.

Oddly enough, because of the widespread impact of systemic fraud and failure, there isn't the same degree of social isolation generally associated with the feeling of being ripped off. Our neighbors, coworkers, and strangers on the morning train commute lost a bundle, too. By the same token, there was also much less self-blame. I attend investor conferences and speak with individual investors daily, and it's rare when one says he or she got greedy.

In the end, the feeling of being violated has had a long-lasting consequence. I think it plays a role in the way the market acts on a day-to-day basis. It contributes to the wild gyrations and knee-jerk reactions to corporate earnings, economic data, and geopolitical events.

There are so many emotions and reminders of the best of times and worst of times for stock investors of this generation. For all of those that negatively impact your mind and your approach to the market, none seems to have a deeper impact than holding on to those old losers that linger in your portfolio. Every time you gaze at these losers that are anchoring your portfolio, any newer efforts to make money seem to be mitigated. Those losers you just can't seem to get rid of will continue to haunt you and laugh at you every time you look at your portfolio.

Hook, Line, and Sinker

The Captain Ahab syndrome isn't relegated just to holding stocks that are screaming sells; it also applies to incorporating methods that just aren't working either.

I understand the need to be amenable, to be able to bend somewhat when conditions in the market dictate. The system I'm teaching in this book could be outperformed from time to time by an array of other systems and approaches, but over the long haul, companies that are doing the right things should see their share prices rewarded. Still, during the late 1990s I abandoned logic for a time to ride the incredible waves, and while it paid off for my clients for a time, it also backfired down the road.

Nonetheless, I was able to come to my senses before things got disastrous. Yet I saw, time after time, when clients refused to take the loss—in fact, more often than not, when investors were down on a stock in 2000 to 2001—the first thought was to average down rather than bite the bullet. At that time many investors found systems and approaches that enabled them to remain stubborn.

After the period that brought us books that touted the Dow rocketing to 20,000 and 30,000 in a matter of years came the doom-and-gloom period: systems that say the market should be lower, that the Dow will never be able to rally higher until it comes down and test 5,000. People are so pissed off and turned off by the stock market that they have taken to theses kinds of tomes with religious fervency.

The biggest problem I see with many investors, from professionals to novices, is their overreliance on charts. I get into charts in greater detail in the next chapter, but for now I want to mention there are charting methods and systems out there that are ridiculously self-important and complicated.

The notion that the share price of a company with thousands of employees in dozens of countries, which generates billions of dollars in revenue, can be predicted by logarithms or is preordained to go down in a three-step motion, then rebound in a two-step motion, and then repeat the process over again is far-fetched. Yet there are legions of folks who have bought into these theories.

I guess it's par for the course in this day and age. *The Da Vinci Code* sold so many copies in part because it took readers on a ride of hidden messages along with cloak-and-dagger maneuvering among the characters. The topic was controversial but there have been books out with similar themes (as witnessed by all the lawsuits against the author, Dan Brown) that didn't ring up a fraction of the sales.

People are enamored with the notion of things being written in the stars or things being preordained.

Embracing systems that haven't worked in a long time, or embracing methodologies that aren't working, is borderline madness. Ironically, I see evidence of this kind of thinking on Wall Street every day. The stock rating downgrades that come after the underlying stock or sector has already declined by 50 percent are commonplace on Wall Street. These guys have systems, very elaborate systems that add every kind of possibility into the equation and only subtract common sense. Maybe it's because they speak to company directors and develop personal relationships; maybe it's because they have very rigid parameters for making adjustments; or maybe it's because their outlooks are supposed to be long term (although I'm not sure what the exact amount of time is that constitutes "long term").

I also think many of the analysts at these large brokerage firms suffer from the kind of arrogance that experts in their field suffer from. These guys and gals, once elevated to rock star status, see themselves as extensions of the prestigious firms they work for. It's easy to get a big head, to believe in your work even in the face of facts and actions that would say otherwise.

I know how easy it is to be swayed by the crowd. When it comes to jumping on the bandwagon, I've done my share in the past and will in the future, but I would never bet the farm on hype or mass hysteria.

The flip side is when the Street sticks with a theme that has been totally rejected by the market. I think, more often than not, it's the contempt of the little guy that makes these Wall Street guys move so slowly.

Another problem is when there is no accountability for being completely wrong. Wall Street analysts don't have to face the clients. Brokers do. In fact, there is a major movement afoot to take accountability away from brokers, too, through managed accounts in which they are recommending an investment scheme in which they have no direct involvement. This means you can't get upset with the broker, but you'll never be able to ask the folks behind the managed plan what the heck they were thinking.

Analysts and now brokers have a corporate veil to hide behind. You can't escape the mirror of personal reality. Buying in to a system hook, line, and sinker is perhaps the ultimate display of capitulation.

Home Run Swing

Not every investment is going to take you to the bank; in fact, some will bankrupt you if you don't accept when they are wrong. When an investor bets it all on one stock, she is going for the home run, and more often than not the only other alternative is a strikeout.

> Though amid all the smoking horror and diabolism of a sea-fight, sharks will be seen longingly gazing up to the ship's decks, like hungry dogs round a table where red meat is being carved, ready to bolt down every killed man that is tossed to them.
>
> —*Moby Dick*

People are frozen by fear and angst and not sure where to turn. Many investors fear that the fate awaiting them is greater and even more diabolical than just staying the course, no matter how tattered and unfruitful it has been. We're not talking about the road less traveled here. When it comes to money, or should I say losing money, intelligence and common sense are the high road. And virtually every time, tossing out the philosophical angle to investing is the right road, too.

The myopic approach to the market is evident in so many aspects of the market, not just holding a stock that goes from $100 a share to $10 a share, or adhering to systems that say the U.S. market is going to go up or down a certain amount no matter what the economic backdrop or political situation, or, let's not forget, the status of corporate earnings. The Captain Ahab syndrome also extends to distribution of funds and balance of portfolios.

I continue to see too many people load up. They are buying a ton of stocks in the same sector or just one stock in hopes of hitting it out of the ballpark. The home run swing comes from those people who want to make it all back overnight. In many ways the home run swing is as much a defensive mechanism as an offensive mechanism.

Anyone who has been to a gambling casino has probably seen the home run swing in action. You know, when you're at the blackjack table at 11:00 at night, when the crowd has thinned a bit and only the diehard and desperate are still at it, someone walks by and takes the seat next to you. The person has a dazed and haggard look and tosses $300 on the table and asks for chips in $25 denominations.

This newcomer then plays a few hands at $25 and proceeds to win one but then loses a streak of hands, perhaps as many as four. What happens next is the home run swing. Assessing what's left, this down-on-his-luck gambler bets half his stake. He gets a face card and the dealer gets a face card. He gets an 8 and the dealer gets a 2. Now he's thinking, man, I should have bet the whole thing.

The dealer has to take a hit (in casinos the dealer has to hold with a total of 17 and must take hits until that number or a greater total has been reached) and proceeds to get a 9, bringing the house total to 21. Talk about bad luck! I'm sure anyone who has been in a casino can identify with this. So the gambler goes for it, he bets it all—the home run swing. Maybe the next hand is a winner, but the mentality has already set in and it's home run or bust the rest of the way out—and the casino doesn't go bust.

The thing is, people still want to load up. Especially since 2000, it has been so hard for me to get people to consider buying just a few shares of a stock that has a fantastic future rather than loading up on a low-priced stock. I haven't done a formal study, but I know from being in the market every day for the last two decades that you'd rather buy a stock going through $100 a share than one going through $10 a share. The caveat, of course, is if the stock going through $100 is doing so based on solid fundamentals. But it's not just a matter of convincing folks to buy $100 stocks. Those with the Captain Ahab syndrome love to load up on stocks trading for $10.

Back in October 2002 a $35 stock was an expensive stock, at least for those who measure value simply based on the share price. If you're honest with yourself, I'm sure you would have reconsidered all the cheap stocks that were out there—you know Lucent was cheap, JDS Uniphase was cheap, Microsoft was cheap, and Intel was cheap, in terms of their respective share prices. At least the latter were companies with the resources to mount some kind of business rebound.

There were also many other stocks out there during the market meltdown that continuously attracted buyers based on past glory and past hype. Ironically these names actually moved even lower. In the meantime companies with solid fundamentals couldn't get investors to buy their stock even though their shares were lower, too, as the entire market suffered during the meltdown. One such name is FedEx, a very familiar household name, whose shares were sinking with the broad market, but once they hit the bottom it has been almost a straight line higher. The stock is up 300 percent and counting. (See Figure 4.3.)

Conclusion

Extensive studies have been done that show how much more the pain of losing money impacts a person than the joy of making

FIGURE 4.3   FedEx Takes Off

Chart courtesy of Prophet Financial Systems (www.prophet.net).

money. It is a scientific fact that people shut down when they endure a monetary loss. Then there are the kinds of losses investors have taken since 2000, crippling losses that create long-term bitterness and anger. In an effort to skip the finalization of such a crippling loss, many investors have become like Captain Ahab. They put on the blinders and only care about the stocks they own. They believe, almost in a psychotic manner, that their stocks will come back.

If you own a stock that has bitten the dust, if management is coming and going so often you suspect there is a revolving door, or if the company has hit the skids and management hasn't been replaced, then it may be time to wake up and smell the coffee. If a company isn't growing the top line, isn't growing margins, isn't giving promising guidance, isn't winning market share, and the stock keeps dropping lower and lower and lower, and you refuse to sell, then, mate, you are spending time going after the elusive white whale—which for you is trying to break even on a stock that isn't coming back.

. . . from hell's heart I stab at thee; for hate's sake I spit my last breath at thee.

—Captain Ahab in *Moby Dick*

When a company becomes broken, the healing doesn't come overnight. The fact of the matter is, it can take years after a rare reversal of fortunes to see a positive impact on a stock's share price.

Taking a loss is tough, but it is the only way to get back on the road toward really making money in the stock market.

Following these maxims will help you avoid the Captain Ahab syndrome:

- Companies that don't pass the fundamental test outlined in this book must be sold.

- When you're down 50 percent, holding these stocks can only become a haunting reminder of past failures in the market or of the market letting you down.

- Consider different systems for picking stocks.

- Stocks aren't preordained to follow sequential patterns; they don't automatically go up three times, then down two times, then up three times.

- Stocks aren't preordained to follow the numerical patterns outlined by nature (birds-fly-south-for-the-winter stocks). Like humans, stocks move to patterns that aren't outlined in the pattern of a shell.

- Reggie Jackson had some of the best home runs in history but also the most strikeouts. Stop focusing on the majestic home run because the missed swings are huge and take a heavy toll on your portfolio.

Remember, sometimes the noise that is making you hold a disaster is coming from inside, emanating from your heart, and drowning out the common sense in your mind. Emotions can't be totally avoided but they can be mitigated, and doing so begins with recognizing the writing on the wall.

PART TWO

TOOLS AND RULES

Pretty as a Picture

Using Charts

They say pictures are worth a thousand words; these days pictures are worth billions in investing dollars that move in and out of the market based on past behavior in the stock market.

In this era of elaborate scavenger hunts, hidden messages in famous paintings, and forensic thrills shown nightly on television, many people would like to play the stock market using fancy tools without knowing or caring about the facts of the companies they're investing in. Like Tom Cruise's character in *Minority Report*, these investors like to whiz around charts with a lot of bells and whistles to come up with moneymaking ideas.

The use of charts to determine probability has long been a part of many endeavors outside the stock market, whether predicting population trends or illustrating the weather. In the stock market charts are part of technical analysis, which is the use of historic price movements to predict future price movements.

In the 1990s, technical analysis through the use of charts became extremely popular, and charts continue to be the primary investment tool for individual investors. However, the professionals on Wall Street have only *grudgingly* given credence to the use of charts. The majority of professionals still consider the *implementation* of charts in the decision-making process to be nothing more than voodoo.

The great thing about charts, particularly during a roaring bull market, is they allow you to suspend common sense. If the chart says a stock is going higher, then the stock is going higher, no ifs, ands, or buts. Whether the stock deserves to change hands at newer and higher levels is inconsequential. In short, the chart justifies a stock being higher and so the stock goes higher. New highs beget new highs, which occur as part of a breakaway bull market anyway, but the move supports the use of charts and the charts validate the move. The roaring bull market provides the perfect symbiotic relationship. That is why so many investors and even some professionals began to incorporate charts in their decision-making processes. The funny thing was, and still is, that few investors *consider the consequences* of negative chart formations when the time comes. The same folks who *bought* on technical breakouts didn't *sell* when the stock is breaking a series of key support points.

I don't blame charts for the trillions of dollars investors lose. I blame the exclusive misuse of charts—ignoring clear sell signals, eschewing fundamentals and plain old common sense. I believe charts have a role to play, albeit in conjunction with fundamental analysis, to successfully outperform in today's stock market. Unfortunately too many individual investors are relying solely on their charts to make investment choices. It's really nuts. I actually believe that people who rely solely on charts have lost more money in the market on their own in the last 10 years than all the losses from corporate malfeasance and Wall Street's complicity combined. The interesting thing about technical analysis is that it *can* be really simple. Following are some of the typical pitfalls of relying only on charts for your information.

Eye of the Beholder

Too many people treat charts as a science, rather than art, yet many folks see different things when viewing the same chart. For me, charts give an idea of where a stock price can *potentially* go if a series of things happen. The thing about technical analysis is it doesn't consider the fundamentals or facts of a company. The charts can make a sloppy company with poor execution look like the greatest stock in the world, or the greatest company can look like junk on the charts.

Another problem with charts is that they're open to interpretation. There are some rules to charting, but for the most part their value lies in the eyes of the beholder. I've spoken to investors about charts that they've hit me with. The jargon and words sounded good on paper, but in the end they were using the charts as excuses to hold stocks or buy more. And yet there is no denying the uncanny coincidences of stocks to come out of certain formations and make moves that are later justified by fundamental news.

Charts tell a story about supply and demand, human behavior, and psychology. When I look at a chart, I feel like I'm looking at a history book, and history does repeat itself, although not in a fashion that can be so easily predicted. I know when the company is a young whippersnapper, and I can see when a company is going through growing pains. I can see when the stock somehow becomes a favorite of the hot money crowd and there is ridiculous speculation. Charts tell *some* important parts of the stock story.

I love charts, but I am also afraid of the influence charts have on investors. It pains me when people think they know the stock market because a couple of chart formations have worked for them in the past. It bothers me to no end when someone loads up on a stock armed only with the confidence that the chart looks good. I also can't believe how many times people will let moneymaking opportunities pass them by until the chart looks good.

Because there are so many people relying so much on charts, technical analysis has a greater impact than it's ever had. So monitoring charts has become a useful tool for gauging emotions and human behavior. Whether professional investors or sophisticated pundits have disdain for average individual investors and their ability to play the stock market, based on charts, there is no denying their collective influence—particularly on a short-term basis.

Remember, emotion can lead to terrible mistakes in playing the stock market. When the crowd is making those mistakes, you can use charts either to take advantage or simply to get out of the way. Of course, fundamental work supersedes technical work, but there are times when the charts are screaming that a stock is a buy, based on a breakout with strong volume, or a sell, based on serious risk.

In a nutshell, fundamental analysis tells you *what* to buy and technical analysis tells you *when* to buy.

You can make decisions based on chart patterns or signs that could help you take your emotions out of the game. Often folks will ignore internal developments that suggest a company isn't executing, is losing market share, is losing pricing power, and so on. Charts can help underscore the declining fortunes of a company. By incorporating both fundamental and technical work, you have a one-two punch that can make you see the light.

Of course, there are going to be times when the chart is saying one thing and fundamental data says another, telling you a completely different story. In this circumstance you should defer to the facts first—they tell a better story of the future than the charts, which tell a historic story, and they hint at the near-term direction of a stock.

I've spoken with many fund managers and expert investors who would never give charting any credibility in public or with their clients, but they do glance at the charts from time to time. I think they consider charts much the way many investors do, as a means to back up a hunch or investment they've already decided on. In fundamental work the numbers are the numbers. They aren't subject to vastly different interpretations (although their rationalization could be twisted).

Charts are great tools, but so is a jackhammer. Use either of these the wrong way and it's curtains. In fact, you'd be better off stubbing your foot with a jackhammer than getting caught using only charts with your real investing money. (If you are using only charts for trading, then there is less risk—but I think playing the market only as a so-called trader is a road to disaster, too.)

Charts are subordinate to fundamental research. No matter how complicated you make your chart work, please don't forget this. Charts are to be used to gauge trading range and supply and demand points, and as a proxy for the emotions of the crowd.

Types of Charts

There are several different kinds of charts, including line area and percent, but the three most prevalent are point-and-figure, candlesticks, and bar charts, all of which have special features desired by folks following the market on a minute-to-minute basis. For me the wide variety in charts is almost silly. In the end, the information they are communicating is the same, just revealed differently.

I want you to use bar charts initially. You can get exotic and fancy later, but the bar chart is easy to interpret and to do studies on without confusion.

Point-and-Figure Charts

Point-and-figure charts use a series of Xs and Os to filter out what adherents consider inconsequential sessions to derive these charts (see Figure 5.1). I know of many investors, especially professionals, who swear by these charts in part because they deliberately take out the first 10 to 20 percent of a move, which could be occurring on pure, raw emotions, and trigger buy and sell signals after the trend is firmly in place. My friend Tom Dorsey of Dorsey Wright is a renowned genius in the use of these charts, and he still advocates swift action should there be abrupt changes in the pattern.

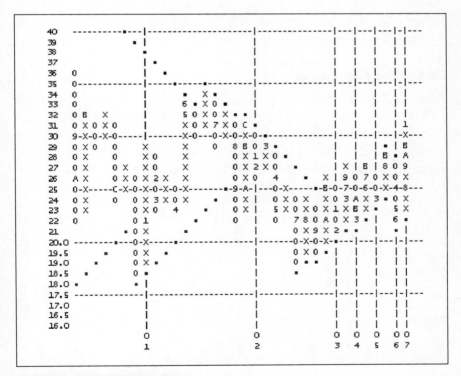

FIGURE 5.1   Point-and-Figure Chart
Chart courtesy of Dorsey, Wright & Associates.

Candlesticks

Candlestick charts were developed in Japan and are also known as Japanese candlesticks (see Figure 5.2). During the Sengoku period, 250 fiefdoms in Japan were being consolidated, and this opened up trade. During that period the Dojima Rice Exchange, generally considered to be the world's first futures market, was established to buy and sell rice that was stored in warehouses throughout the country and ultimately bound for delivery in Osaka. Several historic figures since the seventeenth century have used this charting method to make money and gain fame. In the United States the best source of information on candlesticks is Steve Nison.

Bar Charts

Surely you remember bar charts from first grade or the latest spreadsheet report generated by the folks in the accounting department at work. Stock market bar charts trace the entire trading range of a particular session with lines to denote where the stock opened and closed (see Figure 5.3).

Learning the Lingo

Although you could very well create your own language for technical analysis—for instance, instead of *resistance* you could call it "roadblock" and instead of *breakaway gap* you could call it "busting out of the blocks"—you may have to communicate these ideas with others, and certainly others will communicate

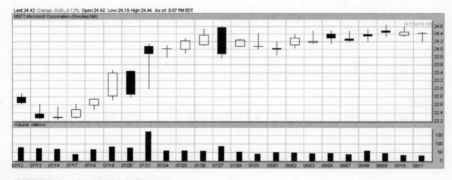

FIGURE 5.2 Candlestick Chart
Chart courtesy of Prophet Financial Systems (www.prophet.net).

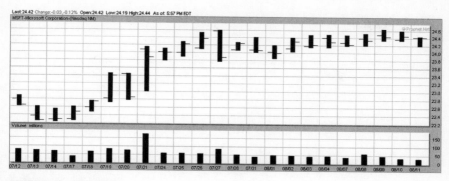

FIGURE 5.3 Bar Chart

Chart courtesy of Prophet Financial Systems (www.prophet.net).

technical ideas and information to you as well. So a common language is helpful.

There are several terms associated with technical analysis, most of which are misused these days, and so they've become an inappropriately prevalent part of the vernacular of investing. When stocks aren't really breaking out but we are told they are, then investors could make poor and costly decisions. Even those professionals who don't use technical analysis in their work often use terms associated with technical analysis. For instance, a breakout should only be called when the stock has broken out to a new 52-week high, yet we hear all the time that a stock has "broken out." Eclipsing certain chart formations, like moving through the top of a channel or closing above a key resistance point on the chart, may be called a breakout, but in reality a breakout is a monumental move to a new 52-week high.

Resistance

Resistance is the point on the chart where the stock failed to break out once before and pulled back, typically 10 percent or more.

I've chosen a six-month chart of Caremark (stock symbol CXM), which had been on a serious roller coaster, but once it broke out through resistance the stock gained solid momentum and made a major gain. (See Figure 5.4.) The resistance point was created when the stock failed to clear through $51 in late February. Later, in March, the stock again failed to clear $51, confirming this was a serious point

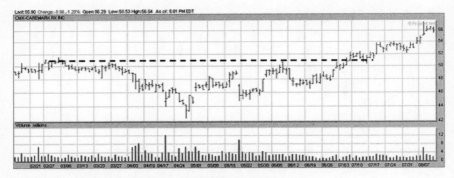

FIGURE 5.4   Caremark: Resistance Point and Breakout

Chart courtesy of Prophet Financial Systems (www.prophet.net).

of resistance. In fact, when the rally failed at resistance for the second time, the stock tumbled hard. That same resistance point held in May and later in June. The fact that this staunch resistance point held for several months made the eventual breakout monumental.

Support

Support is the point on the chart where the stock stumbled but found terra firma and began to rebound. Typically the rebound results in a rally of 10 percent or more.

The stock example in Figure 5.5 is Sears Holdings (stock symbol SHLD), which developed a couple of support points during the six-month period from February to August 2006. One key support point was created when the stock gapped higher in May 2006.

FIGURE 5.5   Sears Holdings: Extensive Damage When Key Support Fails

Chart courtesy of Prophet Financial Systems (www.prophet.net).

Later the stock pulled back to that point but no lower. The support line held (more or less—it doesn't have to be perfect) until early July, when it failed to hold and resulted in a sharp decline that sent the stock much lower.

Note: Resistance becomes support and support becomes resistance. This intriguing occurrence is far more than coincidence. For my next example I use ImClone (stock symbol IMCL), the company at the center of the Martha Stewart scandal in which the domestic diva was accused of trading on insider information. The case centered on whether she dumped her shares of ImClone after receiving a tip from the then ImClone CEO Sam Waksal.

For his part, Waksal eventually received a seven-year prison sentence of his own for selling his stock and directing members of his family to do the same. Because of an extravagant lifestyle (sound familiar?), Waksal was in a dire position. He knew that a deal that was in the works to sell some of the company to Bristol-Myers for $2 billion would go down the drain when news came

---

Erbitux

This super drug made ImClone one of the hottest biotech companies in the world and made Sam Waksal very rich (he made $60 million in 2000 and $70 million in 2001). His new-found wealth and fame from ushering in the cancer miracle drug drove him into the ultrawealthy circle of the world that Martha Stewart inhabited.

Erbitux is a so-called epidermal growth factor inhibitor. It disrupts the growth of cancer in healthy cells, thereby stopping its advance and eventually killing the cancer. The drug was put on the fast track of approval by the FDA in 2001, adding to the allure that sent the share price of ImClone from less than $3 a share in 1998 to $80 a share in early 2000. Since the scandal, Erbitux has been approved for patients with metastatic colorectal cancer who have not done well on certain kinds of chemotherapy. The drug has also been approved for head and neck cancer, and the company is working on many more uses of the drug, including expanded use in earlier cases of colorectal cancer. Currently the drug costs patients about $10,000 a month.

out from the Food and Drug Administration that the company's super cancer drug, Erbitux, would need more testing before it could be approved for patient use.

Waksal panicked and sold his shares ahead of public dissemination of the news. Martha Stewart was never tried or convicted of insider selling; she went to prison for "lying" to investigators.

Since then, the share price of ImClone came all the way back and has been as much as $20 higher than the point where Sam Waksal and Martha Stewart sold their shares (could you imagine pining away in prison for dumping a stock that ultimately rebounds to the point where you sold it?). It has been lower as well. The volatile nature of the stock has created important swing points. Parallel lines that were once resistance, then shifted to support, and later became resistance continue to occur in charts of the stock.

In the chart of ImClone in Figure 5.6, it is clear that $39.50 is a magical point. First it held as resistance, an impenetrable upside hurdle for the stock. Later it served as support, and when the stock dipped below the line in early July 2006, it was a major red flag. The stock tested the number again as resistance and failed to cross over, subsequently tumbling by more than 28 percent less than a month later.

This chart also displays another example of how support and resistance points switch once the stock has crossed through in either direction. From here on out $34, which held as support and later became a serious resistance point, will be an important number.

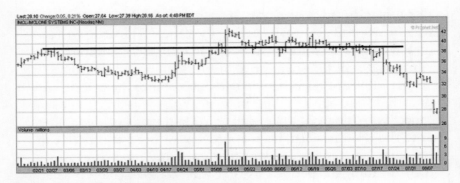

FIGURE 5.6   ImClone: Resistance Becomes Support

Chart courtesy of Prophet Financial Systems (www.prophet.net).

Breakouts

A *breakout* occurs when a stock closes above resistance and continues to rally higher.

A breakout is easy to spot: It's the point where the stock finally clears a longtime stubborn resistance point. A true breakout comes when the stock is moving to a new 52-week high on stronger-than-average volume. However, we hear the term used all the time to denote when the stock simply cleared a key upside hurdle.

Gaps

Gaps are created when a stock opens significantly higher or lower than where it was quoted in the preceding session.

The thing to remember about gaps is that once they are created, they're usually filled down the line. When I say they're filled, I mean that the space created by the major disparity between an opening price and the previous day's closing price will eventually be retraced and the gap will in effect be closed.

Take the chart of Yellow Roadway, the giant trucking company formed from the merger of Roadway and Yellow Freight (Figure 5.7). Its shares have become very volatile in recent years as the strong economy has helped the fundamentals while higher gas prices have hurt the bottom line. Let's take a look at the downside gap created on March 23 when the stock opened for trading at $40 a share after closing the preceding session at $45.

FIGURE 5.7   Yellow Roadway: Downside and Upside Gaps
Chart courtesy of Prophet Financial Systems (www.prophet.net).

From the moment this gap was created I knew there would be a time when it would be closed. However, bottom fishing was out of the question, as it always is. There are a lot of folks out there trying to catch fallen knives, and it makes no sense. Sure, most major sell-offs these days are driven by excessive emotions, but that doesn't make the coast is clear when a stock has been hammered. Usually there will be additional selling pressure to come.

So there was the gap and immediately $45 became the point where the gap would be closed. The point where a gap will close becomes staunch resistance (see the dashed line in the chart). As we see in Figure 5.7, the stock eventually was able to rebound all the way up to fill the gap, but then suddenly reversed back to the downside. This happens often enough to be more than random, so keep it in mind in the future.

Interestingly, there was also an upside gap created during this time frame when the stock opened above $41 on April 25 after closing at $39 the session before. This gap was filled, too, but the stock didn't reverse immediately. However, the stock meandered around $39 and eventually did rally higher, once again proving how gaps play a critical role with respect to near-term direction of stocks. Gaps also give you a sense of how high or low a stock could go over a short period of time (less than one year).

Stocks that have a history of downside gaps should be avoided. Typically this reflects inconsistent management. After all, those big downside openings aren't just intriguing chart patterns, they represent the fact that the stock got hit hard—hammered! No matter how much of a roll a company's fundamentals get on, when management has messed up so badly that huge chunks of value are wiped out in single days, then there is always a chance there will be future missteps.

Figure 5.8 shows California Micro Devices (stock symbol CAMD), a stock that has had the stuffing knocked out of it more than once (marked by the arrows on the chart). The interesting thing is that this stock has been able to climb off the canvas. However, as it stands now, I wouldn't touch the stock with a 10-foot pole. If two years go by and the stock hasn't cratered, then I will take a look at the fundamentals and reevaluate. But it has been my experience that companies that have had two major

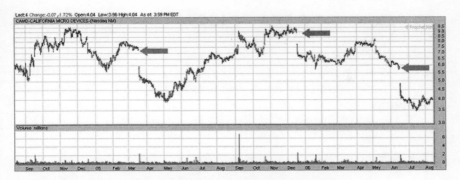

FIGURE 5.8   California Micro Devices: Repeated Huge Downside Gaps
Chart courtesy of Prophet Financial Systems (www.prophet.net).

gaps to the downside within any two-year or shorter time frame are simply too risky. Repeated gaps are like rattles on a rattlesnake—beware!

Summary

When I'm asked about a company or a stock, the first thing I do is look at the chart. I'm not looking for patterns or indicators; I'm simply looking at how successful investors have been with the stock over a series of time periods. Charts tell you:

- About past mistakes.
- About management's ability to execute.
- Where a stock may have been overvalued.
- Where a stock may have been undervalued.
- Where there could be supply.
- Where there could be demand.

I look at six-month, one-year, and then multiyear charts to give me a sense of the upside or downside and also to gauge the degree of supply along the way. Remember, there are going to be sellers at each pivotal resistance point on the upside (folks who bought the stock at that price early on and pledged to get out once they were breaking even). This explains why true breakouts result in huge spikes higher: All the sellers have already sold their shares on the way up, and the weak sisters were out long ago; anyone who has the stock here is going to hold, and that will magnify the impact of any buying.

Turning Charts into Road Maps

Now that you have a general sense about what charts are and how to look at them, let's focus on using the charts in your decision-making process. Charts aren't a magic elixir, no matter how fancy they look or what Internet propaganda says, but they are important and will help your decision-making as to when to buy and when to sell. Look at technical analysis (the ability to decipher charts) as a skill you have to learn. At the end of the day, fundamentals should be 80 percent of your investment decision-making process, while charts and understanding the crowds could make up the remainder.

So What Exactly *Are* Charts, and How Can I Use Them?

There are several important elements in technical analysis charting, including the ability to identify and understand chart formations and indicators, price history daily and historic volume, along with different views framed by using an assortment of time intervals. (I always look at the 52-week chart first and then adjust to better understand recent trends. When the stock is nearing a 52-week high, it is important to adjust the chart back far enough to get a gauge on where the next breakout could land the share price.)

The list of would-be indicators is a mile long, and that's just official stuff. The reality is you could probably find an indicator or two to justify behavior that in your heart and mind you know is incorrect. A number of charting Web sites provide great tools. Following is a list of key indicators found on ProphetChart (www.prophet.net), a site I happen to use in my day-to-day work.

Accumulation/distribution line

Advance/decline line

Arms Index

Average true range (ATR)

Bollinger bands

Chaikin Oscillator

Chaikin Volatility Indicators

CP Volumentum Trend

DeMark Indicator

Detrended price oscillator (DPO)

Directional movement index (DMI)

Ease of movement

Haurlan Index

Keltner channels

Linear regression

McClellan Oscillator

Momentum

Money flow index (MFI)

Moving average (displaced, exponential, and simple)

Moving average convergence/divergence (MACD)

Moving average envelope

Negative volume index (NVI)

On-balance volume

Parabolic stop and reversal (SAR)

Positive volume index (PVI)

Price channel

Price oscillator

Rate of change (ROC)

Relative strength index (RSI)

Short-term Index (STIX)

Stochastic oscillator

Stoller Average Range Channels (STARC) bands

TD Moving Average

Time series forecast

Ultimate oscillator

Upside/downside ratio

Volume

Volume accumulation

Volume oscillator

Volume ROC

Wilder's volatility index (WVI)

There can be so many indicators on a chart it would make your head swim. I swear sometimes it seems like all the stocks that begin with "T" find a way to rally on Tuesday. I'm being a little tongue in cheek, but the reality is there are a bunch of signs and each matters to someone. You could have three signals saying "buy," four saying "sell," and two others saying "punt." It can get very confusing, to say the least.

Choosing Your Indicators Wisely

Figure 6.1 shows an example of how a lot of indicators can be very confusing. In this example, there are only five different indicators. I know people who incorporate two, three, even *four times* that amount. Those charts look more like works of art than tools for investing. Jackson Pollock would have been proud.

The following sections outline some of my favorite indicators.

Moving Averages—Directional Trends and Changes

I love *moving averages*, which are computed by taking a series of days' prices, adding them, dividing their sum by the number of days, and plotting the results to form a continuous line across the width of the chart. There are several types of moving averages (displaced, exponential, and simple), but my favorite is the exponential moving average.

Typically, when plotting moving averages, the system you're using will give you a chance to install various time periods. Since the 50-day and 200-day moving averages are universally used and recognized, you should include those. I also add the 20-day moving average to the mix, although more technicians go with the 10-day moving average.

Moving averages act as swing points and support and resistance points. When stocks clear key moving averages, they commonly

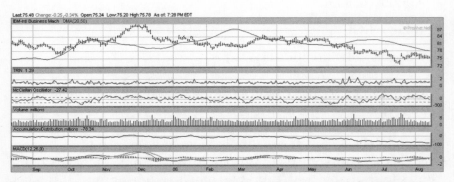

FIGURE 6.1   Chart of IBM with Trend Line, Volume, Oscillator, Accumulation/Distribution, and MACD Studies

Chart courtesy of Prophet Financial Systems (www.prophet.net).

pick up momentum, whereas when they fail to cross the moving average, the stock price is likely to tumble hard and fast. More often than not, the 50-day moving average will be in between the 20-day and 200-day and act as a kind of swing point. If a share price is declining and goes below the 50-day moving average (on a closing basis), then there is a high probability the stock will continue to decline to the next moving average. The same is true when the share price is moving higher and closes above the middle moving average (typically the 50-day); in that case, it is highly likely the share price will continue higher until it touches the next, higher moving average. This is even more likely when there is strong volume (I like to see 50 percent more than the daily average volume), which acts as a confirmation of the breakout through the moving averages.

When all the moving averages are violated (have been cleared), then there is usually a dramatic move, as shown in Figure 6.2. In late September 2005 Maxim (stock symbol MXIM) slipped below all three key moving averages. The stock didn't crumble but the writing was on the wall, and the next time all three moving averages were violated (early October), the move was a harbinger of serious downside to come. Now the lowest moving average was resistance, as indicated by the first arrow on the chart. This resistance held several times before the stock succumbed to a traumatic decline, gapping lower in late October and diving to new lows. Once the stock was in a decidedly downward spiral, there were several attempts to break out that saw the stock get above

FIGURE 6.2   Violating All Three Key Moving Averages

Chart courtesy of Prophet Financial Systems (www.prophet.net).

the 20-day moving average, but it failed at the 50-day. I've high-lighted four such occasions on the chart.

This is why most stock traders consider the 50-day moving average a vital trading tool. The goal of this book is to help you think like investors rather than day traders who chase each twist and turn of the stock market, but I also want to make you aware of the different ways people attempt to play the stock market. With that in mind, you have to understand the short-term implications of the 50-day moving average. It is the key moving average, in my opinion, with respect to significant directional changes in the share price of a stock (although I know some brilliant chart masters who swear by the 20-day moving average).

What are the uses of each of these moving averages?

- The 20-day moving average is great for plotting and getting ahead of short-term moves.

- Typically, 50-day moving averages signal major directional changes and help confirm when a stock is breaking out or breaking down.

- The 200-day moving average gives you an idea of where a stock can go once it clears the 50-day moving average on the upside, or how far the stock could go should the 50-day not hold as a support point.

In the example in Figure 6.3 (American Tower, stock symbol AMT), you can see in hindsight where a trader could have made

FIGURE 6.3 The 50-Day Moving Average as a Swing Point
Chart courtesy of Prophet Financial Systems (www.prophet.net).

money rather than losing it, simply by reacting to the relationship of the stock and the 50-day moving average. A trader could have bought or sold the stock with the notion of exiting that trade within 48 hours. The first three arrows indicate points where the stock slipped under the 50-day moving average and then swung back around and broke out. The last arrow is an example of how the 50-day moving average can also be used to short a stock (i.e., to bet that a stock is moving lower).

Moving Average Convergence/Divergence

Developed by Gerald Appel, the *moving average convergence/divergence* (MACD) takes two exponential moving averages and puts a premium on the data from more recent sessions rather than older data. By matching the newer trend versus the older trends, the MACD allows the trader to gauge the current status of a stock or other financial instrument and predict directional changes.

The MACD appears at the bottom of the chart, under the volume plot. It trends along a centerline, which becomes a trigger point. You can decide on which set of days you would like to plot; I use the 26-day and 12-day moving averages, but some folks use shorter periods to try to pinpoint microscopic directional changes. Again, the reason this system was developed was to give greater credence to recent momentum than to older bias in the underlying stock or financial instrument.

There are two signals you get from the MACD:

- *Divergence* occurs when the MACD is moving in one direction while the stock or financial instrument is moving in the other.

- *Crossover* is when the MACD crosses through the centerline; this denotes a possible significant directional change.

In Figure 6.4, you can see where signals from the MACD could have made a trader a lot of money or even saved a trader a lot of money. In May the MACD crossed above the centerline and signaled a significant rally to come. Later, in July, the MACD slipped below the centerline, signaling a major decline to come.

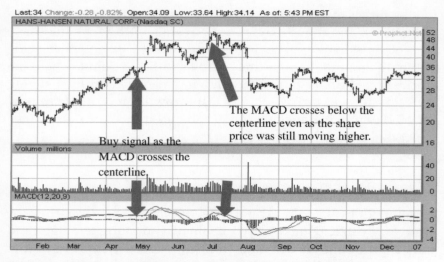

FIGURE 6.4 **MACD as an Indicator of Overbought and Oversold Conditions**
Chart courtesy of Prophet Financial Systems (www.prophet.net).

Rate of Change (ROC)

The *rate of change* (ROC) indicator is designed, as the name suggests, to pinpoint directional changes in share prices before they actually occur. There is a zero line, also known as a centerline, and that is the point where directional changes occur. As the ROC begins to trend in one direction, it is seen to be a harbinger of changes in the share price of the stock.

The ROC is a good tool for detecting shifts in momentum to the upside and downside. See Figure 6.5 for an example of this.

FIGURE 6.5 **ROC as an Indicator of Overbought and Oversold Conditions**
Chart courtesy of Prophet Financial Systems (www.prophet.net).

Chart Formations

When it comes to evaluating charts and the different formations, these days it seems like looking at a work of art—the interpretation is in the eyes of the beholder. To be honest, people have made reading charts too complicated. You can mostly eyeball a chart without any fancy lines and the story will unfold right before your eyes.

Now I'll share my favorite patterns and formations with you.

Double Tops

A *double top*, summarized in Table 6.1, is one of my favorite chart formations, mainly because it is easy to identify and it really seems to work. However, this pattern is overused and misdiagnosis often leads to unnecessary losses. The pattern seemed to be ubiquitous in the years following the market's peak in 2000. And even though investors think they see the pattern as often as the Loch Ness monster is spotted, I just don't see the pattern that much anymore.

THE SETUP The double top occurs after a stock has made a major move to the upside and tickles a point where the rally ran out of gas in the past. (A true double top happens after a stock has peaked at a new 52-week high, but there are also double top formations below the high—they just aren't as dependable.) Typically the stock has rallied hard to the upside on strong volume and then it reaches its Heartbreak Hill.

There is some profit taking, and for the most part the stock begins to pull back on innocuous volume and little news. Then there comes a point when the slide becomes worrisome. Some chart purists argue that at that point, the stock is vulnerable, but they can't confirm whether a double top has been established until the point on the downside, the swing point, has been breached. I don't subscribe to that notion; all it does is allow folks who are trading based on technical analysis to hold on to hope longer than they

TABLE 6.1 Double Tops: Seeing the Turn before It's Too Late

Type	Predicts
Reversal formation	A move to the downside

should. It is also a way for people to ignore news and other facts that have negative implications.

For example (see Figure 6.6), it is entirely possible that purists would have waited for Nike to move to $76 or lower after the double top was formed at $91.50 on December 16, 2005 (matching the previous high established on June 24), because that's how far the stock pull back after establishing the previous top. The reality is that a key resistance point was $88, and if you recall, resistance becomes support (and vice versa); so once it was violated, a nimble trader could have pulled the plug. By doing this the trader could have saved a lot of day-to-day pain and grief.

Moving ahead as the stock began to rebound, the new key resistance points were $85, the high on June 24, 2006, before the stock plunged, and the aforementioned $88. Of course $91.50, the top, was the ultimate resistance point; once the stock moved through that level, it was off to the races. There are traders who try to make day-to-day moves based on all the little nuances of charts; it's an all-day job, to say the least, and in the end not rewarding enough for the time and effort involved. On the contrary, simply holding Nike over the past few years would have been very rewarding, and buying and selling the stock using broader technical parameters would have been a profitable and less stressful approach.

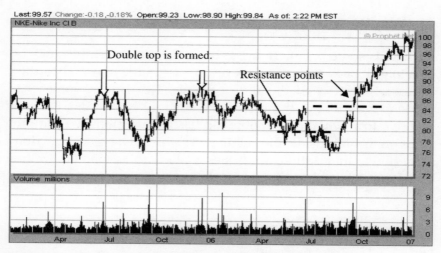

FIGURE 6.6   Resistance Becomes Support and Later Resistance Again
Chart courtesy of Prophet Financial Systems (www.prophet.net).

I prefer that the readers of this book become investors, but if you are endeavoring to avoid major sell-offs, then it's fine to use charts to assist in decision-making. You have to be vigilant to get back into quality names that you sold because of broad-based selling or a temporary pullback.

Let's look at one more chart to get a better handle on the double top and the implications of this formation. This time I've chosen D.R. Horton, one of the nation's largest homebuilders; the stock enjoyed a fantastic run during the boom period of the housing market from 2002 to 2006 (see Figure 6.7). What is interesting about homebuilders stock prices is that they generally aren't volatile, but the combination of the historic surge in home values fueled by 45-year low interest rates, a desire to avoid the risk of owning stocks, and also the cocooning of America in the post 9/11 period made the homebuilders hot stocks and wilder stocks than they have ever been before.

Again, it seemed as if the stock stopped dead in its tracks the moment it tickled the previously established 52-week high in January 2006. Once again investors, both technical and fundamental, should have begun to take closer note of the stock and understand that it was going to become more vulnerable. Moreover, when a stock begins to pull back from a double top, it becomes extremely sensitive to news, and if such news is ambiguous or not clearly great, the stock could come down harder than warranted or justified.

Once again the initial pullback took the stock below a key former resistance point, and once again trader types and perhaps fundamental investors should have been sellers. The stock rebounded

The former resistance point has become support and failed to hold—major sell signal.

FIGURE 6.7   Former Resistance Fails as Support and Is a Huge Sell Signal

Chart courtesy of Prophet Financial Systems (www.prophet.net).

momentarily, which was the worst thing that could have happened for reluctant sellers, as they had already rationalized that it was fine to hold the stock during the first pullback so obviously they would still be holders when the share price began to slip again.

In fact, just like the Nike chart, there were three chances to pay heed to that former resistance point, and the third time wasn't very charming, as it became a de facto trapdoor. The ensuing sell-off was sure and steady. The decline in the share price did stop momentarily at the swing point but it was only a pit stop, as momentum to the downside had reached gale force wind.

OTHER DOUBLE TOPS I like to use 52-week charts when determining true trends and chart formations, but there is merit to mapping formations in periods shorter than one year. Some sophisticated day traders even use intraday charts—that is, a chart of a single session—to determine their course of action.

Let's take a look at a 52-week chart that saw a double top formation develop in a three-month period. Figure 6.8 is the actual chart for International Business Machines (stock symbol IBM). The double top was formed when the stock retested highs established in January, visiting them again in late March. Chart purists would have waited until the stock got under $79 before giving the chart pattern the stamp of approval, but aggressive traders who understand that support becomes resistance and resistance becomes support would have abandoned the stock around $82, which had become a very pivotal swing point on the chart.

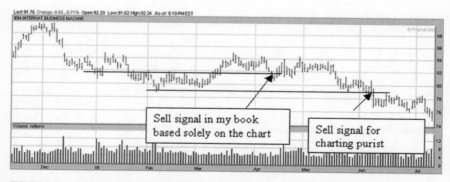

FIGURE 6.8 Acting Fast and Using Trend Lines to Determine Other Formations
Chart courtesy of Prophet Financial Systems (www.prophet.net).

DOUBLE TOP BREAKOUT While double tops serve as important indicators of impending doom or, at the very least, a possible sharp decline in share price, they also serve as a buy signal. Because they are easy to identify and because they work so well, double tops are respected by investors. (You could even argue that a lot of the action that occurs once the formation has been made is self-fulfilling.) That test of a previous high that failed (usually a pullback of 10 percent is required to consider a pullback from the first leg up a "top") brings with it a ton of trepidation and fear.

Knowing this makes the double top breakout much more compelling and attractive as a buy signal. Once a stock gets through a double top, especially if it occurs on stronger than normal volume, it can be off to the races.

Let's take a look at a stock that pierced through a double top and never looked back (see Figure 6.9). GameStop (stock symbol GME) is a very popular video game retailer. The place is like a Mecca for gamers—I know because my son drags me to one often. The company has more stores in my neighborhood than there are Starbucks—so that's saying something!

In November 2005 the stock peaked just under $24 a share, capping off a fantastic rally that had begun at $15 in July of that year. Finally the stock ran out of gas and pulled back. There was even some unsettling news at the start of 2005 that landed the stock just above $18. The stock didn't stay down long and proceeded to rebound back toward $21.

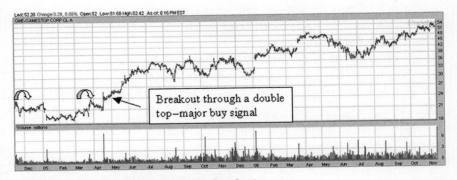

Breakout through a double top—major buy signal

FIGURE 6.9   Easy Buy Signal: Double Top Breakout
Chart courtesy of Prophet Financial Systems (www.prophet.net).

Sure enough, the stock formed a double top on the chart and started pulling back again. However, the stock held at $21 (traders who think the way I do would have been using a stop around $20.50). It then surged on strong volume to close at that top again. This time the stock kept going; it broke out in a very convincing manner.

There are times when the double top breakout fails, when the stock gets above the double top for a day or so but then reverses and comes down. You must be very wary of these kinds of U-turns. These typically occur after the stock is up on good news. The joy that sends the share price higher is followed by a period of "now what?" where investors begin to wonder where the next catalyst is coming from.

It might be nitpicking to suggest using the former double top as a stop-loss point, especially when it has barely been breeched, but you want to use a relatively tight stop-loss at this point to protect profits. Don't forget, I'm talking about a top; that means a lot of people are sitting on a lot of profits, and they are going to be looking for an excuse to get out.

There are also times when a stock spikes on unique, nonrecurring news, news that is unlikely to be repeated. It could be a legal victory, a new drug approval, the departure or arrival of key management, or rumors of a takeover of the company. When these events occur and it looks like the double top is going to be taken out, it is better to sell into the euphoric atmosphere rather than join the crowd. Let's take a look at an example of what can happen when there is a slight breakout of a double top on exhilarating hype.

Saks Inc. is the parent of the famous Saks Fifth Avenue store in New York, and is located in Birmingham, Alabama. The current makeup of the company came about when Profits Department Stores bought out Saks and then changed their name. The stock was underwater for a long time after the deal was consummated, but in the past couple of years the company has gained traction and the stock has responded in kind.

Nevertheless, many investors continue to think that the two companies, along with others that have been acquired and assimilated over years, aren't a good mix and would be better off if separated. This led to serious speculation that periodically added a

---

Missing Out on Big Gains

I'm going to get to the point where we tie in the use of charts with technical analysis, but taking profits is more than just ringing the cash register—it's about guts and convictions. You bought a stock and that stock moved higher, and in your heart you really believe it's going to go even higher still. Yet if the stock pulls back the next day, you begin to wonder if you blew it. To avoid the bout of angst, investors simply bite the bullet and declare victory. You'll often hear that you can't go broke taking a loss, but it's also hard to get rich when you bail out of a winner too soon.

Taking profits is exhilarating, which is why investors cash out too soon, too often. It is also why there is nothing more psychologically damaging than letting a solid profit (double-digit gain) slip away. Watching a big gain go flat and then become a loss is the antithesis of taking profits. It's like getting hit in the head with a cash register and then dropping a huge weight on your big toe.

Letting a winner become a loser saps your guts and makes you a timid investor, one who will pass up great opportunities in order to feel comfortable and safe—a bucolic state that borders on fantasy in the stock market.

---

touch of turbo to the share price. And so it was that in mid-April the stock opened 28 percent higher on scuttlebutt that the long-awaited deal was close at hand. (See Figure 6.10.)

Summary of Double Tops

- Double tops are formed when a stock has retraced a previous rally and reached the point at where that previous rally ran out of gas.

- In order to be a true double top, the stock has to pull back 10 percent or more from the previous high point.

Last:15.82 Change:0, 0.00% Open:15.82 Low:15.82 High:15.82 As of: 4:33 PM EDT

FIGURE 6.10   False Alarm—Why I Take Profits When Deals Are Announced
Chart courtesy of Prophet Financial Systems (www.prophet.net).

- If you are trading or very risk-averse, don't want for the stock to slide to the fulcrum. Find a previous key resistance point and consider that as the stop-loss.

- Double top breakouts are among the best technical buy signals available.

Double Bottoms

Double bottoms are, in my mind, the best and simplest chart formation to indicate a reversal to the upside (see Table 6.2). The opposite of double tops, double bottoms have become a more prevalent chart formation in recent years as so many stocks have tumbled.

True double bottoms occur over a 52-week period, as shown in Figure 6.11. In spring 2005, shares of Federal Express were slipping fast, finally finding a bottom at $80 in late June. After rebounding temporarily, the share price plunged again and dipped slightly under $80, but close enough that a double bottom forma-

TABLE 6.2   Double Bottoms

Type	Predicts
Reversal formation	A move to the upside

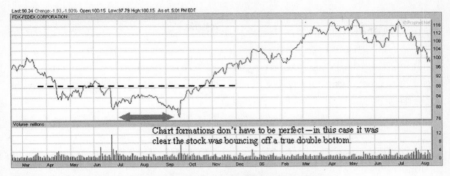

FIGURE 6.11   Double Bottom: Formations Don't Have to Be Perfect
Chart courtesy of Prophet Financial Systems (www.prophet.net).

tion was created and confirmed when the shares closed above $88. Once the stock cleared this hurdle, it was off to the races as the shares ascended another $28, virtually nonstop.

As mentioned earlier, there are chart formations made within a 52-week period that, while not true, still giving prescient directional indications. Figure 6.12 shows a chart of the Dow Jones Industrial Average, which often makes double bottom formations. How many times have you seen someone on television say the market won't rally until it tests the bottom? Whenever the market is moving higher and gaining momentum, and the question is asked about how much traction there is or the validity of the move, you're going to hear at least one analyst a day say, "The bottom has to be tested."

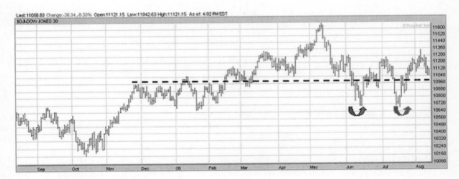

FIGURE 6.12   Dow Double Bottom
Chart courtesy of Prophet Financial Systems (www.prophet.net).

In other words, there *has to be* a double bottom formation in place. In fact, no matter how hot the market may look on a given day or time period, billions of dollars remain on the sidelines unless the index is coming off a double bottom. Once that second bottom has been established, there is a greater sense of optimism.

Summary of Double Tops and Double Bottoms

- Double tops and bottoms occur after the stock has pulled back 10 percent from the top or rebounded 10 percent or more from the bottom and then reversed again.

- These are fantastic formations that are eerily accurate.

- When there is a move above a double top, more often than not it points to a significant rally.

- When there is a move through a double bottom, it is a serious red flag and more often than not points to more pain on the downside.

- Breakouts and breakdowns of double tops and bottoms should occur on 50 percent better than average volume.

Head and Shoulders

Head and shoulders formations are more prevalent during bull markets and especially at points when stocks are making significant breakouts. Head and shoulder formations point out impending doom (see Table 6.3). Like any chart formation, the head and shoulder doesn't have to be perfect; it can look a little like the

TABLE 6.3 Head and Shoulders

Type	Predicts
Reversal formation	A move to the downside

FIGURE 6.13   Typical Head and Shoulders Freefall
Chart courtesy of Prophet Financial Systems (www.prophet.net).

Hunchback of Notre Dame. The formation is created when a previous high is taken out and the rally extents to a new high, thereby
creating a left shoulder and the head.

In the example in Figure 6.13, Tellabs (stock symbol TLAB)
formed the left shoulder in early March when a strong rally ran
out of gas at $14.70 and the stock gapped significantly lower. Later
the stock rebounded and powered to a new high of $16.80 before
slipping again.

The stock pulled back to the neckline (the foundation of the
head and shoulders formation), the previous support point that
had held during the March pullback, and held again (surprise!).
The stock rallied up to $14.70 in June and even got to $15.30 intraday but sank after a week of futilely trying to break out—this created the right shoulder. That was the sell signal. Later the stock
broke under the neckline in the first week in July and it was down-
hill thereafter.

Reverse Head and Shoulders

While the head and shoulders formation is used to predict when a
stock that had been trending higher may be on the verge of
stalling and turning significantly lower, the reverse head and
shoulders is a formation that helps us predict when a stock that
has generally been floundering is on the verge of making a big
move to the upside (see Table 6.4).

TABLE 6.4   Reverse Head and Shoulders

Type	Predicts
Reversal formation	A move to the upside

Indentix (stock symbol IDNX) is a maker of identity scanning equipment, the kind used to pick out terror suspects in an airport, and fingerprint technology used by law enforcement. The stock formed a right shoulder in early March 2004 near $4.40 and subsequently saw the share price roar to $8.80 (see Figure 6.14).

Summary of Head and Shoulders Formations

- These formations are more difficult to identify but are very accurate (though not as accurate as double tops and bottoms).

- Officially a head and shoulders or reverse head and shoulders formation isn't completed until the neckline has been tested.

- Moves through the neckline are considered breakouts and harbingers of major moves. These breakouts should occur on 50 percent or more volume than the daily average.

FIGURE 6.14   Reverse Head and Shoulders Signals Surge to Upside
Chart courtesy of Prophet Financial Systems (www.prophet.net).

Channels

By now everyone knows that stocks trade in a *channel*, as there have been any number of Web sites dedicated to taking advantage of channel trading. Channels are interesting because they form frequently and are fairly steady. As with most chart formations, you could look for a channel over any period of time to help you determine near-term direction of a stock. Remember, long-term direction is ultimately decided by how well management executes its business plan. However, even the best-run company can become overbought and the worst-run company can become oversold. *It's rare but it happens*, and chart formations help you understand when the tide may be turning.

Most trading channels are like two-lane highways; the other parameters are the real barriers, and the centerline is a swing point of sorts. Some people (I hesitate to call them investors) like to try to take advantage of each turn in a stock, so they actually trade the channel—even guessing the moves when the stock (in the following example, an index) nears the centerline.

UP CHANNEL   Figure 6.15 uses the Dow Jones Industrial Average to illustrate the perfect up channel, the implications, the rationale for trading the channel, and the consequence of a stock declining below the bottom trend line.

This channel developed very early on when the Dow bounced off a bottom in October 2005 and began to make a series of higher

FIGURE 6.15   Example of Negative Implications for Failing to Stay in the Channel
Chart courtesy of Prophet Financial Systems (www.prophet.net).

lows in quick succession. And then it took off—the Dow was off to the races, but the bottom of the channel had been established; now we would have to wait for the next pullback.

In January 2006 the Dow began to pull back, and it became clear that the bottom of the channel was going to be tested. Making matters even more compelling, the index was also approaching a very pivotal support point at 10,720 (pivotal because it was once a key resistance point that held back several rally attempts in late 2005).

The one thing to remember with charts is that you have to give leeway, particularly since so many investors are adhering to formations and taking uniform actions; you can't always bail out right at the trend line. In this case the Dow never touched the bottom of the channel but came within its shadow, but it slipped ever so slightly below 10,720. That meant a couple of intense days of waiting for a reversal or a meltdown.

As it happens, the Dow held and turned. The rebound was impressive, but the index couldn't take out the prior high point and began to pull back, again in February, setting up another test of nerves. Once again the channel held and the Dow rebounded. This next rebound probably added confidence to the market, as the Dow had held the channel twice in as many months; maybe the rally was for real.

The next test wasn't on the upside but rather at 10,960, the very spot that the previous bounce off the bottom of the channel had failed. This resistance point became the catalyst for a stronger move higher once the index broke through. Later, in March, the Dow would test 10,960 as support, and hold, again adding conviction to the rally that was already in place since the bottom in October.

By now the channel was firmly in place. The bottom of the channel was tested and held again in April. The next test would also prove the validity of channels, although not in a way that made investors happy.

In May, the Dow began to tumble hard and fast, cutting through the centerline of the channel, after touching the top of the channel, in a matter of days. That is a serious red flag. The catalyst for the move was a general epiphany that inflation was running wild. Although commodity prices were charging ahead, led by base materials such as copper, zinc, and nickel (the penny was actually worth more than one cent, giving Americans a new reason to horde them), the move wasn't new; in fact, the rally was rather old, as was the rally in precious metals.

Nonetheless, there were rumblings out of Washington that the Fed was unhappy, and indeed the Fed went on the warpath, talking down all asset classes with threats of infinite rate hikes. This jawboning went on and on; it was like every day some Fed governor was at a breakfast whining and warning about inflation.

Of course the charts aren't supposed to know or care about stuff like what a Fed governor is saying. Instead the charts just map emotions, and it was clear, even to a nontechnician, that folks were plenty worried. This time the Dow came heading toward the bottom of the channel with force and momentum that it hadn't known before. The orderly market made it easier for the bottom of the channel to hold. It was an invitation for fast money to jump in on slight uncertainty.

However, this time it was different. This time uncertainty wasn't slight but the only sure thing about the market. Investors were worried and voicing fear with their feet and their sales orders. By mid-May the channel was obliterated (see arrow), ripped to shreds, but during this time period, there were still moments of hope.

The Dow held at 10,720, a point that had been resistance once before and had held as support on two consecutive occasions. The pause there and rally attempt gave some hope, but now the former bottom of the channel would be a serious hurdle on the upside. Just as resistance becomes support, support becomes resistance. The bottom of the channel typically is a great upside test of any rally.

When the previous rebound in May failed to get back into the old trading channel, it was the ultimate sell signal for nervous traders. It was time for investors to reassess the stocks they were holding and to perhaps sell the ones they were rationalizing holding in the first place. Let's face it: If you had shares of companies with deteriorating fundamentals and this major sell signal occurred, it would be time to bite the bullet. The main reasons for this are not only to limit your downside but also to have cash once it becomes clear stocks are oversold.

In July we got the technical signal that stocks were oversold—the classic double bottom at that very important number, 10,720.

The more stocks lifted from this point, the greater the momentum became. It takes nerve to buy double bottoms and such, but a combination of this strong technical buy signal coupled with knowledge of great fundamental companies should have emboldened investors into taking action.

BREAKING THE TOP OF AN UP CHANNEL   There are times when the upper part of the channel is broken. This makes for an explosive move and typically occurs on better-than-normal volume. Figure 6.16 shows a chart of NGAS Resources, a natural gas provider whose share price went through the roof, or went parabolic, as my friend chart guru Gary B. Smith would say.

DOWN CHANNEL   Down channels are just like up channels in reverse: Stocks get stuck in a trading range that sees huge resistance at the top of the channel, and once that channel is broken, the share price could zoom to the moon.

In Figure 6.17, Corning Inc. (stock symbol GLW) was heading to the scrap heap along with every other stock associated with the huge telecom buildup that took up to five years to work off and was actually a greater reason for the meltdown in the market than the run-up in Internet stocks, which got more publicity.

Then a funny thing happened: The stock broke out of the top of the down channel and never looked back, rallying to $27 from $1. If one were lucky enough to buy $10,000 worth of stock at the low and

FIGURE 6.16   Example of Up Channel Breakout
Chart courtesy of Prophet Financial Systems (www.prophet.net).

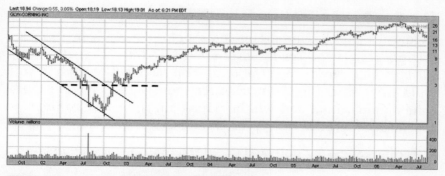

FIGURE 6.17   Example of Up-Down Channel Reversal
Chart courtesy of Prophet Financial Systems (www.prophet.net).

hold for four and a half years, the payoff would have been $280,000. Of course most folks had given up on the stock before 2002 was over, and most of the sellers were people just looking to salvage something. The stock had been as high as $91 in October 2000. Of course, someone was lucky enough to have bought the stock back then, but it took less luck to buy the stock at $3, particularly after the stock had pulled back and tested the neckline, after which it took off again.

Summary of Up Channels

- They can begin as an innocuous series of higher lows and then higher highs.

- Once established, there is a centerline that often acts as a swing point.

- They typically hold three times or more.

- Once the chart becomes extended, the channel is a good way to gauge risk to the downside. Eventually the top of the channel will hold and the stock or index will come down hard and fast.

- Once they fail to hold, the bottom of the channel becomes resistance. If the stock or index doesn't get through in a short period of time, usually less than 30 days, then the ensuing pullback is usually sharp and painful.

The Road Less Traveled

Technical analysis is important and should play a role in decision-making. However, *I cannot stress enough the traps you put yourself into by relying only on charts for investment success.* The truth is, you could trade stocks in the market for short-term gains, but those limited gains could and will be wiped out from time to time by one mistake. As an investor, you should look to charts to provide:

- Trading ranges, or potential upside/downside parameters.

- Backup for fundamental conclusions.

- A way to counter emotional traps. So many market participants are using charts that certain short-term outcomes are going to happen. Don't let them throw you off your long-term game plan, but at the same time don't be oblivious, either.

The charts give us a road map of the past, and that helps to predict the future. But the future isn't a preordained road already mapped out. Use charts and technical analysis as a tool. They are a road map that could hint at supply and demand for stocks and even reflect the past sins and miscues of management. However, the future of a stock, in the long run, depends on the ability of management to deliver the goods. I have stopped out of hundreds of stocks (sold because the stock was down a lot or because it violated a certain chart formation) and regretted it weeks, months, or years later. By the same token, I have found thousands of double- and triple-digit ideas using charts as a determinant of when to pull the trigger.

You have to use charts along with your fundamental work. The combination is unbeatable and will keep you ahead of the crowds.

Chasing Stocks

Chasing stocks is an interesting way to engage in the stock market, as most people associate it with trading instead of positioning for the long term. It can be both. When I say *chasing* I mean buying a stock that has already made a substantial one-day move of 5 percent or more or a double-digit rally over a period of one month or less. Let's face it: You're not going to get in at the absolute bottom and you really don't want to, because anyone who has done that probably missed in the previous 20 attempts to catch the bottom. I've played double bottoms in the past but mostly for trades. At the end of the day, if you happen to pick the bottom it is hopefully by accident. So to a certain degree we are always chasing—you may not be buying a sharp spike higher, but once a bottom has been put in you are buying the stock at a higher level. It is the sharp move higher or lower that generates the greatest urge to act, and this is where we need a set of rules and guidelines.

Watching hot stocks gallop along and hearing about how well others are doing is the adult version of peer pressure; it makes us want to get in the game ourselves. This is less of an issue for folks looking to buy a stock and hold it for a while. In fact, I've had clients tell me a stock I recommended hit my target too fast, and they would underscore this observation by saying they weren't traders. In other words, it was some sort of crime to make money too fast.

As an active investor you are going to have moments when stocks take off faster than you expected them to. There is nothing wrong with taking the profits if the valuation you thought was fair is reached, and anyone who calls you a trader at that point is probably just a little jealous. In order to take full advantage of the stock market, you are going to want to take 20 percent of your portfolio and buy and sell more frequently. You can label this action all you want, but it's the kind of decisive action that will generate returns in flat to down markets.

Making decisions about the market and individual stocks on a short-term basis (1 day to 90 days) requires the ability to make fast assessments and actions but avoid traps at the same time.

Knowing When to Chase

You are going to grapple with the challenge of chasing a stock after it's made a great one-day move. Sometimes these moves could have come that morning or in the preceding day, and at other times the move could have been in place for months. Outside of knee-jerk selling (dumping stocks without regard for the fundamental picture and how those fundamentals jibe with valuation), chasing is the most emotional of acts committed by investors.

In the case of Apple (stock symbol AAPL) in late July 2006, chasing was warranted, as the stock was down previously for reasons that could only be considered circumspect. (See Figure 7.1.) The

FIGURE 7.1   Buying a Spike of a Stock That's Recovering from a Free Fall
Chart courtesy of Prophet Financial Systems (www.prophet.net).

company had just announced great quarterly earnings results and there were a lot of reasons to believe it would continue to enjoy good fortunes. The company still had a lot of products up its sleeve and was also in position to leverage its newfound audience and introduce them to its other product offerings outside the iPod.

Chasing Apple on July 20 and the days immediately following the earnings announcement would have been smart, and while I admit it's easy to say after the fact, you have to buy stocks based on future potential and the assumption that management will be able to take advantage of those opportunities. Investors who bought the stock on July 20 were up 25 percent by September 15.

I could give you thousands of examples of where chasing a stock would have been the right thing to do. The key with chasing stocks is to make sure you are chasing a stock that's up on tangible news and not part of some hype campaign that will only ensnare you and destroy your portfolio. A great earnings report and higher guidance aren't going to be reflected in the share price in one session. Even if the stock is up 10 percent, there probably is going to be more room in the stock. There are numerous factors that will send a stock price higher. Take advantage of some of these and avoid others.

Case Study: Chasing Earnings

When it comes to earnings and chasing stocks, you want the best possible setup. Ideally you want the stock to already be depressed—in other words, you want the share price to reflect the limited expectations about the company. When a stock is already trading higher and there's good news, that news tends to be mitigated. In fact, if the earnings results are good and the stock spikes the day the news is released, it isn't uncommon to see the stock tumble back lower in the ensuing days and weeks.

On August 10, 2006, Brinker International (stock symbol EAT) posted its financials for the quarterly period that ended on the last day of June (its fourth quarter). The earnings, excluding special items, came in at $0.75, versus the consensus estimate of $0.65. It's not every day a company beats the general consensus by a dime, so that in and of itself was huge, and there was no way it would be reflected in the share price in a single session.

Heading into the earnings announcement, the stock was drifting lower and lower and looked dead in the water. (See Figure 7.2.) This is the perfect setup, a stock that has come down gradually. This was a reflection of indifference, so the sellers didn't have an ax to grind, they had simply lost faith. This is great, because once the stock begins to move higher, there won't be an entrenched campaign to keep it down. The short position was 6.6 percent of the float, kind of high but not a jihad—just a few folks who wanted to ride the stock as low as it would go.

To understand just how little faith there was in the stock, the shares closed at $32, just eight cents off the low of the session, down $1.14 the day before the earnings were released. The next morning the stock opened at $33 and it was off to the races. By September 15, buyers at the open on August 10 were up 27.3 percent. I bet 95 percent of all hedge fund managers would give their left arm, or maybe their Presidential Rolex, for that kind of return in just one year.

Of all the reasons to chase a stock, none is better than chasing

FIGURE 7.2   Buying Up for Great Earnings
Chart courtesy of Prophet Financial Systems (www.prophet.net).

earnings, particularly if the stock isn't already orbital and if the valuations suggest the stock is still undervalued.

Chasing Stocks (Brokerage Upgrades)

I must say Wall Street researchers have become a scary lot. These guys are walking around like gazelles on the African plains, wondering when they're going to have to run for their lives. Once upon a time Wall Street analysts were king of the jungle; they were the lions that kept the story going and investors excited. Of course, this position was abused and now analysts have been bumped down the food chain. To be sure, I see better reactions to upgrades and downgrades, but it's amazing that the Dow marched from 7,600 to 12,000 and there were hardly any strong buys. In fact, most of the ratings on individual stocks were middle-of-the-road stuff like "market performer" or "neutral."

And you get the feeling, when they decide to upgrade a stock, they're like gazelles migrating across a great river infested with crocodiles. Ironically, this development is turning out to be good for investors. Back in the day, buy recommendations were a dime a dozen and strong buy recommendations were commonplace, even when there were no fundamentals to validate such ratings. These days you have to send out a search party to find a strong buy, and only after the coast is clear are we seeing new buy recommendations from the Street. That fear of being on the wrong side of a stock has made the buy rating more believable, such that under the right circumstances the buy rating is worth chasing.

Just as it's better to chase stocks propelled by earnings when they are at or near a low, so too is better to chase brokerage upgrades when a stock has been languishing.

Real-Life Example

On the morning of September 12, 2006, there were eight brokerage upgrades from eight different firms. The action in the share prices of these stocks over the next week is a perfect template for how to play brokerage upgrades. Of the upgrades listed in Table 7.1, only two stocks were already significantly higher from the year-ago period. Of the six that were lower over the course of the previous

TABLE 7.1 A Typical Day of Brokerage Upgrades

Company	Symbol	Firm	Rating (Upgrade)
IPSCO	IPS	UBS	Buy
NATCO Group	NTG	Matrix Research	Buy
Advanced Micro	AMD	Lehman	Overweight
Steris	STE	Key Banc	Buy
Applied Materials	AMAT	Credit Suisse	Outperform
Genentech	DNA	Robert Baird	Outperform
Matria Healthcare	MATR	First Albany	Buy
Lone Star Tech	LSS	Bear Stearns	Outperform

year, only one didn't make a substantive rally in the days after the upgrade.

On September 11, 2006, IPSCO (stock symbol IPS) shares closed at $87.20, down $5 for the day but still higher than a year earlier when the shares were changing hands at $66. Essentially the firm was trying to catch a falling knife. Perhaps sensing that they had missed the initial move higher, this was a chance for the analysts to get in the game at a reasonable price, or at least that's the way it appears. A week later the stock was still struggling to gain traction, trading well below the $91 share price reached on the day of the upgrade. (See Figure 7.3.)

NATCO (stock symbol NTG) was also already in a strong uptrend when the stock was upgraded to buy from neutral at UBS. Like IPS, this stock was under recent pressure, but the share price, which closed at $30.68 the day before, was still much higher than the $23 it fetched a year earlier. The stock got to $31.90 the day it was upgraded but resumed its horrific slide later in the day and in the immediate days to follow. (See Figure 7.4.)

Matria Healthcare (stock symbol MATR) was trading at $44 in March 2006 before getting slammed a few times and landing at $20 in June. The stock was upgraded by First Albany, which is a fine firm but doesn't have the ability to generate excitement beyond its own corner of the world. Still, the stock rallied the day of the upgrade and held up over the next several days. (See Figure 7.5.) This was a difficult stock to chase based on the mix of pros and cons.

Last:87.25 Change:2.12, 2.50% Open:85.45 Low:85.42 High:87.81 As of: 4:04 PM EDT

FIGURE 7.3   IPSCO

Chart courtesy of Prophet Financial Systems (www.prophet.net).

Last:31.03 Change:0.10, 0.36% Open:30.75 Low:30.39 High:31.50 As of: 4:02 PM EDT

FIGURE 7.4   NATCO Group

Chart courtesy of Prophet Financial Systems (www.prophet.net).

Last:26.42 Change:-0.12,-0.49% Open:26.57 Low:26.26 High:26.71 As of: 11:20 AM EDT

MATR-Matria Healthcare Inc.-(Nasdaq NM)

FIGURE 7.5   Matria Healthcare
Chart courtesy of Prophet Financial Systems (www.prophet.net).

Matria Healthcare—Pros

- There was some insider buying at $20.43, but the insiders were also buyers in April at $27.50 to $30, so their timing wasn't so hot. The company's top line was growing exponentially, as was the gross margin. (See Table 7.2.)

Matria Healthcare—Cons

- A history of horrific declines—the stock gapped lower three times in the first half of 2006.

- High valuation—while I actually seek out higher P/E stocks for trades (i.e., stocks with higher price to earnings ratios), they have to be in up trends. This stock was getting crushed and still had a P/E ratio of 51, more than twice the industry average at the time.

The stock hit a pivotal resistance point where it filled a large gap. More often than not, when this happens, stocks pull back again.

TABLE 7.2   Matria Healthcare Income Statement

Income Statement	6/30/06	3/31/06	12/31/05	9/30/05	6/30/05
Total revenue (in millions)	$82.6	$80.9	$48.6	$46.3	$44.8
Gross margin	67.8%	67.5%	58.8%	58.7%	59.4%

The stock was already commanding a high valuation, so that mitigated the fact that the fundamentals looked so great, but it didn't discount the fact—stocks deserve to trade with higher multiples when management is doing the right thing.

That being said, you would incorporate the chart along with the stellar fundamentals and conclude that the stock became a buy once it closed above $26.

Upgrades on Stocks That Are Down Year over Year

There were seven stocks upgraded on September 12, 2006, that were trading at or below levels from a year earlier. Of these stocks, six were able to sustain the momentum of the upgrade and become viable trading ideas. Chasing this bunch was a smart idea.

Advanced Micro

Advanced Micro (stock symbol ADM), the chip maker that has steadily gained on its giant rival, Intel, saw its shares come down hard as Wall Street braced for a pricing war between the two companies. The stock rallied 7.8 percent from the close on September 11 to an intraday high on September 12. During the same time period, the Semiconductor Index was up 3.3 percent. (See Figures 7.6 and 7.7.)

The stock had some momentum behind it when the upgrade occurred, but the share price was at about the same level as the year-earlier period and down hugely from just six months prior. Wall Street upgrades work best when they aren't nebulous ("overweight" is similar to a "buy"), but the fact of the matter is if Wall Street really likes the stock, analysts should simply say it's a buy or strong buy. Moreover, Wall Street isn't great at picking bottoms, and their upgrades have a more sustained effect on the underlying

FIGURE 7.6   Advanced Micro

Chart courtesy of Prophet Financial Systems (www.prophet.net).

FIGURE 7.7   Semiconductor Index

Chart courtesy of Prophet Financial Systems (www.prophet.net).

share price when that same stock has already experienced a significant move higher.

Applied Materials

Applied Materials (stock symbol AMAT) is the largest maker of semiconductor equipment and has long served as a proxy for the industry. (See Table 7.3.) The stock has suffered despite numerous opportunities via new standards and the evolution of chip making, but there was a general sense that the worst was over, and that's why the shares were already in motion to the upside before the upgrade. This stock was already a screaming buy based on the top line of the income statement and other fundamental factors. (See Figure 7.8.)

TABLE 7.3   Applied Materials Income Statement

Income Statement	7/30/06	4/30/06	1/29/06	10/30/05	7/30/05
Total revenue (in millions)	$2,543.4	$2,247.7	$1,857.6	$1,718.1	$1,631.9
Gross margin	48.1%	46.5%	45.1%	44.2%	44.0%

FIGURE 7.8   Applied Materials
Chart courtesy of Prophet Financial Systems (www.prophet.net).

Steris

Steris (stock symbol STE) gapped up significantly more than 4.4 percent on the upgrade, and the stock managed to rally another point on the upgrade by Key Banc. (See Figure 7.9.) To tell the truth, not all brokerage firm upgrades carry the same weight. Key Banc isn't known as a research powerhouse and the firm doesn't have the retail firepower to get behind a stock, either. The result is that the company's upgrades and downgrades don't have the influence of other larger wire houses and specialty firms.

Montpelier Re

Montpelier Re (stock symbol MRH) is a property and casualty reinsurer and insurer whose financial situation fluctuates with the weather. The stock opened at $19.10 after closing the previous session at $18.65 and hit a high of $19.70 a couple of days later. (See Figure 7.10.)

Last:24.55 Change:-0.20,-0.81% Open:24.73 Low:24.53 High:24.80 As of: 11:41 AM EDT

FIGURE 7.9 Steris
Chart courtesy of Prophet Financial Systems (www.prophet.net).

Last:19.51 Change:-0 ,-0.05% Open:19.57 Low:19.30 High:19.66 As of: 4:12 PM EDT

FIGURE 7.10   Montpelier Re
Chart courtesy of Prophet Financial Systems (www.prophet.net).

Lone Star Tech

Lone Star Tech (stock symbol LSS) makes steel tubes, and after a wave of acquisitions in the industry, the company stood as the lone (no pun intended) U.S. player. The analyst from Bear Stearns said he liked the stock because the company was close to completing its planned acquisition of a Chinese steel tube business. Considering the huge premiums fetched by NS Group and Maverick Tube, the rivals that were taken over by foreign buyers, the analyst's note made it clear this was as much a takeover play as anything else.

The stock continued to rally after the upgrade, in part because the rumor was plausible, and the fact that such a well-respected firm had a favorable opinion added the right dose of credibility. (See Figure 7.11.)

Genentech

Genentech (stock symbol DNA), a pioneering biotechnology company, was also upgraded on September 12, 2006. Robert Baird

Last:51.35 Change:0, 0.00% Open:51.29 Low:50.63 High:51.59 As of: 11:16 AM EDT

FIGURE 7.11   Lone Star Tech

Chart courtesy of Prophet Financial Systems (www.prophet.net).

lifted its rating on the stock to "outperform," joining the majority of its peers that already had favorable ratings on the company's stock. The upgrade came on the heels of news that the FDA had asked for a substantial safety and efficacy update from its E2100 trial to assess the risks associated with the combination of Avastin and chemotherapy in patients with metastatic breast cancer.

It was interesting that the stock reacted the way it did, free-falling from $82.07 at the close on September 10. The stock got as low as $76.80 and finished September 11 at $78.33, down 5.0 percent for the day. (See Figure 7.12.) The news shouldn't have been so shocking—after all, the company posted a magnificent quarter on July 11, only to see its share price get pummeled the next day on scuttlebutt of disappointing news coming from the FDA that would delay the approval of Avastin for use in treating breast cancer.

It is almost nuts that the same news item could slam the stock more than once despite a remarkable earnings report and tremendous long-term potential, and yet that was the case. Is it

Last:79.26 Change:0.25, 0.32% Open:79.70 Low:78.98 High:79.73 As of: 11:16 AM EDT

FIGURE 7.12   Genentech
Chart courtesy of Prophet Financial Systems (www.prophet.net).

any wonder the stock was upgraded? I wonder why there were still any holdouts at that point.

The company beat the consensus earnings estimates for the June quarter by $0.09. The numbers looked great, as did the direction of the margins. One could quibble that the gross margin hit some form of Heartbreak Hill around 70 percent, but there was a healthy year-over-year improvement in the June quarter. (See Table 7.4.)

The stock continued to edge higher after the upgrade, but the real challenge was still ahead. There were now three sizable gaps to the downside—obvious red flags and impediments to a sustainable rally. The problem for the company is that earnings

TABLE 7.4   Genentech Income Statement

Income Statement	6/30/06	3/31/06	12/31/05	9/30/05	6/30/05
Total revenue (in millions)	$2,199.0	$1,986.0	$1,893.1	$1,751.8	$1,526.9
Gross margin	69.4%	69.6%	70.4%	68.8%	65.8%

adjustments had to be made to previous assumptions of greater Avastin sales as its new launch for use against breast cancer was pushed to sometime in 2008, after the new trial and after procedural red tape was cleared at the Food and Drug Administration.

Traders will probably toil into the stock until it breaks out of the downtrend that it has been trapped in since peaking in December 2005.

Case Study: Chasing the Hype

There are so many times when we knowingly jump on the bandwagon of a hot stock or fantastic story and hope to make a lot of money in a short period of time. There is nothing wrong with jumping on the hype bandwagon, but there is something wrong with believing the hype.

When you take a look at the one-year chart (ending September 20, 2006) on Pacific Ethanol (stock symbol PEIX), there are two valuable lessons to be learned. One is about chasing and one is about investing to get in ahead of the crowds. There is another lesson from a longer-term chart (seven years) on avoiding getting caught in the chasing trap—in other words, the hype.

Pacific Ethanol is a marketer and producer of renewable fuel sources, such as corn, to replace fossil fuels. In 2005 the company began to generate revenues and finished the year with total revenue of $87.6 million versus revenue of just $19,764 in 2004, and yet during this entire period of revenue building the stock didn't attract much attention. The share price ticked higher as investors who were aware of the story were able to buy the stock without attracting much attention from the fast-money crowd.

The story was in all the newspapers in 2005—but not on the stock pages. The story was on the political page and maybe the environmental page. In 2005 Congress passed a bill that called for an increase in ethanol use by refineries to 7.5 billion gallons by the year 2012. In addition it had already been mandated that methyl tertbutyl ether (MTBE) be removed as an additive in 2006, which created more opportunities for other possible additives for the octane boost.

The stock had been trending higher since 2004 when it climbed completely off the canvass and began an unprecedented two-year rally. (See Figure 7.13.)

Last:15.27 Change:-0.71 ,-4.44% Open:16 Low:15.18 High:16.12 As of: 6:09 PM EDT

FIGURE 7.13   Pacific Ethanol, October 2005 to August 2006
Chart courtesy of Prophet Financial Systems (www.prophet.net).

A person could be excused for not discovering the stock in 2004, but once it began to generate revenues from zero, if you had the chance to look into the stock for any reason, there were fundamental reasons to own some shares. The momentum crowd wouldn't have been interested because there wasn't enough volume, although the uptrend was solidly entrenched.

Then all of a sudden the stock was hot. It began taking off in January 2006 and became a fast-money crowd favorite, with the excuse that ethanol would become the ultimate alternative fuel. Just think of the hype factor:

- The U.S. wouldn't be reliant on foreign oil.

- The stuff worked—it was actually the fuel in Henry Ford's first car.

- Regulators were pushing for cleaner fuel and would grease the wheels. In fact, even President Bush got in on the act in a nationally televised speech in which he touted alternative fuels.

The stock made the kind of rally rarely seen since the height of the Internet craze, climbing to $42 from just $9 in a matter of months, and still a lot of folks continued to buy in to the hype. We mentioned the stock to clients but only on our trading service, and we got out too soon, something I highly recommend when chasing the hype.

The stock peaked, and then it happened: The decline was just as rapid as the rally. The slump in the share price actually occurred before the sell-off of crude oil in the fall of 2006. I think one of the reasons for the pullback was greater light on the true benefits of ethanol. As it turns out, the overall cost for this alternative fuel is higher than that of fossil fuel. When taking into account the amount of energy it takes to turn corn into fuel, the economic benefits begin to wane.

Obviously, chasing this stock in early 2006 made for a lot of fun and generated a lot of money, but I think more money was lost (see how the volume peaks at the top) than made on this stock by the time 2006 came to a close.

One thing to keep in mind about story stocks—companies with a lot of promise but a bumpy road map to profitability—is that once the crowd discovers them, there will come a point when the company will have to generate profits in order to maintain or justify the valuation that had so generously been built into the share price.

When chasing stocks that are riding a wave of hype, also keep in mind the source of that hype. If it's stuff in the headlines, topical stories that come and go like the weather, remember that headlines change, and the fast-money crowd will be looking for the next hot-button issue.

Pacific Ethanol could wind up being a grand slam investment as there are factors in place that assure revenue generation (government regulations, higher prices for fossil fuels, and grassroots demand for alternatives), but profitability is going to be an issue. More than likely, however, this stock and other players in the ethanol space will replace fuel cell names as the trade of choice whenever higher fuel prices dominate the front page of newspapers and not just the fanatical pages.

There was another clue as to how to play Pacific Ethanol, and that was to pull up a long-term chart. In this case a seven-year

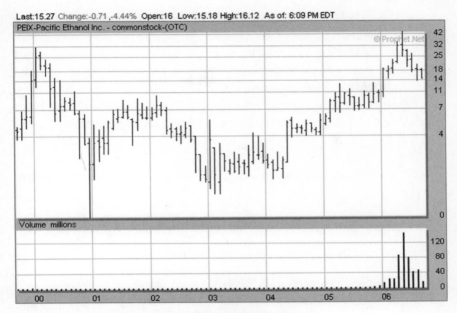

Last:15.27 Change:-0.71 ,-4.44% Open:16 Low:15.18 High:16.12 As of: 6:09 PM EDT

FIGURE 7.14   Pacific Ethanol, late 1999 to September 2006
Chart courtesy of Prophet Financial Systems (www.prophet.net).

chart would have given a hint to just how high the stock could go. (See Figure 7.14.) At the same time, the aftermath of that last great rally was the perfect cautionary tale about the risk associated with holding this stock too long. Back in 1999 the stock began a mind-boggling move that saw it rocket from $4 a share to $32 in a matter of months. By 2001 the stock was trading well below $4 a share. It's fair to say that the story was well ahead of reality.

The Antithesis: Buying Dips

The opposite of chasing stocks is buying the dip that follows a stock that is free-falling for any variety of news, from earnings results to brokerage downgrades. This goes back to the notion of trying to pick the bottom, but in the face of something awful—after all, the stock wouldn't be dipping if there wasn't a reason. Sure, investors overreact, and that's why sharp declines look so attractive, but unfortunately most of the people who buy stocks to the downside are looking for immediate rebounds. This very rarely happens.

So buying the dip is the closest that most investors will ever get to bungee jumping. Bungee jumping is a lot safer, unfortunately. There are times to go out and buy the dip the moment it occurs, but for the most part you are going to avoid stocks that have been hammered if there are any of these accompanying factors:

- Truly poor earnings results and subpar guidance

- A sharp reduction in earnings guidance between earnings reports

- Massive departures of upper management

However, stocks could be buys if the downside driver was:

- A change in opinion by a Wall Street firm

- A negative mention by the media

- Geopolitical or topical news that doesn't change the fundamentals of a company

Right now too many investors are focused on buying dips. My phone rings off the hook when a company gets hammered. People can't wait to get in, and usually they are asking what the news is after they've pulled the trigger. While it is true that stocks can and do make minute bounces after being trashed (i.e., down more than 5 percent in a single session), going after these moves isn't worth the effort the majority of the time.

This buy-the-dip mentality can be traced back to the 1990s when investors were instantly rewarded for buying stocks that were down—for any reason. In fact, from 1997 to March 2000, the knee-jerk buy on any dip was the most rewarding of all approaches to the market. People made a lot of money buying stocks on weakness, and for the most part they bought without regard to news or any other factors. These tactics don't work anymore!

Case Study: Buying the Dip on Renewed Hope and Hype

Sometimes a story is so sexy that when investors envision the potential and crunch the numbers, strange letters appear on their calculators because there are too many digits on the screen. Wow, this company could make a gazillion dollars! One such company that has been able to rev up investors not once but twice is Infospace (stock symbol INSP).

Infospace was founded in 1996 by Naveen Jain, who by all accounts was one of the most charismatic characters of the Internet boom period—and that's saying something, since there are hundreds of guys from that era who have a place reserved for them in the Snake Oil Salesman Hall of Fame.

Jain once told an interviewer that Infospace would be the first publicly traded company to hit market capitalization of $1 *trillion*. Talk about triggering an error reading on your calculator. As it turns out, the price did reach $1,200 a share in March 2000 when it enjoyed a market capitalization that exceeded that of many big (read: real) companies, including one down the road from it called Boeing.

Eventually the company crumbled under the same wake-up call that destroyed the entire space, and eventually Jain and his wife were ordered to pay the company $247 million for dumping stocks even while his silver tongue was working to get people to buy the same stock.

By the time the judgment was rendered against Jain, the stock was already beginning to climb back as the company was beginning to live up to its early promise as an innovator in the search space and also an online Yellow Pages publisher. The stock shifted into a higher gear, however, upon the ruling against Jain, which was seen by investors as some sort of affirmation that it wasn't the company but the guy running the company that caused the stock to implode in the first place.

The stock took off from $15 and made its way to $52 by late 2004. (See Figure 7.15.) The stock was back, or at least the belief was back, and investors were prepared to throw caution to the wind and ride this puppy up to $1,200 a share.

It wasn't just a company that was getting its act together that brought investors back into the fray. The company remade itself into a middleman for ring tones and other services for the wireless industry. Wow, just think, there are about 400 million cell phones out there and if each person paid $10 a month, times 12 months, and so on, the potential was off the charts and off the calculators again. Once the stock began running like a locomotive, that old

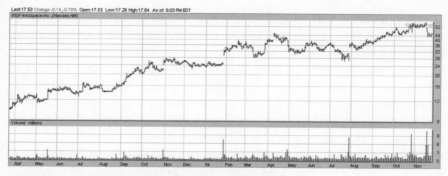

FIGURE 7.15   Infospace, March 2003 to November 2004
Chart courtesy of Prophet Financial Systems (www.prophet.net).

emotional feeling among investors that they couldn't lose came back, too. Just a couple of years removed from being totally written off (the stock had trolled around at $3 a share in late 2002), the stock was back and so, too, was a feeling of invincibility.

And then it happened: The company began disappointing investors on a regular basis. But most investors stayed the course, and there were always folks willing to buy the weakness.

There were major free falls in November 2004, January 2005, February 2005, April 2005, and July 2005. (See Figure 7.16.) Still, the allure of story was powerful, and the story was fantastic; I even had a buy on the stock thinking it was going to score big with its ring tones. The cautionary tale from the fundamental perspec-

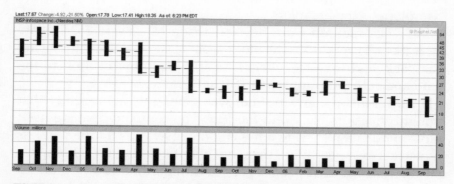

FIGURE 7.16   Infospace, September 2004 to September 2006
Chart courtesy of Prophet Financial Systems (www.prophet.net).

tive is that potential is nothing if there isn't the skill to make it come true. The company wasn't dreaming of conquering the world; it really was positioned to take advantage of one of the hottest consumer trends in the world. It just didn't happen.

I gave up on the stock in the summer of 2005, but it found terra firma later that year and begin to climb back, albeit with less oomph than before, but obviously there were folks buying the dip. But history repeated itself; the stock began falling in May 2006 and was totally annihilated. On September 21, 2006, the company reported it had lost Cingular, as the telephone giant was going to pursue ring tone deals directly with record companies.

When to Buy the Instant Dip

Unnerving news that doesn't change the fundamentals and probably will not have an impact on earnings but sends a stock spiraling lower anyway creates great buying opportunities.

On August 10, 2006, security forces in England busted a plot to blow up 10 airplanes heading to the United States. The plot included an assortment of airlines, and all airline stocks were down in trading that day, but the shares of British Airways (stock symbol BAB) seem to take the biggest hit. The stock, which was trading at an all-time high, was slammed from $75 a share to $69 in two days.

It was an unnerving period, to be sure. Security measures at airports were ratcheted higher just as people had finally become used to the extra scrutiny, and now boarding a plane would be an even tougher ordeal. I flew to Dubai a month after the incident and watched firsthand just how complicated and even comical getting through security had become. While I was waiting in line to be scanned, there was a security guy pulling things out of bags and yelling to the long line of travelers reminders about items that were prohibited. These were the items he was actually pulling from baggage and showing to the crowd:

"No juice."

"No water."

"No glue."

"No applesauce."

Obviously there were serious concerns about flying and whether the public would pull back on late summer plans, or whether there

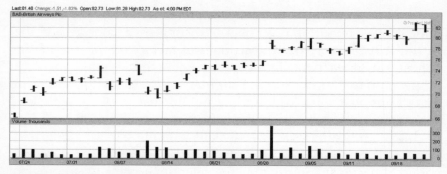

FIGURE 7.17   British Airways
Chart courtesy of Prophet Financial Systems (www.prophet.net).

were plotters who hadn't been found and were still prepared to go ahead with their mission, or whether there simply were other undiscovered plots. There were reasons to rationalize that this latest would-be terror plot to use airplanes as weapons of destruction and fear could hurt demand for air travel. But that would have been a poor assumption.

Instead, the share price of British Airways stabilized and rebounded for a 20 percent move in a few weeks. (See Figure 7.17.)

Chasing Stocks over the Long Term

You are going to be in the stock market for the rest of your life, and stocks will go up and down. But you will not become rich by guessing that a stock isn't going to move higher because it's already made a good move. Great businesses grow over years, decades, in fact. What may look like the ninth inning to you is really just the second inning.

When the stock market came unglued in 2001, virtually every single publicly traded company saw its shares hammered, including brick-and-mortar businesses (i.e., businesses that you can actually touch and feel—for all the talk about Enron, how many times did anyone walk or drive into an Enron gas station?), businesses that figured to be around until the end of time. Case in point: Yum! Brands, the company that owns Kentucky Fried Chicken, Pizza Hut, and Taco Bell, to name just a few.

There are hundreds of businesses that we know will be around until the end of time, in part because we spend a lot of our money there. Sometimes investors consider this fact and think about buying the stock, only to talk themselves out of it because the stock is "too expensive." Still, these same people make that weekly, maybe even daily, visit and spend their money at these establishments. It simply makes sense to be a part owner of these establishments if you are willing to part with your hard-earned cash there.

When it comes to any investment, the thing you want to focus on is future value and not how much the value has already changed. Interestingly, people have come to grips with this concept when it comes to real estate. People always think their home is going to increase in value. Yet so many investors believe they missed the move, that a stock has already moved higher and therefore they're late to the party. That is a short-term mentality that makes the stock market the casino so many individual investors say they fear in the first place.

The fact of the matter is that you are going to build a portfolio of stocks and buy over time. Your goal is to own individual stocks that are going to trend higher and higher over time. There will be bumps in the road, but don't talk yourself out of prosperity by looking behind. Instead, look ahead. There is no ceiling for how high a stock can go. If you and everyone you know are spending your money somewhere, then there is a great chance that that company's stock is going to go higher and higher.

Let's take a look at Yum! Brands. If I told you to buy this stock at the end of 2002, your first response may have been "The stock is up 43 percent in the last year, it's too late." Look at Figure 7.18—it wouldn't have been too late.

The stock meandered a bit in 2002, and you may have been angry that I had given you a bum stock tip that actually saw the share price pull back. But during the course of the year, you would have bought the stock (you should accumulate stocks in great companies over time) and had an average daily cost of $21. At the end of 2003 the stock was changing hands at $34.

By then I would have been back in your good graces, so you would have had a buddy call me to find the next hot winner, and I would have said to him, "Try some Yum!" His reaction would have been "You gave that to my buddy and the stock is

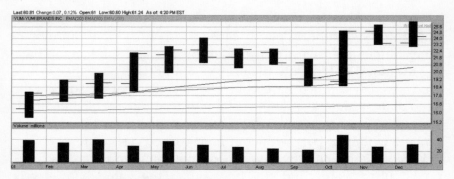

FIGURE 7.18   Yum! Brands, 2001 to 2002
Chart courtesy of Prophet Financial Systems (www.prophet.net).

up 48 percent in the past year alone—I missed it." Oh really? Look at Figure 7.19.

Another year goes by and you keep eating at Taco Bell, but the food tastes even better since every time you pay for your food, you know that you are also paying yourself as a part owner of the company. By now a few more people learn about this notion of buying what you know and they want in, too. They say there is no way they are going to chase the stock, but I ask them why not? Is the company any less attractive if the upside potential is actually greater than it was a year earlier? If you like the food, maybe the billions of people around the world who haven't had a chance to try it yet will, too. So they go ahead and buy the stock at $34 at the

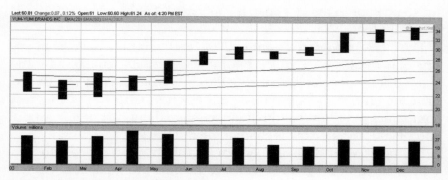

FIGURE 7.19   Yum! Brands, 2003 to 2004
Chart courtesy of Prophet Financial Systems (www.prophet.net).

beginning of 2004, and by the end of the year they're up 35 percent. (See Figure 7.20.)

By now I think you get the picture, literally. The message doesn't stop with Yum! Brands; we could go through this exercise with most of the publicly traded companies that you come in contact with in your daily life. Okay, so you chase the stock at the beginning of 2005 at $46 and by November 2006 the shares are changing hands at $60, an increase of 30 percent in less than two years, the kind of move that generates real wealth in your portfolio. (See Figure 7.21.)

Don't talk yourself out of owning stocks because they've made great moves. The fact is you want stocks that are moving higher rather than lower.

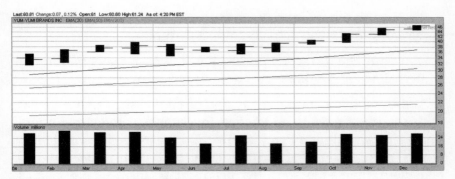

FIGURE 7.20   Yum! Brands, 2004 to 2005
Chart courtesy of Prophet Financial Systems (www.prophet.net).

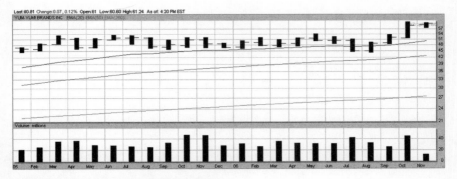

FIGURE 7.21   Yum! Brands, 2005 to 2006
Chart courtesy of Prophet Financial Systems (www.prophet.net).

Summary

When is it okay to chase?

- It's okay to buy a stock that is higher if it's higher because the company is executing, improving the top line, and expanding the bottom line. You can chase a stock after a great earnings announcement and solid guidance.

- It's okay to chase stocks for a trade after a brokerage firm has issued an upgrade, but make sure the stock isn't already up big. Wall Street firms are often late to the party, and when they say buy at the top, it's time to consider selling into strength.

- It's okay to chase hype as long as you know it's only hype and you're willing to take a quick profit or quick loss.

- It's okay to buy the dip when it is unlikely the news that drove the stock lower will actually impact earnings.

- Don't buy the dip when the stock is down on really bad fundamental news. Fundamentals don't improve overnight.

At the end of the day, it's okay to chase if the stock isn't fully valued. You don't have to be the first investor in at the very bottom. There isn't an Admiral Perry Award, and the extra risk simply isn't worth trying to make an extra buck or two. With respect to dips, take your time—the so-called dead cat bounce, where a stock bounces after a sharp decline, is also too risky a move for the effort.

The Level Playing Field

We are undoubtedly a society obsessed with righting wrongs. From grade school activities in which there are no losers and no winners to the notion that we should penalize the most successful folks and reward the least successful folks through tax hikes and cuts, it seems like the nation is bending over backward in an effort to be fair. But we must ask ourselves if we are really taking a step forward or if we are making adjustments that are against the nature of mankind or the nature of capitalism with respect to financial markets.

We use the phrase *level playing field*, but the reality is there is no such thing. Soccer and football fields are actually crowned in the center, allowing water to drain to the sidelines. In golf, the only flat spot on most courses is the area where you tee off. There has even been talk of changing basketball courts by raising the rim or making big guys play farther away from the basket.

This concept of fairness also grips the stock market. There is a huge movement to get the folks investing the least amount of money into the market the same information as investors risking millions of dollars. I think it's noble and wonderful but it has actually hurt all investors, including the small investor. Instead of information flowing freely to all, information has dried up, and it's actually more difficult now to get the buzz on a company. In addition, investors are relying more and more on message boards and chat rooms to learn about stocks and make investment decisions.

I believe in fairness but I'm also a realist. If someone pays $200 for a theater ticket and I pay $100, I expect him or her to have a better seat than me. Sure, I would be upset if the person wore a hat and I couldn't see over it, but the truth is my anger would be exacerbated to some degree by the fact that person has a better seat.

I think the notion of fairness is driven in large part by jealousy toward those who have more money and better contacts than the rest of us. The problem is that attempts to hamstring them have only hamstrung the entire market. It's gotten harder for all of us, and you just know the rich people are still getting better information than you are.

For a long time Wall Street didn't have any rules, and there were incredible moments of boom and busts. Along the way there have been rule changes and additions, but as time goes on, there is always the need for newer rules and newer regulations. I'm worried that the lawmakers and gatekeepers have gone in the wrong direction. When you invest in the stock market, you're going to win some and lose some. This is a lesson many of our children are not learning in gym classes that have eliminated such things as winning or mean-spirited games like dodgeball.

For all the bluster of those officials who believe they have leveled the playing field through a series of new laws and tough talk since 2000, I believe seriously important, stock-moving information continues to float around, and certain people are making a bundle on that precious information. You and I won't ever be in those circles, but by establishing a system and monitoring the market, we can see signs that key news and developments are on the near-term horizon (more on this in the tape-watching section).

As for the rules that have been established through the efforts of Eliot Spitzer, the SEC, Arthur Levitt, and others to protect investors, I think on balance they have actually hurt the market and small investors. Not that the intent wasn't positive, but the unintended consequence has actually put more of an onus on investors to dig up information as opposed to relying on their broker or financial adviser. Moreover, the cost of staying compliant with the new rules has forced a lot of small public companies to delist and go private (making it harder to raise money and generate effective distribution of risk).

Backdrop

Let's take a look at the history of the rules of the stock market and how the market has come to an impasse of too much regulation.

The Securities and Exchange Commission (SEC) was formed after a series of events that may sound eerily similar to the events that unfolded in the stock market from 1995 to the present. In 1929, the stock market crashed; in fact, that fateful moment when the wheels came off is still known simply as "the crash." After an unprecedented bull market that saw the nation gripped by the tales and opportunities to make fortunes in stocks, it all came to a grinding and painful halt.

The bull market leading up to the crash, driven by easy-money loans in which investors only had to put up 10 percent of the funds while borrowing the other 90 percent, lasted a full eight years. Once the dam broke in 1929 and the collective calm returned in 1932, stocks were down 83 percent. Needless to say, there was serious outcry from the general public. Hmm . . . this all sounds very familiar.

In 1932 the U.S. Senate Banking and Currency Committee, headed by Ferdinand Pecora, began looking into the reasons for the crash and ways to prevent such a debacle in the future. It became known as the Pecora Hearings and paved the way for the Security and Exchange Act of 1933. The Act required companies to file statements with the Federal Trade Commission (FTC) as well as to provide prospectuses to investors.

(To say the titans of Wall Street were not amused by the Act would be the ultimate understatement. They fought back with the Wall Street strike, which included boycotting new issue offerings but ultimately didn't work.) In 1934 the SEC was created and the first head of the agency was Joseph Kennedy.

The interesting thing about the SEC Acts of 1933 and 1934 was that these were the last major changes in rules that had an immediate impact on the stock market and investor behavior. Sure, there have been a bunch of new laws and rulings from the courts, the SEC, and federal legislatures since then, but not a lot of sweeping changes.

The Fox Watches the Henhouse

The choice of Joseph Kennedy was intriguing and controversial, as well. Kennedy's family made their living importing scotch and running a saloon. The generally accepted view is that the family continued to sell scotch, illegally, during prohibition. Kennedy ran a bank at age 25, became a stockbroker at age 30, and made a ton of money (legally) manipulating stocks in stock pool schemes that these days would be called pump and dump scams.

Urban legend has it that Kennedy decided not only to close out his long positions in the market but also to sell stocks short (betting there would be a decline in value) after getting a stock tip from a shoeshine boy. Of course that isn't unlike the hype over stock-picking cab drivers and other regular folks that were turning Wall Street and stock investing on its ear.

There were rules that governed insider trading and removed fixed commissions (one of the pillars of the individual investor movement that created the self-directed approach I promote in this book), and there were also changes in reporting and accounting.

As an interesting aside, back in 1937 the McKesson brothers of McKesson and Robbins were caught artificially inflating their accounts receivable and inventory records. The company reported revenue that was $19 million more than actuality but allowed them to pocket $3 million—a lot of money now, and a fortune back then. I love this story for several reasons:

- The company's accountant was Price Waterhouse and Company. The same Price Waterhouse that was one of the so-called Big 3 accounting firms that missed many of the scandalous accounting acts that punctuated the wave of corporate malfeasance that rocked the stock market and destroyed public confidence.

- The scandal resulted in new rules that made accounting firms more accountable (most didn't even bother to visit their clients and just took their word about financial statements and fiscal health) and also made audited financials a permanent fixture for publicly traded companies.

- In 1999 McKesson had to restate its revenue and earnings results for that year, 1998, and 1997. The news sent the company's share price tumbling, and by the end of the day it lost $9 billion, or half its value the day before. The reason for the restatement came from the new software division of the company acquired through the acquisition of HBO and Company. Sort of ironic that the company would lose so much value because another company lied about its books.

Tourniquet Too Tight

Public participation in the stock market soared in the 1990s. More important, investors were forgoing their brokers and playing the market via Internet and on-line brokerage accounts. Thus the self-directed revolution had begun. Along with this revolution, which turned Wall Street's steadfast truism upside down, came a sense that there was a party that would go on forever. Also during this period it seemed like everyone lost their common sense and most of us committed several of the seven deadly sins; some committed all of them.

1. *Pride.* As the money piled up so did pride, a lack of humility that made us all believe we were geniuses. I once sought a meeting with a Wall Street legend and put him on my service for free. He mentioned to me a few weeks later that I needed more New York Stock Exchange ideas, and I thought he was stupid. At the rate the market was going, the NASDAQ Composite would be trading higher than the NYSE within months. By the time I realized he was right, the tables had turned and I couldn't get 98 percent of my clients to bite the bullet on any NASDAQ stock or even consider NYSE stocks.

2. *Greed.* "Greed is good" is the famous line uttered by Gordon Gekko (played by Michael Douglas) in the movie *Wall Street.* This became the mantra for everyone in the market. With stocks climbing through the roof, visions of unlimited wealth

danced in the heads of the most ordinary of folks, many of whom had never dared or cared about being rich or super rich. Of course all the villains from that era—the former heads of Adelphia, Enron, and Health South, to name a few—were already very wealthy people when they decided they needed more.

3. *Envy.* On Wall Street it was all about envy, ogling the stuff the other guy had and doing what it took to get that stuff or better. Admiration, once a quality of gentlemen and gentlewomen working on Wall Street, was swept away by the battle for the biggest toys. The green-eyed monster was alive and well, and not just on Wall Street. I'm sure the person at your office who came to work in the latest sports car and credited his stock-picking prowess didn't have a lot of real friends, but always made the watercooler talk mean-spirited and spicy.

4. *Wrath or anger.* Although it was a freewheeling time, one that brought back memories of the Roaring Twenties or Sodom and Gomorrah, there was an undercurrent of anger and meanness. In the business world the cutthroat leaders and ruthless CEOs (think Chainsaw Al Dunlap) became the most admired folks.

5. *Lust.* If Jimmy Carter didn't have a problem with lust in his heart, Wall Street would have been the place to be in the 1990s. It wasn't so much a sexual thing as much as it was a lack of self-control. To be honest, a lot of folks pushed the pleasure envelope as far as they could, thinking that like the stock market, any adverse aftermath could be repaired as fast as a hot NASDAQ stock rebounded from a rare poor session.

6. *Gluttony.* "Get in my belly" was the call of a character in *Austin Powers: Gold Member.* For many investors it was only the beginning, as the appetite for so many folks knew no boundaries.

7. *Sloth.* From a religious point of view, this is known as responding slowly to God. From an investing standpoint, it was being slow to respond to the realities of the stock market and

its rapid demise. Certainly, once the bloom was off the rose, one could say it was divine intervention. Yet not enough investors saw the writing or got the message. In fact, nothing drove my desire to write this book more than the fact that so many investors are in the market or coming back to the market with the same exact habits and approach that sank them the last time around.

New Rules, New Roadblocks

So we all lost our way in the 1990s, and during that time those in charge of shepherding us seemed to be looking the other way. Let's face it: In any endeavor where a lot of money could be made, there will be people trying to cut corners and cheat the system. But what happened in the 1990s was simply a lack of regulatory guidance. To be honest, I think the SEC had been spending too much time and money going after small brokerage firms, bringing RICO lawsuits against any firm that didn't have a national footprint. In the meantime the big boys, those same firms that made more money in one day than all the penny-stock scam artists made in a year, were devising system after system that moved deeper and deeper into the gray area.

The rich got richer and weren't afraid to strut their stuff. The insiders got the straight dope while everyone else had to feel like a dope. Just think of all those e-mails where an analyst touted a stock in public and then trashed it with his real clients and buddies. It is absolutely amazing that this was allowed to go on. The sad thing is the remedies have been nothing more than a Band-Aid while some of the knee-jerk responses have actually done more harm than good.

Regulation FD

Agency: Securities and Exchange Commission.

Action: Final rule.

Summary: The Securities and Exchange Commission is adopting new rules to address three issues: the selective disclosure by issuers of material nonpublic information; when insider trading liability arises in connection with a trader's "use" or "knowing possession" of material nonpublic information; and when the breach of a family or other non-business relationship may give rise to liability under the misappropriation theory of insider trading. The rules are designed to promote the full and fair disclosure of information by issuers, and to clarify and enhance existing prohibitions against insider trading.

Effective Date: The new rules and amendments will take effect October 23, 2000.

Executive Summary: We are adopting new rules and amendments to address the selective disclosure of material nonpublic information by issuers and to clarify two issues under the law of insider trading. In response to the comments we received on the proposal, we have made several modifications, as discussed below, in the final rules.

Regulation FD (Fair Disclosure) is a new issuer disclosure rule that addresses selective disclosure. The regulation provides that when an issuer, or person acting on its behalf, discloses material nonpublic information to certain enumerated persons (in general, securities market professionals and holders of the issuer's securities who may well trade on the basis of the information), it must make public disclosure of that information. The timing of the required public disclosure depends on whether the selective disclosure was intentional or non-intentional; for an intentional selective disclosure, the issuer must make public disclosure simultaneously; for a non-intentional disclosure, the issuer must make public disclosure promptly. Under the regulation, the required public disclosure may be made by filing or furnishing a Form 8-K, or by another method or combination of methods that is reasonably designed to effect broad, non-exclusionary distribution of the information to the public.

Source: Securities and Exchange Commission

Reg FD, as it is affectionately known on the Street, was designed to create fairness. The thought was that by making sure information was fairly distributed, the playing field would be leveled. But instead of the same tide of information lifting all boats, the quality of work by Wall Street analysts suffered—mightily. There are academic studies that show just how dramatic was the free fall in accuracy in predicting earnings results. There was also a major exodus from "buy" and "strong buy" ratings to "hold" and even "sell" ratings. (Currently there are birds on the Audubon list of missing species that have been seen more frequently than the "strong buy" rating on Wall Street.)

In addition, corporate information flow dried up like the surface of the Bonneville Salt Flats, with the dry cracks and sagebrush to boot. Sure, some corporations disdained the thought of dealing with the general public and lost interest in telling their stories. Other corporations are so afraid of speaking for fear of regulatory infractions that they've muzzled their executive staff. So instead of a dam of overflowing information we have a stream of cautious comments that serves nobody.

Reg FD wasn't a magic elixir for the market, which began to tumble hard earlier in the year (see Figure 8.1).

I never had a problem with analysts having close ties with the companies they cover. On the contrary, I think it is essential that an analyst could make a phone call and get the straight scoop. Of course, that doesn't mean there should have ever been exclusive relationships based on the fact that a brokerage firm took a company public. That is blatantly wrong. But now the laziest analyst has access to the same information as the most gung-ho analyst. In

FIGURE 8.1   Untying the Hands of Analysts
Chart courtesy of Prophet Financial Systems (www.prophet.net).

an industry that was built on hustle, now there is a serious lack of urgency to make stock rating changes or offer an opinion that ventures too far from the norm.

A lot of folks continue to gripe about Reg FD, including many mutual fund companies that lament the quality of research from the Street. Moreover, analysts who want to get ahead of the crowds have to make assessments based on the tone of the conference call and the wording employed by management during presentations and interviews (I endorse this technique as well, though only as a small part of the decision-making process). By the way, analysts are still meeting one-on-one with companies and still gleaning greater insights, but there are few gems of information exchanged during those meetings.

Ironically, because it isn't unlawful for analysts to print or publicize so-called information (in fact, professional analytical organizations mandate that their members share such information with their clients and the general public), they still sniff around and try to coax such information out of management. By the end of 2005 there were only six cases citing violation of Reg FD, brought by the SEC against public companies:

Raytheon, 2002

Secure Computing, 2002

Siebel Systems, 2002

Schering Plough, 2003

Siebel Systems, 2003

Flowserve, 2005

Yes, Siebel Systems ran afoul of rule Reg FD *twice*, an amazing feat considering that thousands of publicly traded companies, or 99.99 percent, have avoided making the mistake even once. Siebel Systems actually took the SEC to federal court and had the backing of the U.S. Chamber of Commerce (which took the position that Reg FD violated the First Amendment) to fight the authority of the law. Needless to say, Siebel lost and Reg FD lives on. Its proponents claim the minuscule number of cases reflects the success of the regulation, but I don't agree.

By the way, of the cases brought against companies for violating Reg FD, only the Siebel case resulted in a monetary fine ($250,000). At a Merrill Lynch–sponsored luncheon in November 2001, when Tom Siebel told the gathering about upbeat sales numbers, the news at the time wasn't common knowledge, and it sent the company's share prices zooming more than 20 percent.

Oh, there is one more twist to this situation: On the same day regulation Fair Disclosure went into effect, so too did rule 10b5-1.

Rule 10b5-1

Agency: Securities and Exchange Commission.

Action: Final rule.

Summary: The Securities and Exchange Commission is adopting new rules to address three issues: the selective disclosure by issuers of material nonpublic information; when insider trading liability arises in connection with a trader's "use" or "knowing possession" of material nonpublic information; and when the breach of a family or other non-business relationship may give rise to liability under the misappropriation theory of insider trading. The rules are designed to promote the full and fair disclosure of information by issuers, and to clarify and enhance existing prohibitions against insider trading.

Effective Date: The new rules and amendments will take effect October 23, 2000.

Rule 10b5-1 addresses the issue of when insider-trading liability arises in connection with a trader's "use" or "knowing possession" of material nonpublic information. This rule provides that a person trades "on the basis of" material nonpublic information when the person purchases or sells securities while aware of the information. However, the rule also sets forth several affirmative defenses, which we have modified in response to comments, to permit persons to trade in certain circumstances where it is clear that the information was not a factor in the decision to trade.

Source: Securities and Exchange Commission

Essentially, 10b5-1 was established to help combat illegal insider selling. For years, corporate officers bought and sold stock ahead of major material news and for the most part got away with it. The defense worked so well and was so transparent that the SEC wanted to put an end to it. Once again the would-be solution wasn't foolproof.

There is a loophole in 10b5-1 that allows insiders to sell their shares even if they aren't in a position of material insider information. The caveat is the insider has to already have a written selling plan in place before becoming knowledgeable of this information. These days virtually every corporate insider has a written plan to routinely sell shares. Most point to the downfall of the market and the need to diversify their holdings as the rationale for having these plans. But it's also good for them to be able to sell stock ahead of bad news—bad news they know is coming and the rest of the world doesn't.

Information should flow freely from publicly traded companies into the financial arena. In the past, problematic news and developments were known initially by a select few, but ultimately the word made the rounds and the impact on stock prices was mitigated. These days, shocks to the system result in extraordinary share price declines because it feels like a ton of bricks when disappointing news is released to everyone at the same time. One could argue that news that made the rounds slowly lessened the impact, consequently softening the blows to stocks that make the average investor panic and flee.

Material knowledge is locked away these days like the Hoover Dam holding back millions of gallons of rushing water. The veil of fear has replaced the veil of secrecy that once modulated the impact of bad news. In short, Reg FD just hasn't been worked for the market or investors.

Sarbanes-Oxley Act (SOX)

Agency: Securities and Exchange Commission.

Action: Supplemental information on proposed rule.

Summary: On July 30, 2002, President Bush signed into law the Sarbanes-Oxley Act of 2002. Section 302 of the Act requires us to adopt rules implementing specified statutory certification requirements for principal executive officers and principal financial officers by August 29, 2002. On June 14, 2002, we had proposed to require a specified certification by a company's principal executive officer and principal financial officer. In addition, we had proposed to require a company to maintain procedures to provide reasonable assurance that the company is able to collect, process and disclose the information required in the company's quarterly and annual reports, as well as current reports on Form 8-K, and also to require periodic review and evaluation of these procedures. This document contains supplemental information regarding those proposals in light of the enactment of the Sarbanes-Oxley Act of 2002.

Section 302(a) of the Sarbanes-Oxley Act of 2002 provides that the Commission shall, by rules that become effective not later than August 29, 2002, require, for each company filing periodic reports under Section 13(a) or 15(d) of the Exchange Act, that:

The principal executive officer or officers and the principal financial officer or officers, or persons performing similar functions, certify in each annual or quarterly report filed or submitted under either such section of such Act, that—

1. The signing officer has reviewed the report;

2. Based on the officer's knowledge, the report does not contain any untrue statement of a material fact or omit to state a material fact necessary in order to make the statements made, in light of the circumstances under which such statements were made, not misleading;

3. Based on such officer's knowledge, the financial statements, and other financial information included in the report, fairly present in all material respects the financial condition and results of operations of the issuer as of, and for, the periods presented in the report;

4. The signing officers—

    A. Are responsible for establishing and maintaining internal controls;

B. Have designed such internal controls to ensure that material information relating to the issuer and its consolidated subsidiaries is made known to such officers by others within those entities, particularly during the period in which the periodic reports are being prepared;

C. Have evaluated the effectiveness of the issuer's internal controls as of a date within 90 days prior to the report; and

D. Have presented in the report their conclusions about the effectiveness of their internal controls based on their evaluation as of that date;

5. The signing officers have disclosed to the issuer's auditors and the audit committee of the board of directors (or persons fulfilling the equivalent function)—

A. All significant deficiencies in the design or operation of internal controls which could adversely affect the issuer's ability to record, process, summarize, and report financial data and have identified for the issuer's auditors any material weaknesses in internal controls; and

B. Any fraud, whether or not material, that involves management or other employees who have a significant role in the issuer's internal controls; and

6. The signing officers have indicated in the report whether or not there were significant changes in internal controls or in other factors that could significantly affect internal controls subsequent to the date of their evaluation, including any corrective actions with regard to significant deficiencies and material weaknesses.

Source: Securities and Exchange Commission

The Sarbanes Oxley Act established the Public Company Accounting Oversight Board (PCAOB), another quasi-government agency that will set policy and yet somehow be almost completely out of sight of the public. The bottom line is these guys have been given a mandate to go out and flog corporate executives who run afoul of the rules and guidelines of the Act.

At this stage of the game, even the most ardent cheerleaders of SOX are beginning to acknowledge the unintended consequences of the Act. The problem, however, is how slow these people have been to unwind the negative aspects. As it stands now, in my opinion, this Act was the ultimate knee-jerk reaction to a business problem. While there is no denying the cries for justice and blood-letting among investors in 2001 when the Enron scandal was unfolding, there is equally no denying that the *remedy* has been worse than the offenses that ushered the law into being in the first place.

In 2002 there was dual legislation working through Congress to address corporate and accounting scandals in the wake of Enron and WorldCom, as well as Arthur Andersen, the accounting firm of both companies. Because legislators were asleep at the wheel during the massive buildup of these houses of cards, they knew they would have to come down hard, very hard, not only through punishment but also through a new set of rules. The new set of rules, while draconian to be sure, was also a way of providing the real overseers of financial markets with less culpability in the future.

In the Senate, Paul Sarbanes, a Democrat from Maryland, was pushing through a bill that was seen as very extreme by the business community and the Republican party. Initially when the would-be legislation began making the rounds, most folks didn't think it would fly. After all, Enron, though a horrific story of blind ambition, greed, and arrogance, seemed like a one-off, a singular event, just one company that figured out how to beat the system (temporarily). Enron tilted the scales toward an extreme overreaction by lawmakers, but then came WorldCom. This one-two punch of almost $200 billion in houses of cards and fraud was enough to grease the wheels and trigger the quick adoption of that draconian bill along with the bill from Republican Mike Oxley of Ohio.

The point of the bill was to restore public confidence in the financial markets. The way of achieving this would be to go after corporate executives with a vengeance if they ran afoul of the rules. Moreover, accounting firms would also be held to more accountability, and yet severing the consulting aspects of their work for the companies would also hamper their roles of performing accounting duties for. If the public wanted a pound of flesh, it got it and then some.

There would be criminal and civil penalties of the highest magnitude for companies that violated the SOX Act. Complying with the Act, however, was more than a shot across the bow. It in effect became a penalty just for being a publicly traded company. It was understandable how our lawmakers either underestimated the cost to companies, large and small, of complying with SOX, but it is almost fascinating that the SEC didn't figure just how harsh the financial impact would be. Instead, a bunch of new rules designed to deter the handful of dishonest corporate executives of publicly traded companies were rushed into place and the result has been devastating.

Provisions of SOX:

- Certification of financial reports by chief executive officers and chief financial officers.

- Auditor independence, including outright bans on certain types of work for audit clients and precertification by the company's audit committee of all other nonaudit work.

- A requirement that companies listed on stock exchanges have fully independent audit committees that oversee the relationship between the company and its auditor.

- A ban on most personal loans to any executive officer or director.

- Accelerated reporting of trades by insiders.

- Prohibition on insider trades during pension fund blackout periods.

- Additional disclosure.

- Enhanced criminal and civil penalties for violations of securities law.

- Significantly longer maximum jail sentences and larger fines for corporate executives who knowingly and willfully misstate financial statements, although maximum sentences are largely irrelevant because judges generally follow the Federal Sentencing Guidelines in setting actual sentences.

- Employee protections allowing those corporate fraud whistle-blowers who file complaints with OSHA within 90 days to win reinstatement, back pay and benefits, compensatory damages, abatement orders, and reasonable attorney fees and costs.

Source: Wikipedia, www.wikipedia.com

The problem is that most of the companies that have been adversely impacted by SOX aren't household names. There was a good article in the *Orange County Register* about some companies that have had to deregister; in effect they are no longer publicly traded companies. The names of some of these companies included:

- Anacomp

- On Cure Medical

- Procom Technology

- Troy

- Niagara Corporation

These were all viable companies that provided jobs to their communities. Now they must toil in a new reality where they will not be able to reap the rewards of being publicly traded. It is estimated that 60 to 70 percent of all job creation comes from small business—small businesses that are now faced with trying to grow and expand without a vital bloodline of monetary access. That access has been turned off.

Thus far hundreds of formerly publicly traded companies have had to deregister, or "go dark," while many other companies have simply been delisted or kicked off the public markets.

And despite the pleas from these businesses, and the growing acknowledgment of financial experts and lawmakers about the negative aspects of the Act, there is still resistance to changing the law.

One of the biggest proponents of the law is Arthur Levitt, at the helm of the SEC when the Act was in the works and a major backer of the reform movement; many consider it his shining moment. So even as the evidence mounted to the contrary, Levitt continued to use a bunch of macro data points, mostly empirical stuff, to claim the effectiveness of the Act.

The Fox Watches the Henhouse Part II

On August 3, 2001, President Bush appointed Harvey Pitt to head the SEC. In many respects his appointment was reminiscent of the Kennedy appointment in the sense that as a Washington, D.C., lawyer and lobbyist, Pitt knew and probably took advantage of the gray areas of the rulebook. His tenure was a disaster, ending after just 15 months when he resigned after a series of gaffes that included questionable job appointments (most noticeably William Webster to an agency investigating a company of which he was a board member).

The thinking was to get the ultimate insider in the game on the side of the good guys, but in the end it was all "turmoil," which Pitt mentioned in his resignation letter.

Arthur Levitt was appointed to head the SEC in July 1993 by President Clinton. He had always been an advocate of the general public and rights of small investors. There is no denying that his intentions were always to help the individual investor. The list of accomplishments during Levitt's tenure (found on the SEC Web site, www.sec.gov) points to his philosophy of leveling the playing field as a way to make the stock market a better place.

Key policy successes include:

- Strengthening the independence of auditors and the profession's self-regulatory functions.

- Improving the quality of financial reporting, including strengthening the oversight role of corporate audit committees.

- Leveling the information playing field through Regulation Fair Disclosure, which requires companies to release important information to all investors at the same time.

- Creating a regulatory framework that embraces new technology and promotes competition through the order handling rules, which dramatically reduced the cost of buying and selling in the NASDAQ market; and Regulation ATS, which provided regulatory flexibility for electronic markets to innovate.

- Reforming the municipal debt markets by eliminating pay-to-play and improving price transparency.

- Requiring the use of plain English in mutual fund investment literature, public company communications with investors, and SEC communications with the public.

- Sanctioning the NASDAQ market for price manipulation and mandating improved self-governance.

- Preserving the independence of the private sector standard setting process.

- Commencing vigorous Internet fraud detection and prosecution.

- Working closely with the criminal authorities to prosecute securities fraud.

- Improving broker sales and pay practices.

Source: Securities and Exchange Commission

Unfortunately, crafting the rules and attempting to make things fair to the investor have only made things unfair to businesses. It's not just small companies that have been negatively impacted by the Act; the largest of corporations have also paid a financial price that is exponentially higher than anything proponents of the Act expected. American International Group reported that in one year alone it spent $300 million to comply with the laws of the Act.

The Act goes from good public policy to the equivalent of bringing a submachine gun to a fistfight via Section 404. This part of the plan calls for management to design and assess the effectiveness of its internal controls and for auditors to assess management's efforts. The problem with the Act is that this exercise has become more art than science. That may sound a little bohemian or romantic even, until one considers that if there are mistakes people could go to prison for up to 20 years.

At the end of the day it all boils down to the CEO and the CFO signing the line that is dotted. Companies that may do business in two dozen countries through 50 offices are asked to sign off that there isn't any hanky-panky anywhere in the system. Just think about that for a moment. Anyone who has supervised a handful of people understands how tough it can be to vouch for those people at all times, particularly any nefarious actions that are obviously going to be masked.

Some regional manager in Akron, Ohio, could fall behind his quota and take desperate measures, maybe thinking that sharpening the pencil one time could be adjusted later and nobody would be the wiser. Eventually it creates a domino situation that causes some guy in the Ivory Towers in Manhattan, New York, to get into serious hot water. It is interesting that the Act hasn't netted a lot of offenders, the biggest being Richard Scrushy of HealthSouth, and he beat the rap. This is one of the sad ironies of SOX.

No doubt there should be laws that hold corporate officials to greater accountability. Investors want blood—they want people who cost them their hard-earned money to pay stiff penalties. Talk about the thin line between love and hate. It's one thing to have the people you bet your money on come up short, but it is something entirely different when they deliberately come up short because they were lining their own pockets.

The investing public is much like the French during the reign of Marie Antoinette. Although scholars differ on whether she actually uttered the infamous line "Let them eat cake," she is the ultimate symbol of the disdain that the rich and powerful have always had for common folk. When common folk get the chance to turn the tables, they do it with a fury. These days Sarbanes-Oxley stands as the would-be guillotine for any modern-day Marie Antoinette who dares to trample on the sensibilities of investors.

But all the Act has done is stifle risk taking among large businesses, driven small companies to delist and deregister, and severely hampered their ability to raise money or generate wealth. All of the major initial public offerings in the world in 2005 occurred outside of the United States; historically 9 out of 10 used to happen in New York.

Summary

There are rules that govern things like how much money an investor can borrow (margin), and these rules are good as they help save you from self-destruction, especially when times become maddening. Then there are rules that have slowed information to a crawl; there are rules that have spooked corporate officials into taking cautionary approaches to business. The amount of money lost and innovation that has been dragged down will never be quantified, but it's astronomical.

In a much-cited paper, "Economic Consequences of the Sarbanes-Oxley Act of 2002," Ivy Xiying Zhang says that the market lost $1.4 trillion from the time the Act was proposed until it was finally approved (http://w4.stern.nyu.edu/accounting/docs/ speaker_papers/spring2005/Zhang_Ivy_Economic_Conse quences_of_S_O.pdf). At the end of the day we want the businesses we invest in to be bold and strive to be more dynamic than their industry. There isn't any public confidence in a lot of the new rules, as witnessed by the tons of money made by corporations but not reflected in their share prices.

The one thing you have to understand as an investor is that there will always be bad guys and gals lurking about, looking for loopholes, legal or otherwise. I don't think the stock market is going to be able to really take off until provisions of SOX are revised or omitted. Investors will come back to the market in droves when the world comes back to the U.S. markets in greater numbers, and that isn't going to happen with the hurdles put into place by the new rules.

In the end, time will also play a role with respect to confidence in the market. I don't think any new scandals will emerge (what else could these scoundrels have thought of, anyway?) but of course there is a wait-and-see attitude among investors. The key is that you should never become too complacent. You're always going to have to do your homework to stay ahead of the crowd and even ahead of unscrupulous corporate operators.

Furthermore, there should be tighter laws to combat predatory shorting of stocks, which has wreaked havoc on small-cap companies.

In the end, the nation is awash in an effort to make things easier, which goes against nature. The osprey has big talons that allow it to snatch fish out of the water—a sad thing for those fish that fall prey, but a necessary part of nature. The movement to make nice has resulted in our children playing games where there are no winners or losers and prohibiting games like dodgeball where people could get hurt psychically or emotionally. It is a terrible way to train for a future where there will always be winners and losers, especially in the stock market, where nice can be a four-letter word.

Fairness for the little investor is fine, but it shouldn't come at the expense of the big investor, and it certainly shouldn't come at the expense of limited communications for all and impossible conditions for small companies that are seeking to participate in the capitalistic dream of being a public company.

PART THREE

ACT AND GET RICH

Watching the Tape and Market Manipulation

T he *tape* is a catchall term that includes all aspects of information flow. Since the advent of the ticker tape, there have been numerous developments in sources of information. It's one thing to know the news surrounding the stocks in your portfolio; it's altogether different to see news coming.

Being able to read between the lines of all the information flowing during each session is the essence of "watching the tape." Unlike yesteryear, where the tape was a homogenous flow of quotes and news over a slender strip of paper, these days it incorporates all sources of information and data. Being able to monitor and interpret the tape will go a long way toward making your investment experience richer.

Things happen for a reason. Stocks don't trade twice their average daily volume on no news. In many instances, though, the news isn't out and you could take advantage of that. Sharp price changes (which can be as small as 1 percent moves if all the other stocks in the industry aren't moving or are moving lower), as well as noticeable increases in volume for the stock and its underlying options, are anomalies. When there are anomalies in the stock market it's a harbinger of things to come, 95 percent of the time.

The most important thing to understand is that people know things you don't, despite all the rules and regulations that are supposed to flatten the playing field. Important moneymaking information is flowing, and while the news itself may not be known, the actions to capitalize off the news are right in your face.

So What Exactly Is the Tape?

There is an actual tape, the linear heir to the original ticker. It's that zipper on the bottom of the screen when you watch financial television. It's also used to relay other types of information on television beyond the realm of the stock market, including sports scores and traffic updates.

Watching the stock market tape during the day is a great way to forecast news and stock-moving events. Components of the tape include:

- Price movement

- Volume changes

- Anomalies versus the industry or broad market

- Options activity

Every single day, major news items and brokerage upgrades or downgrades are telegraphed by the action in the tape. I see it every day and from now on you'll be on the lookout for these signals, too.

Telegraphing Brokerage Rating Changes

On September 13, 2006, I asked Brian, our analyst who covers the advertisers, what was happening with Interpublic Group (stock symbol IPG). He wasn't sure, but agreed that the action was curious. He had a "hold" rating on the stock but the shares had been coming on strong, so he was already digging around. The next day at 7:30 in the morning I got an e-mail from Brian: Wachovia initiated coverage with an "outperform" rating.

Someone had known this upgrade was coming. I don't know where the information was leaked from—perhaps the brokerage firm, or perhaps someone at the company told a friend. But there is no doubt in my mind the news was leaked.

Wall Street is a leaky place. This is how I find a lot of my trading ideas. I'm not in the loop, but the loop can't hide the volume. The share price began to appreciate on August 28, when the volume spiked and the stock closed above a key resistance point (right under $9), as shown in Figure 9.1. Astute technical traders may have used that as a "buy" signal; for the rest it should have been a signal to take a closer look. If you already owned the shares, it was a plus.

I'm not picking on Wachovia; somehow the word is getting out for every brokerage firm when there might be an upgrade or downgrade of a particular stock. I'm not saying every change in opinion by brokerage firms can be detected the day before, but many are telegraphed. This often offers opportunities to make or save money.

Yahoo! Finance and other web sites offer lists of the most recent actions from brokerage firms, which I find extremely helpful. Remember, when all the brokerage firms are bearish, the only way they can go is positive, although they do it through baby steps such as raising ratings to "neutral" or "hold" from "negative" or "sell."

If you see peculiarity in a stock—let's say it's trading higher while others in the same sector are trading sideways or lower—even then, you begin to dig. If there hasn't been an upgrade in

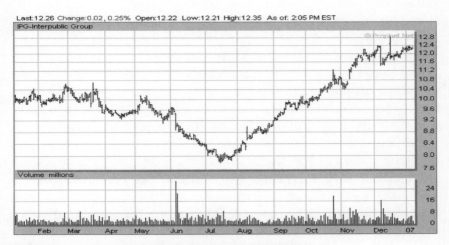

FIGURE 9.1   IPG Stock Began Rising before the Rating Change
Chart courtesy of Prophet Financial Systems (www.prophet.net).

some time, then making an assumption that one is coming isn't a leap of faith.

Telegraphing Corporate News

Sometimes the tape tells us something is brewing, and then the news comes out from the company. The following article is interesting, to be sure. But the action in the stock in the days before the press release suggests that it may not have been news to everyone.

> BURLINGTON, Mass.—(BUSINESS WIRE)—Sept. 13, 2006— iRobot Corp. (NASDAQ:IRBT—News) today announced a new addition to its family of home robots, the iRobot® Dirt Dog™ Workshop Robot. The rugged robot is designed to pick up small nails, dirt, sawdust and other debris that accumulates in garages, basements and workbench zones. Priced at $129.99, the workshop robot will be available at www.irobot.com starting Sept. 15.

The daily trading volume in the shares of iRobot (stock symbol IRBT) began to climb in the second week of September, getting progressively higher beginning Monday, September 12, when the stock began the week changing hands at less than $18 a share and spiked, on a surge in volume, to close at $18.50. The next day the stock was quiet until the close, when the shares surged again, closing above $19.

The company presented at an investor conference on September 12, but we don't think any significant news was unveiled. Yet the wheels of motion were in place—someone knew something from the beginning of the week, and now more people knew. You and I weren't in the loop, but clearly something was going on.

On September 13 the company announced a new product and the stock spiked to $20. By the end of the week shares were changing hands at $23 and reached a high of $24. (See Figure 9.2.)

The key to watching the tape and being swayed by the action isn't just the movement of the stock, but the combination of price movement and unusually high volume. There have to be a lot of players in the stock, and better yet, they have to be making big bets.

Last:22.89 Change:1.92, 9.20% Open:21.21 Low:21.10 High:23.94 As of: 1:33 PM EDT

FIGURE 9.2   iRobot: The Company Does Better than the Movie
Chart courtesy of Prophet Financial Systems (www.prophet.net).

Be Aware of Head Fakes and Unfulfilled Dreams

When you are engaged in the market and looking for short-term gains based on reading the tape, there is a powerful temptation to get in ahead of the crowd. Just as one can jump the gun and buy a stock that is on the cusp of a breakout but doesn't break out and instead turns lower in a hurry, so too can one be victimized by tape readings that are compelling. A stock may see a spike in volume but with no news, and many investors jump into the fray only to be disappointed days later. You have to be very careful of these head fakes.

I have been the victim of so many head fakes I've lost count. I have also been deliberately set up a few times. I don't get as many of the calls as I used to, but in the early 1990s my office was like hot-stock-tip central. This is before the Internet became a major communication force. Back then, Wall Street Strategies was a vital vehicle in getting the word out; our clients were always looking for action and the inside edge. So we got a lot of credible phone calls about possible events that would move stocks, such as pending but unannounced takeovers and other major news.

At one point I was so well known for having big news items and takeovers before they became official that I was dubbed the Rumor King. There was a time when the SEC would routinely send me forms to fill out to find out if I was personally long (owned) some of the takeovers we called ahead of time, or if I knew someone on the inside. At first the forms were unnerving, but later on they became almost a badge of honor, like trophies. I disliked that moniker, the Rumor King, to no end, but it got us noticed and got me on television. Over a period of time I was able to express my skill set beyond my expertise in takeovers, so it worked out fine.

During this period where we called so many takeovers and got so much good information, not just from the tape but also from our network and anonymous phone calls, we also got a bunch of junk, too. The one area to be especially on alert for false signals is in the small-cap and micro-cap arenas.

It's easy to take the bait when there is a spike in volume, especially on a low-priced stock or a stock that isn't widely covered by the Street. It's one thing when a large-cap company hints something is brewing and it turns out to be a brokerage upgrade, but when you know the news could be even more significant since brokerage firms don't cover a stock, it makes the action more enticing.

When it comes to these small-cap and micro-cap names, one has to be very careful about taking the bait simply because it looks like the train is pulling out of the station. The most important thing to remember is that large companies generally don't turn around overnight, and it's almost impossible for smaller companies with fewer resources to adjust fundamental deficiencies overnight or in a matter of months. The fact is, bottom-fishing these names or taking the bait of false breakouts isn't worth the risk.

Secure Computing (stock symbol SCUR) specializes in network security solutions, an area that experienced meteoric growth in the 1990s but fell off a cliff as tight-fisted information technology managers opted to spend money on technology considered mission critical. The stock has a wonderful history of plunging off the face of the earth only to rebound in an amazingly short period of time.

In fact, if there was some sort of official praise for stocks that climb off the canvas (let's call it the Phoenix Award), this stock would have won it a couple of times.

- In January 1999 the shares were changing hands around $28 a share, then took a dive to $3, only to rally all the way back to $28, all within a 15-month time frame.

- From January 2002 to January 2004 the stock went from $24 a share to $3 a share and back to $20 a share.

One of the reasons for the wild gyrations in the stock is the amount of time that the company spends involved in the rumor mill. Since the late 1990s the stock has been said to be an acquisition target, and once a year these rumors resurface. This bit of history set the stage for another head fake in 2006.

On July 11, 2006, the company warned it would miss earnings, guidance previously given to investors. Instead of earnings at $0.10 to $0.12 a share predicted by consensus, the company's new earnings estimate was a range of $0.04 to $0.05 a share. The Street was looking for $0.11, so needless to say, the stock was hammered to $5.10 from $8.10.

The stock immediately rebounded after the earnings warning, and after settling down, it began to climb higher and higher. Outside of the large-volume days immediately following the earnings warning (a common occurrence), the stock began to move in leaps and bounds, and was up 39 percent within a matter of weeks. (See Figure 9.3.) While this kind of action isn't completely unusual, such rebounds generally don't happen that fast.

While the move was fascinating, the fact that it occurred on average volume was always a cautionary red flag, and one reason I wouldn't have jumped into the stock. Yet even after the stock was hit again in early September, it rallied back rather quickly and, again, on no public news. It shouldn't have been a surprise when the gains were wiped out in a single session.

I want you to avoid the temptation of taking the bait from stocks that are trading under $5 a share but at one point used to trade significantly higher.

If the stock in question is a small-cap name or micro-cap stock with no brokerage coverage, you have to proceed with caution

Last:6.58 Change:-0.41 ,-5.87% Open:7 Low:6.25 High:7 As of: 3:24 PM EDT

SCUR-Secure Computing Corporation-(Nasdaq NM)

Volume millions

FIGURE 9.3 Not So Secure: Secure Computing Gives Back Ground Gained on No News
Chart courtesy of Prophet Financial Systems (www.prophet.net).

and try to find the source of the price movement. Obviously, if there is solid news, then it mitigates the risks and adds to the sense of urgency.

Bucking the Trend—Relative Comparisons

The vital part of watching the tape is watching not just for the action by the stock in question, but also how the shares of rivals are reacting.

Let's take an example scenario. A stock is on the move, inching higher right out of the gate, while the broad market labors and the share prices of rival companies more or less languish. There is something brewing. Relative evaluation is important in fundamental analysis and in technical analysis, too.

On September 5, 2006, there was an announcement in the oil patch that shook up the industry. Chevron and Devon Energy, using rigs that tunneled as much as seven miles into the ocean and earth, employing new technologies, made a discovery that could ultimately swell the oil reserves in America. Although neither company would give an exact estimate on how much oil they tapped into, many believe the Gulf of Mexico, where the discovery was made, holds as much as 20 billion barrels.

Needless to say, the share prices of the stocks involved in the discovery enjoyed fantastic sessions. Devon was the number one percentage gainer on the NYSE that day (my clients were long the stock from a month earlier). Going into that weekend I loved the way the stock was acting. It was exhibiting a lot of strength and it seemed like it wanted to trade higher. Yet there was never a spike in volume. Still, something was up, and the reason I knew it (though I had no idea of the magnitude of the news to come) was the stock was bucking the overall trend of the industry.

On August 31, 2006, the share price of Devon Energy (stock symbol DVN) stood at $60.99. By the close of the market the next day, September 1, the shares were changing hands at $64.14, or a 5.18 percent increase in 24 hours. (See Figure 9.4.)

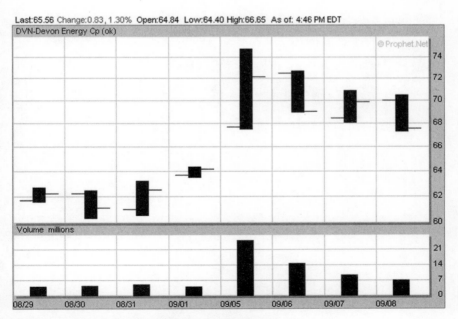

Last:65.56 Change:0.83, 1.30% Open:64.84 Low:64.40 High:66.65 As of: 4:46 PM EDT

FIGURE 9.4   Devon Was Acting Great before It Took Off
Chart courtesy of Prophet Financial Systems (www.prophet.net).

By the same token, the broader energy space was flaccid, not moving much, and in fact many of the key rivals to Devon and Chevron were lower. The Amex Oil Index (stock symbol XOI), which includes Chevron, began trading at 1,158 on August 31 and closed at 1,154 on September 1, virtually unchanged for the 24-hour period. (See Figure 9.5.)

Call me crazy, but there is no doubt rumors were swirling in the right circles about a possible oil find, perhaps even a monumental find.

On the other side of the coin, there are going to be times when a stock is flat or down when the rest of the group is trading higher. This is a cause for alarm but doesn't instantly mean something is wrong. However, if I were considering a stock in a particular sector and it wasn't moving with its peers, I would be concerned.

More often than not when this is happening, there are one or two reasons for the boycott. One, the stock probably put in one of the poorer quarters in the most recent round of earnings releases,

FIGURE 9.5   Oil Was Stagnant, Making Devon's Strength More Compelling
Chart courtesy of Prophet Financial Systems (www.prophet.net).

perhaps even lowering guidance. Two, the stock may be a smaller player in the group and the conventional wisdom is that it will not be able to reap the rewards from macrostimulus to the same degree as its rivals. These situations eventually become so-called value plays if this trend continues over a period of time and the rest of the group enjoys larger market valuations.

The Pile-on Effect

When I say a lot of news is already known to a select group of people, I'm including official news. Just as there are typically signs when a stock is going to make a big move—indications in the form of daily volume, directional bias, and relative action (i.e., the stock versus the stock of rivals or indexes that cover the industry)—there are also signs when a big media piece could be brewing.

Moreover, there are often times when there are so many negative articles and scuttlebutt on a company that one wonders if there isn't a collaborative effort to help or harm the share price of a specific company. Cynics who have been on the Street for years call these stories *plants*, deliberately published to drive a stock lower or higher. For the most part, planted stories are designed to drive stock prices lower.

The topic is coming further out in the open because of the irreparable harm that was done to many publicly traded micro-cap stocks (companies with market capitalization of less than $100 million) in the late 1990s and early part of the new millennium. Most of the micro-cap stocks were hammered relentlessly by short-sellers (folks positioned to profit financially when the share price went lower); as the broader market tumbled they were totally decapitated. The shorts got a lot of help from dubious Web postings, magazine articles, and other negative news pieces in various media.

In the meantime, those micro-cap and small-cap companies (companies with market capitalization of $100 million to $500 million) had no voice and were driven out of business, because their share prices became so low they couldn't take advantage of being public. They couldn't raise capital or generate wealth for themselves, the company, or the shareholders.

Now larger publicly traded companies are complaining about similar shorting programs designed to derail their share prices long enough for shorts to make money. Don't get me wrong; shorting is a great way to make money and to hedge your portfolio. Plus the short crowd is infinitely smarter than the long crowd. But the shorts who spread false rumors and get suspect things published (whether true or not) to help their case are hurting the integrity of our equity market.

One big-name company that is a great case study is Apple Computer (stock symbol AAPL). Apple Computer is the quintessential success story, founded by Steven Jobs. The company has been a trailblazer from day one. Yet, like most technology companies that have burst on the scene in the past couple of decades, there have been periods when the company had to deal with the challenge of a new mousetrap. Or, to borrow a Silicon Valley term, the company found itself in need of a killer app.

The rise in the share price of the company reflected its unique connection with customers, which in turn resulted in unbridled financial success. Shares were trading at $3 at the start of 1998 and by March 2000 were changing hands at $34 a share. Then the market fell apart, demand for technology from businesses and consumers waned, and the stock began to slide, too.

The company's shares finished out 2000 trading at $7.43 and then the stock was cast into a period of purgatory. Occasional the stock would move up, but mostly the shares traded sideways, as the company seemed to morph from a technology business to a design business. Their stuff had always looked sleek and hip, but the technology prowess was missing—there wasn't enough steak to go with the sizzle.

And then it happened: The iPod was spawned, and it was the perfect marriage of design and function.

The stock took off from January 2004, when it was trading at $10.70, and hit a high of $75.50 by January 2006. The ability to come up with a second act is a big deal, as F. Scott Fitzgerald would attest. Apple had a small audience of nerds but is now a global force whose products are coveted by all. The stock was a phenomenon, too, and caught the attention of the shorts.

The stock began pulling back and struggled to gain any upside traction, falling into a classic down channel, forming a series of lower lows and lower highs. The shorts were in control and obviously they had to keep the momentum going.

There was a series of positive news and the action in the share price in June hinted at a possible reversal of the six-month-long slide. That's when some would say certain articles and observations were planted to make sure the stock didn't reverse trend.

Whether these articles or comments that pressured the stock were planted or not, I don't know, but the timing was very fortuitous for the shorts. It should be noted that the short position in the stock climbed to 22.6 million shares in June from 17.6 million shares in May.

June 22, 2006, there was talk that Best Buy was on the verge of offering a wider array of Apple products, especially the Mac (personal computer), which the company hoped could ride the coattails of the iPod. The news sent the share price of Apple through the top of the channel, which you now know is more often than not a "buy" signal. (See Figure 9.6.)

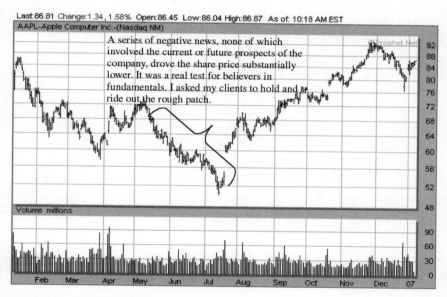

FIGURE 9.6 Apple's Wild Ride

Chart courtesy of Prophet Financial Systems (www.prophet.net).

On June 23, the very next session, momentum was exhausted after the stock crossed $60 and the shares closed near the low of the session.

On June 26, the shares opened under pressure as an article in the weekend version of the *Wall Street Journal* questioned the transparency of the company and indirectly insulted the intelligence of shareholders as folks willing to buy at the word of management. I took the weakness that ensued that next Monday session as an opportunity to mention the stock as a long idea to my clients, as I just didn't buy in to the notion that the company was any more secretive than any other. I certainly didn't buy in to the notion that there was a nefarious motivation behind this veil of secrecy.

The stock climbed ever so slightly off the canvas as the session went on. It looked like the entire episode was over and the stock would pick up from the upward momentum created the week before.

On June 27, the share price of Apple got slammed, and without any apparent news, the stock stumbled hard.

On June 28, an analyst from American Technology Research came out with a note that Apple would have delays in two highly anticipated products, the new Nano and the widescreen video iPod. The stock moved to its lowest point of the year.

What is very interesting about this onslaught of negative opinions and questions about integrity is that there was a real problem that was never mentioned. All the hunches centered on execution problems and corporate secrecy. None of the finger-pointers seemed to know about Apple's impending option-backdating scandal, which was significantly more detrimental to the integrity of management than some short-term product delay.

On June 29, at the close of trading, Apple revealed it was launching an internal probe of how it disturbed its stock option rewards. The company was the latest in a long line of companies that may have backdated options to generate maximum profits for insiders. The practice is illegal.

By June 30, the stock, which had closed at $58.97 on June 29, finished the session at $57.27.

By July 17, the stock had reached a low of $50 a share.

During this meltdown period there were other negative stories about Apple. The pile-on effect was in full operation. Needless to say, I had a serious problem on my hands trying to convince clients to hang in there. I lost one large client but gained the trust of many others as the stock began to rebound. The public was about to see a series of reminders that management wasn't resting on its laurels.

An active trader should have been out of the stock on July 23, when momentum dried up and the stock pulled back ahead of a three-day weekend. Investors should have stayed the course, as there was never a change in the company's fundamentals.

The charts are wonderful tools, and each type of market participant should use them. But be careful not to fall victim to deliberate campaigns to shake out the weak sisters. The weak sisters are those investors who are not well informed and are moving in and out of the market at the whims of each tick, a technique better suited for surfing than for investing in the stock market.

Obviously, the less you know about a company, the more likely you'll be one of those weak sisters. At this point in the evolution of the stock market, certain people with agendas that aren't nice know it's easy to get the average investor to become an unwitting accomplice in their schemes.

If you are using steadfast stop-losses, then you are going to be manipulated and sell stocks you should be holding. By the same token, you will also chase stocks (with undeserved high valuations) higher and get caught holding the bag. The last leg down in Apple stock was purely emotional. It was investors who never read the balance sheet, coupled with hot money that needed to deliver results sooner rather than later.

Apple came back fairly quickly, shaking off lackluster news from rival Dell Computer and a general malaise at the time about technology companies.

Don't Carry a Grudge: Reentering Former Losers

One aspect you are going to have a tough time with, as most investors do, is buying a stock that cost you money in the past, especially if the past is only a week ago. A lot of investors lost a lot of money as the share price of Apple Computer was melting down. Volume on down days was noticeably greater than volume on up days in the stock market. (See Figure 9.6.) Any combination of factors made folks bail out of the stock. Whether it was news that questioned the integrity of management, reports that questioned the execution of management, the timing of new products, the possibility of lost market share and stronger competition, or just whether some were unnerved by the stock options scandal.

The question now was when to get back in to the stock. First, you had to know there was never any fundamental news during the entire period the stock was melting down to justify the substantial loss of market value. Let's take a closer look at the series of events to be sure. (See Table 9.1.)

There was an assault on Apple, and while not everyone involved wanted to deliberately harm the stock, there were others who absolutely wanted the stock to come down, which it did, leaving a lot of investors on the sidelines with losses when the stock came roaring back.

So now investors were on the lookout to buy the stock and were waiting for the right signal from the tape for a clue. The clue, in this case, came through loud and clear but you had to move quickly.

There was the "buy" signal from the chart and also the sense that a worst-case scenario was baked into the company's shares heading into the quarterly earnings announcement on July 19 (the

TABLE 9.1   Taking a Bite Out of Apple

Issue Raised	Reality
Transparency	This is kind of interesting considering the fabulous gatherings headed up by Steve Jobs; there is always rapt anticipation for these gatherings. Beyond product development, the company does as much as any other tech company, in my opinion, to communicate its progress.
Competition	Apple has blown away would-be competition with its iPod, and the onus has to be on other companies to actually take market share before investors should react negatively.
Option scandal	While it isn't reassuring and is a reminder of the loss and fast ways of the 1990s, the stock option scandal isn't new per se. Its discovery is new, but the actual infraction is old news.

company posted its financial results after the closing bell). Remember, throughout the sell-off there was no evidence the company's fundamentals were deteriorating.

On July 18, 2006, the day before the company was to release its earnings, the stock closed higher for the second day in a row.

On July 19, the stock pierced through the short-term downtrend on convincing volume (read, in flashing lights: "buy" signal . . . "buy" signal)—in fact, the volume was the best in over a month. There is no doubt smart investors were taking a position ahead of the earnings report.

On July 20, the stock gapped open 13 percent higher than the previous close as investors celebrated a 48 percent increase in earnings and a 61 percent surge in shipments of notebooks. The stock never looked back, and additional stories about increased competition and poor management become background noise.

The shares of Apple were in a perfect down channel, as seen in Figure 9.7—not fun if you're long, but a great way to watch for a chance to reenter. It isn't always realistic that you will buy off the bottom of the channel—that's mostly a move for day traders. The ultimate "buy" signal came when the stock traded through the top of the channel on strong volume.

FIGURE 9.7   Buying Simply on the Chart, When the Stock Broke through the Down Channel

Chart courtesy of Prophet Financial Systems (www.prophet.net).

Watching the Puts and Calls

Stock options are a good tool for playing the stock market when you're a buyer and an even greater tool for managing investments when you are writing (selling) them. I'm not going to get too deep into stock options from a strategic point of view simply because I'd be doing you a disservice; there are so many esoteric ways to incorporate options into your investment scheme that describing them would take an entire book.

Suffice it to say, I worry when investors buy stock options as their only method for engaging the stock market. If you are doing this then you are playing the market, not investing, and the game is more akin to Russian roulette than Monopoly. Still, I understand the appeal. The returns are right up there with winning the lottery—some days options are up several hundred percent in a single session.

When you're watching a stock that has seen a spike in volume and there is no news from the company or any of its rivals, or any other developments that would have a material impact on the company, it's time to take a look at the options activity.

There are two basic elements of options that you need to understand:

- *Calls* give the holder the right to buy 100 shares in the underlying company for each contract, at a predetermined share price (strike price or strike) and by a specific period of time (expiration date).

- *Puts* give the holder the right to sell 100 shares in the underlying company for each contract, at a predetermined share price (strike price or strike) by a specific period of time (expiration date).

Stock options are contracts that are traded, but they do expire (die on the vine), and this is a point that doesn't seem to dawn on many investors. Sure, you could hold an option to the expiration date and choose to take advantage of the terms of the option, but more than likely you would have already traded it away.

Drivers of Stock Options

The pricing of stock options is science with a fair amount of art mixed in for good measure. We begin with *intrinsic value*, the core value of the option based on the strike price and the actual price of the stock. For instance, a strike price of $35 on a stock trading at $38 has intrinsic value of $3. Then come the layers of premium added through a number of factors:

- *Time premium.* Since time is money, the farther out the expiration, the more expensive the option. In November, the February calls will inherently be more expensive than the December calls, assuming the same exact strike price. You have to pay for the privilege of time.

- *Volatility or volume.* When there is more demand and liquidity, options tend to fetch higher prices and therefore the stock doesn't have to move as much to see a marked difference in the appreciation of the option. When buyers are standing by, the price of a stock option is likely to hold up more than for an option with few to no available buyers.

Because the payoff in options can be astronomical, speculators will often load up on them in hopes of early retirement. However, the really big bets in stock options are from some guy who just got tired of schlepping to the off-track betting parlor. The real action comes from the big boys, those hedge funds and other money manager types who are looking for the big score, too.

Sometimes when scuttlebutt is making the rounds and it's credible, you will see a surge in the options activity. The big boys have the inside track and we aren't in the loop, but they can't hide their buying, despite efforts to do so (it's not uncommon for them to drive a stock lower to shake out the little investor and then load up on the same stock at a cheaper price).

One example of sensing that the big boys knew something was brewing came in the case of Glamis Gold. There was a good article in the September 1, 2006, issue of the *New York Post* that highlighted the odd behavior in the call options of Glamis before the company released news that it had received a takeover offer from Goldcorp (the *Post* got its information on the article from insideoptions.com).

On August 17, 2006, some 21,000 call options changed hands on Glamis Gold, significantly more than the average daily volume of 3,050.

On August 31, the shares of Glamis opened higher, *much* higher, finishing the session up $7.26, or 19 percent. The stock was the number one percentage gainer of the session. My clients were already long on the stock, as we had mentioned it as an idea only a month earlier. In the immediate days after it was featured as a long idea, I had a few calls on the stock because it wasn't "doing anything," just moving sideways. I asked clients to hold the stock, in part due to the fact we felt it was undervalued. But I also liked the way the stock was acting versus its rivals (gold in general was under pressure in the summer of 2006) and I also liked the option activity.

Summary

News like brokerage upgrades and downgrades, articles or stories in the media, and even major news like new products and takeovers are telegraphed through the action in the stock. I call the task of looking for this action *watching the tape*. It involves knowing the average daily volume for the stock and options and also checking out the daily action of a particular stock.

Signs something is amiss or something is brewing:

- Increased volume (normally characterized as 50 percent or more beyond the daily average).

- Sharp price moves without any official news, upgrades, or downgrades.

- Stock is moving in the opposite direction of its rivals.

- Options activity: extraordinary put or call buying.

- Insider transactions—buys are much more significant than sells.

You are going to have to monitor for all of these signs as well as watch the action in stocks in the food chain of those in your portfolio. This is truer during earnings season, as this is the period when most disasters occur.

You don't have to be glued to a computer screen to do this. Just come home and review the volume and put a list together of intriguing companies (there are a ton of systems that currently assemble these lists for investors). Then take a look at the open, high, low, and close for the session. The stocks that open lower and close higher are the ones that should rank highest on your list to do further digging.

I would never ask you to buy a stock for the purpose of holding for a takeover only. You should, however, get in front of the news if the fundamentals warrant the risk.

Staying in the Game by Staying Informed

If a man will begin with certainties, he shall end in doubts;
but if he will be content to begin with doubts, he shall end in
certainties.

—Sir Francis Bacon

To stay *in* the game, you must stay *on top of* the game. This requires more than just looking at charts all night. It means knowing broad market news, industry news, as well as the company news of the stocks in your portfolio. Just looking at headlines and charts will bring you a false sense of certainty. You must be a skeptic and prove things to yourself over and over again. These days there is a ton of information on the stock market. The Internet provides a flow of information that can at times feel like Niagara Falls, and it is intimidating to try to figure out what is good information and what isn't.

Most Internet web sites devoted to the stock market are aggregators of information. These sites mostly have limited messages and wrap those messages around a bunch of bells and whistles. The business for most of these web sites is an advertising model, and many spend more time and money on marketing themselves than generating in-house content.

Then there are the web sites that have the magic bullet solutions to playing the stock market. These black-box web sites rely solely on technical indicators and are focused on making a short-term gain, usually in a day, and trumpeting those gains, often less than $1.00 and 1.0 percent, as trading wins. It's okay to trade, but it should only be 20 percent of you're your investing dollars. Selling a stock because it's up $.90 will lead to lost opportunity and heart-break as that same stock, which could pull back, ultimately rallies significantly higher over a long period of time.

I have clients who use those black-box solutions and use our work, too, the former more so for trading. I'd prefer they didn't use these systems. It enables poor investing behavior and requires investors to be tied to the PC just to make minuscule gains.

Some black-box systems are better than others, but at the end of the day making endless trades each day and being whipped around in the market isn't going to make you rich. You have to own stocks that go from $81 to $130 in a year and a half. You also have to have cash sometimes, you have to go short when the market is in obvious bear mode, and you can dabble in a bit of trading, but look to make a double-digit gain in 30 days or so and not taking pennies in a series of hunches. Trading should never be the majority of your investing activity.

Online Sources

When it comes to information resources, you have three basic types:

- Established resources
- Government resources
- Cutting-edge sources such as chat rooms and blogs

Established Independent Resources

Internet web sites pop up all the time, and there will be a lot more as the market moves to new highs in the future. Cutting through the clutter will be difficult; many of these newer web sites will have bells and whistles and look smart but they won't be smart and won't have much value-added.

I have put together a list of current web sites that I believe are the best with respect to their efforts to help investors, their experience, and their commitment to keep investors informed. These web sites are well financed and have crackerjack staff members.

- www.wstreet.com: Of course I have to begin with my own web site. Its mission and design are to make you money in the stock market and to help investors shed embedded habits that are very self-destructive.

- www.yahoofinance.com: A great way to gather news and keep a pulse on the opinions of the Street. The web site quickly updates news from and about publicly traded companies and lets you know where the professional analysts of Wall Street stand.

- www.bloomberg.com: A very intelligent web site, good global views and learned opinions. At times the content is a little highbrow for the newer investor but it's worth a daily visit.

- www.marketguide.com: Great for ratios, financials, and links to company web sites. This is a great tool for doing your own fundamental assessments of companies and industries.

- www.marketwatch.com: Up-to-date news and explanations of the news. This web site does a very good job at watching the market.

- www.thestreet.com: A ton of up-to-the-minute opinions and analyses of current events. This site offers an array of paid services, too.

- www.economy.com: Somewhat highbrow but great information on—what else?—the economy.

- www.msnmoney.com: Articles on personal finance mixed with timely dissemination of financial news.

- www.prophet.net: Interactive charts for equities and futures.

- www.morningstar.com: The king of mutual fund research, this site has equity research, too.

- www.bigcharts.com: Great charting and tools.

- www.ragingbull.com: Lots of chatter. Some of it good, but be careful.

- www.motleyfools.com: Not the powerhouse it once was, but the site has loyal fans and insightful information.

- www.realtimequotes.com: Good for quotes and other features.

- www.smartmoney.com: Smart articles on long-term financial objectives and how to reach them.

- www.forbes.com: Smart articles on individual companies, the economy, and individual stories that bring companies into focus, plus there is my favorite issue, the Forbes 400.

Government and Official Resources

There are also certain web sites that you must save as favorites so you can gather and review information, cut through the clutter of opinions, and come up with your own conclusions. I can't emphasize how important it is that you begin to read the economic releases from the actual sources. Just think how often have you glanced at financial television and someone says, "The market is down on the housing data this morning," and then the market finishes substantially higher.

Don't fall for the initial reactions, because most of the folks who are making instant decisions based on the headlines will more often than not come to regret it. One of the most important abilities you're going to need to become rich in the stock market is to keep a cool head, and the only way to do that is to know the facts—*all* the facts—and to stop letting talking heads interpret the facts for you.

Here is a list of web sites I visit to gather information that I use in my research. These web sites aren't hard to use, and it really feels empowering to have at your fingertips the same information that the pros have. Stop allowing the folks on the news to assess the data for you.

- www.bls.gov: This is the web site for payroll data, unemployment rates, producer price index, consumer price index, U.S. import prices, and inflation calculator.

- www.bea.gov: This is the web site for gross domestic product (GDP) information, personal income and spending, international balance of payment, and trade in goods and services.

- www.federalreserve.gov: FOMC schedule and information, speeches from the Federal Reserve, and in-depth economic data.

- www.census.gov: New residential construction sales, construction data, and additional data.

- www.realtor.org: The source for existing home sales, starts, and related information.

- www.sec.gov: It never hurts to know the rules and regulations.

- www.cboe.com: The Chicago Board of Options has a wonderful web site with up-to-the-minute news and developments.

Chat Rooms and Blogs

The Internet is a great tool and it's simple to access. You can capitalize on information or, at the very least, not be victimized by the spin doctors who often are talking up their books or who can't tear themselves away from an embedded opinion so their version of the news is always going to be skewed. And I'm talking about the professionals who are in business and really want to help. Then there are those lurking to ambush you and your portfolio.

Chat rooms are fine for passing along information and occasionally there is a kernel in the mix that could make you money, but on the whole they are the worst way to go if they're your only source of investing information. Like blogs, chat rooms have democratized the flow of information and opinions, but all too often that opinion is taken and presented as fact.

You have to be very careful of the ulterior motivations of people posting information in chat rooms. There is no filtering system, there is no fact checking, and, most worrisome of all, there is no accountability.

I have only responded to comments made in chat rooms twice; in both instances I was being attacked because I didn't like a particular stock. That's how those chat rooms work; people come on to hype their own positions (or talk up their book, as it's known on the Street), and anyone who would persuade the rest of the chatters to think otherwise becomes fair game for ridicule. Getting raked over the coals is part of the fun of participating in chat rooms. The goals of chat rooms are great, but instead of free-flowing information where investors try to help one another, many chat rooms have become cesspools of vitriolic anger and nonsense.

For now the chat rooms remain a den of tainted information, uninformed facts, and deliberate campaigns to separate investors from their money. The last time I responded to something in a chat room was a few years ago. A client of Wall Street Strategies was long on a stock that some guy was knocking hard in a chat room. When the client entered the fact that he was long and felt good about the idea because I liked it, the nonbelieving chatter went ballistic. I was called a token, a joke, and a few other unmentionables, too.

Although this guy's opinion of the stock in question was different from mine, I really didn't care and wouldn't have bothered to enter any thoughts on the matter into the chat room. But there were serious comments about my race and position in life that compelled me to respond (something I wouldn't do these days no matter how ignorant the comments). I only had to wait a few days, because the stock opened higher one day and took off like a rocket. My client made a lot of money and I took the opportunity to talk smack in that very same chat room.

I never looked into the matter again and wished I didn't bother even then. The point is there will be good information in chat rooms from time to time, but it is significantly dwarfed by horrendous information. Only bother with chat rooms when all other sources of intelligence have been exhausted, and be prepared to look with a jaundiced eye at the reasons and rationales presented. It might be an answer to a question, but it could also be the wrong answer.

Web logs, or blogs, by contrast, seem to be making strides to legitimacy. Unlike chat rooms where folks come in under the cloak of false names and handles, blogs are accountable and therefore I believe the information is a lot better. The blog phenomenon is changing the news business, but there are some worries, too. Most blogs have built-in agendas so the information may be tilted in a certain manner. Also, blogs have limited staff or, in many cases, no staff at all, so they rely on unfettered information and rumors as they race to be the first with the news. Many times that news is incorrect.

Still, blogs are much better than chat rooms as a source of information in general and for stock market information, too. Even so, blogs should only be part of your research and not the sole source of information.

Newspapers and Magazines

There is also a lot of information known in research circles as fuzzy information; these are articles in periodicals and magazines. The daily information from the *Wall Street Journal*, *Financial Times*, and *Investor's Business Daily* is great for learning about stocks. *Investor's Business Daily*, in particular, is great for those trading stocks.

The Wall Street Journal

The Wall Street Journal (WSJ) is a great paper; it covers so much and gets to the bottom of things both financial and political. These days the *Journal* is best at getting beneath the surface, particularly after the new topic has made a big splash. The *Journal* is still the definitive source for accuracy in the world of money. With unfettered access to the big boys, you will know what the official party lines are at the largest funds and with the smartest investors (although it could be argued that the really smart folks don't speak to the media, not even to the WSJ).

Always begin with the "C" section when you read the *Journal*. The key columns include:

- "Heard on the Street"
- "Abreast of the Market"
- "Ahead of the Tape"
- "Long and Short"

Investor's Business Daily

This is a great newspaper and fills a void. It is an actionable newspaper. The stories are short, focused, and topical. The only drawback is the paper creates a trading mentality and helps to push stocks to overvalued levels. William O'Neil has created a great formula for highlighting hot stocks based on relative strength. The thing is, by the time the RS reading reaches its highest point, the stock has already made a sizable move.

Still, for folks looking for trading ideas, historical anecdotes, inspirational stories, and how to list, this paper should be a daily read. It includes these key features:

- IBD 100: A list of the hottest stocks in the market. There is a focus on certain metrics and one sentence to explain the company or current trends at the company.

- "Inside the 100": A column that gives greater detail on newsworthy companies on the IBD 100 list.

- "Investor's Corner": Provides solid insight on several aspects of investing in the market.

Barron's

This is the smartest read for investors, but at the same time it is the most negative. If there is a nugget of negativity in the air, whether it's from an upcoming round of corporate earnings, interest rates, the economy, commodity prices, or consumer confidence, that negativity will be magnified. Be that as it may, the paper is usually on point, albeit not right away. It's not uncommon to read about a great article that predicted news only a year earlier.

In addition, I believe the paper is too conservative and features only the old-guard money managers whose thinking isn't very elastic or distinguishable from one another. Sure, these folks are accomplished, but it would be great to see a larger variety of people with different approaches. The paper is elitist and looking for returns designed for the wealthy. It's fine for the wealthy to be content with annual returns of 6 percent, but the person reading the paper religiously and looking for more is going to be hamstrung.

Key columns and features include:

- "Up and Down Wall Street": Usually written by Alan Abelson, the column is witty but will remind you of that uncle who was the antithesis of the eternal optimist.

- "Reviews and Previews": A glance at the past week and highlights of key goings-on in the coming week.

- "First Feature": Usually a piece on a Fortune 500 company and the cover story; the reporting will be detailed and prescient.

- "The Trader": My favorite is usually written by Michael Santoli and gives good insight on what really occurred during the week.

- "Market Laboratory": A lot of information but only if its not football season and the kids are still in bed.

Barron's has a lot of juice, and each Monday stocks move from the so-called *Barron's* bounce; often traders will try to buy the bounce if that Monday morning move is to the downside. It's a technique I've used in the past when the initial reaction was too harsh, but the optimum word here is *trade*. In the long run these guys are usually right—they can smell a rat inside an individual company long before the rest of us can.

Financial Times

This is a great paper to get a decidedly non-American point of view (some might even say an anti-American point of view) on global developments, considering that the planet is shrinking and the phrase *global economy* becomes more relevant each day. It includes the following key columns and features:

- "FT Companies and Markets": Covers the big business news around the globe but particularly in Europe.

- "The S&P Report": Part of the international coverage, which means U.S. equity coverage.

- "The Market": Takes a look at economic drivers and is usually in the back of the second section; the articles are intelligent and insightful.

Setting Up Your Command Center

Self-directed investors use online brokerage firms or other Internet-based trading platforms to play the market. These sites all have ways to monitor your positions and the stock market. So, too, can you establish watch lists on sites such as MSN.com and Yahoo! Financial. However, I want you to create a wide swath of observation, a platform that will take into account macrofactors and indicators down to microfactors that would have a direct correlation with the stocks in your portfolio.

Ideally your watch lists should be set up in a top-down fashion. You have to know what the broad market is doing and use that as a benchmark to assess the action in your portfolio on a stock-by-stock basis.

Macroview

First, you need to follow the broader indexes. Let's say you own a semiconductor stock that is unchanged for the session, but the Semiconductor Index (stock symbol SOX) was down for the session. Maybe you have a stock that wants to move higher given the right stimulus. Conversely, if your stock was the only one down while all the rivals were higher, then it's time to go back, check the news, check the filings, check for upgrades or downgrades, and make a reassessment. I'm not saying to make a knee-jerk reaction, but move decisively to make sure you aren't in the wrong stock.

It is tough to follow every single stock in a particular group, so watch the indexes that represent the industry (the Dow Jones has a ton of indexes that cover nooks and crannies of sectors).

The *Dow Jones Industrial Average* (DJI or INDU) is composed of only 30 so-called industrial companies, which are supposed to be reflective of the broader market. The knock on the index, besides the fact that it is limited in number and therefore a poor proxy for the broader market, is that the stocks in it are simply lumbering giants that don't reflect the sizzle of smaller growth companies and the changes in their share prices.

Perhaps because of its staid image, the powers that be at Dow Jones spruced up the index in November 1999 with the addition of

Intel and Microsoft. Not just a smokestack index, by adding the two stalwarts of technology the index gained greater credibility from investors and a little oomph, too. Intel was changing hands at $37.50 and Microsoft at $41. These stocks rallied to $72 and $51 respectively but tumbled hard and have actually been a drag on the index for several years.

How ironic that in a move to be hip and relevant the Dow became extra vulnerable to the backlash on technology. There have been additional changes since 1999.

The NASDAQ Composite (stock symbol COMPQ) is the Super Ball of all the indexes; it bounces around and gyrates sometimes to the delight of investors and sometimes to their detriment, but there is never a dull moment. In 1961 Congress asked the SEC to perform a study of all markets, which eventually led to the creation of this electronic market. The first official day of trading was February 8, 1971.

The S&P 500 (stock symbol SPX) is an index of 500 stocks designed to be reflective of the overall market and economy. Stocks are selected based on size ($4 billion market cap minimum), liquidity, and industry. Each company must have 50 percent or more of its shares in the public float and be an operating company. The top five industries as of June 2006 are these:

- Financials, 21.3 percent

- Info techs, 14.9 percent

- Health care, 12.3 percent

- Industrials, 11.7 percent

- Energy, 10.3 percent

The Russell 2000 (stock symbol RUT) contains the 2,000 smallest stocks from the Russell 3000 index. The focus is on smaller-capitalization companies and the average market cap is $540 million.

The Dow Jones Wilshire 5000 actually contains more than 6,000 stocks in an attempt to capture the total stock market and not just be a proxy. Although most of the stocks in the index are NASDAQ-listed, the NYSE issues dominate the market valuation of the index.

- NSYE, 80 percent

- AMEX, 1 percent

- NASDAQ, 19 percent

   Other key indexes include:

- The Biotech Index (BTK)

- The Philadelphia Semiconductor Index (SOX)

- The AMEX Networking Index (NWX)

- The AMEX Securities Brokers/Dealer Index (XBD)

- The S&P Retail Index (RLX)

- The AMEX Oil Index (XOI)

- The Dow Jones U.S. Home Construction Index (DJUSHB)

   There are many other indexes that cover everything from toys to tires, software, automobiles, asset managers, fixed-line telecommunications, reinsurance, distillers and vintners, medical supplies, computer hardware, platinum and precious metals, coal, mining, trucking, basic resources, steel, business training and employment . . . and the list goes on and on. There is no niche of the market that isn't covered. This is fantastic for investors to get a relative read on their holdings.

   You want to discover stocks that look intriguing and check them for the action compared to its average daily volume. Also check them against their rivals by looking at some of their top competitors and an industry index.

Monitoring Stocks by Grouping the Key Players of a Particular Industry

Your screen should be broken into industry groups that form food chains and share other correlations of influence. For instance, I would place auto parts makers above automakers, and I would have steel makers next to the auto parts makers because of the impact of metal prices on the fortunes of automakers. Generally you have to have the biggest players in a particularly industry in your grouping, and then you could also add up-and-comers and other intriguing players.

I'd also have all the transportation niches near each other—the airlines, followed by the cruise liners and the hoteliers and then the gaming casinos. After all, these industries are driven by a strong economy and cheap oil.

Watching the Action

The most important thing you're going to be looking for from your screens is intraday action, things that pertain to possible news. If a company's shares gap open higher by more than 1 percent, then more than likely there is news. However, the stock that opens flat and then begins to come on strong, noticeably outperforming its industry group, is the stock that you want to take a deeper look into. I always check the average daily volume to assign credibility and urgency to the move in the share price. Table 10.1 lists the key elements that should be included in your screens for individual stocks.

The appendix gives you starter groupings. Use these as your foundation and feel free to add or subtract names when you feel others are more appropriate. You have to be able to monitor the market in order to play both offense and defense, so you have to have your monitor established as a tool to help you sniff out opportunities and risks. If you have a system that doesn't hold all the symbols, make sure you have *at least* the top three companies in each key industry group.

If your system isn't robust enough to follow all or an abundance of stocks, then make sure that the stock you're holding is included with companies that most closely resemble it within the industry.

TABLE 10.1   How Your Stock Screen for Individual Stocks Should Look

	Quote	High	Low	Open	Volume	Average Volume	Market Cap
Symbol							

Summary

Your screens must convey more information than just whether the stocks in your portfolio are up or down. You must also be able to sense what industries are healthy and what stocks act like they want to outperform. Scanning this universe will put you in tune with the market in general and help you make faster and wiser decisions. Whenever you think something is intriguing, make sure to look into that company and its three to five closest rivals, and also look at the food chain—companies that may sell the raw materials to make that finished product and companies that distribute that finished product.

Risk and Reward

*K*akorrhiaphobia, fear of failure and defeat, is a greater hindrance to success in the stock market than is greed. But in the stock market there also seems to be a fear of success. I can't put my finger on the precise reason it exists, but it does.

All too often investors are snatching defeat out of the jaws of victory. I see it all the time and I'm sure it's happened to you, too. You sell a stock for no real good reason and then it goes on to be a gigantic winner. Or you are so intimidated by the market and losing money that you simply sell with the crowd over and over again and console yourself for the short period of time when that same stock is a little lower, but feign ignorance or even take it off your screen once it's roared back.

There are any number of risks associated with the stock market; some are tangible and others are emotional. You can get a handle on both with greater knowledge of the market and the stocks in your portfolio. As a self-directed investor, you'll have to modulate the fear of success and the fear of failure and at the same time stop being your own worst enemy.

Understanding Risk and Reward

A simple equation of knowing what the possible upside is versus the possible downside gives us the risk-reward ratio. This is the key to mitigating losses and achieving a balanced portfolio. Taking risk into account isn't a high enough priority for most investors. Investors always know what the upside is and sometimes they know what the downside is on the charts, but too rarely do they know embedded risks associated with the companies in which they've invested.

Individual investors say they don't need help because they've figured it out. Some have come to this conclusion based on a false confidence in the charts, and others have lowered the bar and now consider not losing money to be success. The main source of this chutzpah came and continues to come from investors making big scores in the market despite taking on incredible risk, incorporating faulty asset allocation, and not doing real homework.

I call it luck but it's really more of a curse, because poor investment habits become embedded and tied in to your psyche with a Gordian knot. Don't get me wrong, luck can be a big part of the game, but you want to get lucky for the right reasons and not the wrong reasons. You want to own the number one percentage gainer in the market because the stock was taken over by some company that concluded it was cheap, just as you did. If you won the stock from a tip, consider the score luck and don't let this become your method for playing the market.

Some investors deliberately go for the home run ball every time they come to bat. Each stock in their portfolio has to be a million-to-one play—a company that has the cure for cancer or a technology that will leapfrog anything Microsoft or IBM has on the market. Sure, these kinds of investments are always lurking about, although they're like the lottery with the multimillion-dollar jackpot: We know somebody won, but we've never met anyone who has won.

In baseball, sometimes the *last* thing a manager of a club wants is for a singles hitter (a player who normally hits for accuracy rather then power) to hit a couple of home runs. Why? Well, the home run is infectious; it is the ultimate adrenaline rush, or so I'm told. I remember when former New York Mets player Lenny Dykstra (now a stock guru) was named by fans as the best lead-off hitter in the game—no small feat since Ricky Henderson was also playing at that time—he began to hit home runs.

The excitement of watching him hit those homers all the time energized the team and the fans, but after a while it began to hurt his real talent—the ability to get on base. In my mind he never was the same, and he was eventually sent packing from the team.

As an investor, there would be no greater thrill than to wake up one morning and learn that XYZ Biopharmaceuticals has just been granted FDA approval for a cure for lung cancer. That would be like the most famous home runs in the history of baseball, the shot heard around the world (Bobby Thompson), the Kirk Gibson home run in the World Series when he could barely walk to the plate, and the three-home-run performance by Reggie Jackson, all rolled into one.

It's good to dream, but in the stock market it is so much more important to adjust for and plan for risk and worst-case scenarios.

What is the difference between a professional investor and the average individual investor? The professional investor assesses the risk; in many cases it's the first thing he looks at—what is the worst that could happen? By contrast, individual investors are always counting their chickens first, daydreaming about how high their holdings will go without regard for the possible downside.

In order to become rich in the stock market, you have to consider and master the following:

- Understanding and planning for risk

- Distribution and allocation of assets

- Timing and exit strategy

- Researching and understanding your portfolio

In order to control your risk and reward properly, you have to be able to control your emotions throughout the entire investing cycle.

Riding Out the Bumps in the Road

Handling the ups and downs of the market is the key to success. Mostly handling the downs is the key to success in the market, and the difference between becoming a frustrated day trader or someone who stays cool and creates wealth. If you enter the stock market thinking every stock is going to go straight up, you're in trouble. If you enter the stock market and sell stocks on every dip, you'll be real broke, real fast. I've met a ton of traders who use stop-losses yet have the same amount in the money today that they had three years ago.

You must understand there are life cycles to the market and to each investment you're going to make.

Life Cycle

The life cycle of an investment begins the moment one takes the position (going long or short) and lasts until the moment one exits that position (selling a long idea or buying to cover a short). Each phase of the life cycle carries a certain amount of risk and challenges that must be constantly assessed or reassessed. The main impediment to becoming rich in the stock market is the fact that too many investors are closing positions during the period they should be holding and, to a lesser degree, holding when they should be selling. It is folly to expect any stock to be able to go up in a straight line. Armed with the tools in this book, you will have the confidence to hold companies that are simply under pressure from the crowd.

BUYING This is the easiest part of the life cycle of an investment. Let's face it, anyone can come up with a hot investment idea, and everyone will, at one time or another. At this stage of the game investors should already know the following:

- How much they are looking to make. The upside should be realistic, although at the end of the day a great company is going to return so much more than you've become accustomed to. The key is to hold it.

- How much they are willing to lose. When you take 2 percent profits out of fear of the stock being down the next day, then you are going to have to play it close to the vest on the downside, too, or a 10 percent loser will wipe out five would-be winners.

- Why this idea? Is it a tip, hunch, wild guess, or was real fundamental work used to come up with the idea? With real fundamental work you are prepared to be an owner of the company.

HOLDING Riding the waves is tough. Since 2000 those waves have been so wild and erratic that even staid, dyed-in-the-wool, buy-and-hold types have taken hits and bailed out. Mastering this part of the life cycle of an investment is where you will get your black belt and open the door to riches. Of course, there is a big difference between holding on to hope and holding on to value.

EXITING This is really the hard part, isn't it? We worry about getting out too soon, leaving money on the table, looking at those riches that were within our grasp. Many of the same factors that determined why you took the position will and should determine how you exit. Of course, I want to make sure you enter investments for the right reasons so that you exit at the right time, too.

Types of Risk

Risk is what we take the moment our eyes open in the morning. There is a chance the water in the shower could be too cold or too hot; the former makes for a jarring wake-up call, the latter makes for a possible visit to the hospital. But of course we have knobs that clearly indicate hot and cold, and we also have to ability to feel the water, testing for the moment it reaches perfection.

As the day moves forward the risk increases exponentially. We, however, moderate our lives to adjust for risk. If that nut in the car in front of you looks like he has had too much to drink, you simply switch lanes and move around him, maybe giving him a dirty look as you pass by. You continuously check and assess risk when you drive your car, looking at the rearview mirror every few seconds.

You are always checking, monitoring, and preparing for unpleasant events in your life. You probably dread doctor visits (I know I'm not alone in this), and yet the earlier an ailment is discovered, the greater the chance of curing or fixing those would-be problems. We buy life insurance although we avoid dwelling on the inevitable. For the most part we are always checking and assessing risk in our lives: Can I really jump over this puddle of water or should I just take the longer route and stay dry?

And yet you and the overwhelming majority of individual investors don't feel for the comfort level of your portfolio the way you do in the morning shower to make sure it's just right. Sure, you check out a few quotes, and more and more folks are checking the charts, and that's a start. It should go without saying that when a stock in your portfolio is swerving all over the road like a drunken driver who is five miles from home and has totally let his guard down, you'd better investigate.

Risk in the stock market isn't the actual action of a stock or of the stock market. Risk is a measure of *probable outcome* and the resulting response of a stock should unplanned but highly possible developments occur. It's great to know the potential of a company and assume what the upside payoff is going to be—we all do that. But you also have to assess the worst-case scenario when you buy the stock and throughout the life cycle of the holding itself.

Company-Specific Risk

There are different types of risk that you are going to have to account for as an investor or even if you want to be a so-called trader. The first kind of risk is the risk associated with the business of the stocks in your portfolio. During the great movement of self-directed investors in the 1990s, there was little care about what the actual business was or whether a company was doing a good job. Back then *earnings* had become a bad word, as the new paradigm put a greater emphasis on spending money rather than making it.

I remember one of the most exciting and heavily traded companies during the era was HBO and Company (former stock symbol HBOC). Most of the investors in the stock thought the company was a provider of cable television programming, even though it is in actuality in the information technology (IT) industry, providing services to the health care industry. The company eventually merged with McKesson and Company.

It was a hot stock and made a lot of money for a lot of investors (some of my clients were long the stock when the takeover was announced), but few knew what the heck the company did. Nor did they care. During that time, I would say (not entirely tongue in cheek) that not only could ignorance be bliss but it could be very profitable, too. Too many investors are banking on the return of such a period, but I don't think it's going to happen for a long time.

So we begin with knowing what a company does and then go from there. We have to understand how the company makes its money and how likely it will be able to do so in the future. We must understand the industry that a company operates in and understand the inherent pros and cons of that industry.

ONE-TRICK PONY There are other forms of company-specific risks, such as being a one-trick pony. There are a lot of good companies out there that have limited products and therefore limited upside potential. One that comes to mind is TiVo (stock symbol TIVO), a company with such a groovy product the name has been added to the lexicon of television watchers.

The business has been great and something I think anyone who grew up in the 1970s wished for at one time or another, just to ditch the commercials (ironically, I love commercials these days). In a world of two-income households and 500 TV channels, the ability to program the TiVo and let it find your entire list of favorite shows is a wonderful value-added. Those who sing the product's praises even say it improves the quality of life.

The stock has the same kind of cult following; folks continue to equate the cool product with great fundamentals, and see huge profits. The company has experienced steady top-line growth since 2001. The fact is the product has been a big hit, but after five years the company still wasn't profitable. (See Table 11.1.) Moreover, competition continues to increase and the company is racing against the clock to find new uses and partnerships to maintain its edge.

Although revenues continue to improve, the rate of improvement has slowed and the stock has been deadline for a couple of years and trapped in a narrow range since 2001. (See Figure 11.1.)

TABLE 11.1   Full-Year Financial Results for TiVo

Year End	1/31/2006	1/31/2005	1/31/2004	1/31/2003	1/31/2002
Revenue	$195.9	$172.1	$141.1	$96.0	$19.4
Operating income/loss	$(37.4)	$(75.8)	$(22.5)	$(57.1)	$(151.5)

FIGURE 11.1   Share Price for TiVo since October 2000
Chart courtesy of Prophet Financial Systems (www.prophet.net).

Other potential company-specific issues include:

- Young or inexperienced management. I'm talking about companies that are new to the public scene. Often an expert in their particular field runs them, but that person may have no idea how to handle analysts or investors. These guys make the first bump in the road a mountain rather than a molehill.

- Thin product pipelines. These harm companies in biotech and technology and can lead to vicious cycles of boom and bust for individual companies. In these highly competitive fields it's all about what's up your sleeve. Just as these companies are unveiling the next big thing, investors are saying "That's great, what's next?"

- Business models that aren't as effective as they once were. I think this has hurt companies like Dell and Lexmark in recent times. No business model can be effective forever, and companies that rest on their laurels pay heavy prices. Keep in mind that business models not only have to adjust to the ever-changing realities of the marketplace but also have to be tweaked to fend off competition.

- Poor images. These seem to haunt many companies whose share prices can't shake misdeeds of the past. The corporate scandal is the scarlet letter and a brand that takes years to remove or diminish.

BUYING SCANDAL-SCARRED STOCKS   There has been a series of stock market scandals since the late 1990s, including the accounting scandals at Enron and WorldCom as well as the more recently un-veiled stock option backdating scandal that artificially inflated the incomes of corporate officers by billions of dollars. In the over-whelming majority of these cases, the stocks were usually ham-mered and left for dead. Yet there are large groups of investors, both professional and individual, who focus exclusively on beaten-down stocks. For many of these players, the harsher the re-action by the market, the more compelling the stock becomes.

It's a tough racket, trying to guess when the worst is over for these companies, but one thing is certain: The problem isn't re-solved the day after the stock bites the dust. When a company has been cooking the books, it takes time for a true financial picture to emerge. It takes significantly longer before the company gets any traction in the belief department, which makes earnings and other developments ineffectual in helping the company's image.

The first step to curing these situations is to bring in new man-agement, but changing the corporate culture overnight is virtually impossible, and the Street understands this. However, there has to be a management change if the stock is ever to command a fair value, let alone a premium valuation. Larger companies tend to re-bound faster than smaller companies guilty of similar infractions.

The bottom line is that trying to assume when a company will emerge from a deep-rooted problem, especially a problem involving ethics, is the ultimate guessing game. If you want to play with these hand grenades, I suggest relegating them to trading vehicles only, at least for the first year after the news hits. Many have made nice re-bounds from the ultimate low, but those scenarios typically play out over a long period of time; the knee-jerk bounce for a 30 percent profit or more just doesn't happen. But stocks do come back.

One great example of this situation is none other than Interna-tional Business Machines (stock symbol IBM), the company that was synonymous with U.S. capitalism during the second half of the twentieth century. IBM was the big business. Past leaders of the company are legends in the business world. Yet somehow the company lost its way. While the company is adamant that Thomas Watson Jr. never said "A worldwide market of only five electronic computers exists" in 1953, it cannot deny it was asleep at the wheel as Bill Gates and his crew were cobbling together a com-pany they called Microsoft.

IBM was fighting a decade-long antitrust battle in the 1980s, and that may have sidetracked management, but complacency was the order of the day. So too, it seems, were funny accounting techniques. The company was already the subject of rampant speculation about shaky accounting, and the share price was already sliding when the bad news finally hit.

In 1993 IBM posted the then-record largest quarterly loss in corporate history. That July the company posted a loss of $8.1 billion because it had to write off $8.9 billion. Yet the day the earnings were announced, the stock rallied three points! That's because investors were actually bracing for the worst and got something a little better, if you can believe that. The stock traded in a range between $8.80 and $9.60 until it broke out that November. The stock went on to climb to $124 a share by the end of 1999, an increase of 1,300 percent. The IBM story is the perfect example for when to invest in scandal-riddled stocks.

One of the hardest things I have convincing individual investors of, mostly because so many pundits get it wrong and espouse it all the time, is the notion that a great company could have an overbought stock while a poorly run company could have an oversold stock. When IBM was falling apart, a lot of the selling was disgust that one of the most fabled companies in American history had botched it so horribly. When the final nail in the coffin came via one of the worst quarters any publicly traded company had ever experienced to that time, the news was already factored into the share price.

Buying when the dawn is darkest can work. This is why IBM was a screaming buy despite common and popular wisdom at the time.

- When IBM posted that infamous quarter, the stock was already at an 18-year low.
- Just before the earnings release, IBM hired Lou Gerstner in April of that year. A well-respected executive, Gerstner had run RJR Nabisco for four years.
- The company had a lot of room to make significant changes and a history of corporate excellence to rely upon.

Figures 11.2 and 11.3 illustrate that the worst was already built in to the stock and some smart buyers began to build positions. The long-term rally underscores how the risk was warranted.

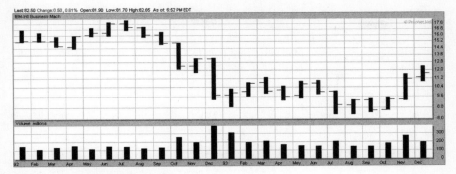

FIGURE 11.2   IBM, 1992 to 1994
Chart courtesy of Prophet Financial Systems (www.prophet.net).

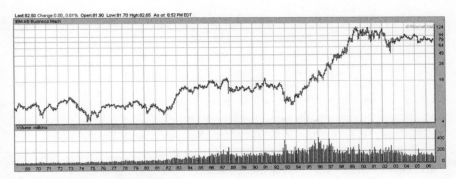

FIGURE 11.3   IBM, 1968 to 2006
Chart courtesy of Prophet Financial Systems (www.prophet.net).

There aren't a lot of companies out there that could pull off the trick that IBM did, although other scandal-scarred stocks may eventually make for great investments. The fact of the matter is there are always good companies that go begging for valuation, so you really don't have to force the issue if there is a question of credibility. For each IBM equivalent, I could show you scores of companies that haven't been able to come back from a serious drubbing because of a substantial loss of credibility. So if you're holding on to a stock because you remember it was once considered a great company, your stock market emotional IQ is well below genius.

Table 11.2 lists some companies that endured bouts of questionable accounting and never saw their share price come back to even.

So insider information is illegal and the playing field is level?

TABLE 11.2   Scandals Where Scars Are Still Visible in the Share Price

Scandalous Scoundrels	Year Scandal Revealed	Highest Share Price Year Scandal Broke	Lowest Share Price in the Aftermath	Highest Point since Hitting Rock Bottom
Cendant	1998	$40.00	$10.10	$42.00
Xerox	2000	$49.00	$ 3.75	$15.80
Time Warner	2002	$26.30	$ 8.70	$19.40
Tyco	2002	$60.00	$ 7.00	$35.70
Bristol-Myers	2002	$52.00	$19.50	$30.70
Duke Energy	2002	$38.30	$12.20	$31.00
Computer Associates	2002	$38.70	$ 7.40	$31.70
Qwest	2002	$15.10	$ 1.00	$ 9.20
AIG	2005	$73.40	$49.90	$71.00

Think again. Not only is insider information alive and well, it occurs in plain sight. (By the way, there is work to do to stop predatory shorting of small-cap stocks—if indeed there is a place for legislation, it's there.) You have to be prepared to monitor the stock market, not necessarily to day-trade but to identify actions that could harm your portfolio or make you a lot of money.

Industry Risk

The best industry to use when discussing inherent industry risk is the biotechnology space. Let's say you're a buyer of biotechnology stocks. Have you planned for all possible series of events? What happens to the share price of XYZ Biopharmaceuticals when the FDA doesn't approve that wonder drug? How many shares do you own? What percentage of your portfolio is in the stock? Was the stock already up big time and, if so, did you take any defensive measures?

The example of the hypothetical company, XYZ Biopharmaceuticals, isn't an exaggeration. Routinely, biotech companies receive news from the FDA or from clinical trials that take the company back to square one, literally! Needless to say, when a company has to go back to square one, the stock does, as well.

Although the biotech space has been a favorite place for speculators, investors frolic there amid land mines that could have incredible collateral damage to the entire space, as in the 1980s when cures for septis shock were going to change the world of medicine. Then there was the difficult period for the space after the human genome was mapped out.

MAPPING THE HUMAN GENOME AND HUMAN INVESTING PATTERNS In 1998 Dr. J. Craig Venter and the Applera Corporation formed a new company called Celera Genomics (stock symbol CRA) to sequence (map) the human genome. This venture began with great fanfare and hope. After all, we aren't talking about a hot stock from a company making ugly shoes. The fact of the matter is there continues to be great hope that by sequencing the building blocks of human life, new medicines and treatments will be designed, tailored specifically for various ailments from cancer to heart failure.

The company's stock was a monster! The shares entered heights that were simply unprecedented. Sure, during that period we saw other stocks of companies with no earnings make it into orbit, too, but few people knew when or if this company would ever even have revenue.

Here's the stock timeline:

- The company went public in 1999 and didn't initially zoom out of the gate, but once the chatter began, the stock started to lift off its base at $6.

- In March 2000 the company published its sequencing of the *Drosophila* (fruit fly). The excitement leading up to the news drove the share price to $258 a share. (See Figure 11.4.)

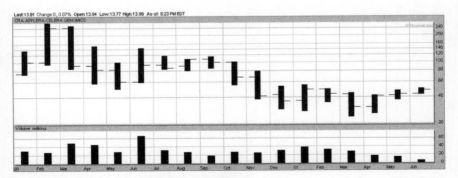

FIGURE 11.4   CRA, January 2000 to June 2001
Chart courtesy of Prophet Financial Systems (www.prophet.net).

- In June 2000 the company completed the first half of its efforts to map the entire human genome. That month saw the biggest surge in volume, and the share price bounced from a low of $60 in the preceding month to a high of $120. (Although it didn't directly affect the share price, one interesting aside was the lack of differences between the genome of the fruit fly and that of humans.)

- In February 2001 the company published the human genome sequence in *Science* magazine. By this time the excitement had passed. Nobody believed there would be immediate super cures from the efforts of the company and there was still the question of how money would be made, if indeed money could ever be made.

- In January 2002 Dr. J. Craig Venter stepped down as president of Celera Genomics. The stock finished the month changing hands at $20.75 a share and has never been that high since.

The moral of the story is that with great hype can come great rewards, but also fantastic risks. Take a look at the long-term chart of Celera Genomics (Figure 11.5) and pay close attention to the bottom bars, the graphing of the volume. It is clear that most of the volume occurred during the run-up in the share price, which means there was a significant amount of buying. As the share price began to crumble, the volume slid, too, a sign that there were fewer sellers

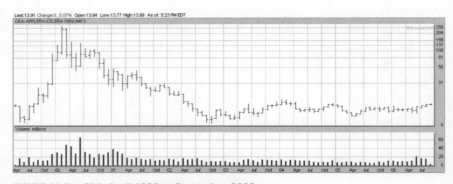

FIGURE 11.5   CRA, April 1999 to September 2006
Chart courtesy of Prophet Financial Systems (www.prophet.net).

on the way down than there were buyers on the way up. That means people held on and held tight. They held on based on ego and pride; their emotions got the better of them.

These means there are still a lot of investors holding the bag; they own Celera Genomics at $250, $150, and even $50 a share. At this point the company probably would have to come up with a cure for cancer for those investors to break even or make money. Investors who jumped on the bandwagon in 1999, 2000, and 2001 had a wild ride, but how many of them ever stopped to ask: What's the worst that could happen?

Sure, it was a fun ride, for those folks who got in and out, yet realistically even Sir Isaac Newton would have jumped back into the stock, even if he had made a fortune on it at the beginning of the hysteria. The thing with this kind of stock, one that's flying off the charts, is to make sure you only have a certain amount of your portfolio at risk. And that doesn't mean having three other biotech stocks, but to be able to be long other less exciting stocks in different industries while a certain portion of your portfolio is sizzling.

DNA: BUILDING BLOCKS OF A WINNER In 2000 only 20 percent of biotechnology companies were profitable. That number has improved, but the fact of the matter is most biotechnology companies are still not turning profits. Of course there have been incredible winners in the biotechnology space including Genentech (stock symbol DNA). The first biotech company to go public, it was taken over and then spun out again as a separately traded company.

The returns from the stock have been like the shot heard round the world, plus Kirk Gibson and Reggie Jackson's heroics, all rolled into one. By the same token the number of pure disasters in the space has cost investors billions of dollars. In 2002 the share price of Genentech languished around $14 for most of the year; by October 2005 the share price tickled $98, a 600 percent increase. (See Figure 11.6.) This move occurred during a time when many investors were actually out of the market.

Most of those investors weren't comfortable with the backdrop of the market. The overwhelming majority of investors didn't consider value to be a determining factor for investing (which is a fallacy that continues today), just the fact that the market had been rocked and was still a little jittery. Even after the stock

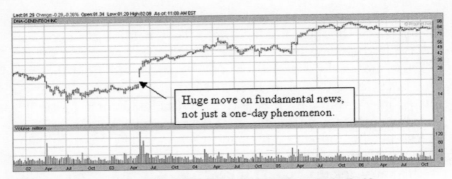

Huge move on fundamental news, not just a one-day phenomenon.

FIGURE 11.6 Genentech Stock Gaps Open and Has Huge Room to the Upside

Chart courtesy of Prophet Financial Systems (www.prophet.net).

gapped open much higher in April 2003 and climbed above $21 (heretofore a major resistance point), there was still a ton of upside potential.

The company has had monumental milestones throughout the years, although there have been periods of drought. The bigger developments were:

1997: Rituxan

2004: Avastin

2006: Lucentis

There are varying degrees of risk in every single stock that trades in the market (see Table 11.3). At the end of the day it is the general consensus of risk that determines the direction of the price of the stock. After all, sellers must believe that a stock is moving lower or that the risk of that happening is greater than that the stock will not move lower. Buyers should be making similar assessments, rather than simply being buyers of weakness or looking for a bounce.

Execution Risk (Company-Specific)

Unlike baseball, where a manager or pitching coach has the ability to pull a pitcher out of the game after he's faced just a single batter, investors have to watch poor management flub it over and over

TABLE 11.3   Different Industry Sectors Have Different Inherent Risks

Industry	Risks
Biotechnology	Low/no revenues, FDA approvals, intense competition, thin pipelines, volatile stock movements
Semiconductors	Swift business cycles, deep declines in demand, depreciating pricing power, volatile stock movements
Homebuilders	Interest rate, highly cyclical, historically low valuations
Truckers	Gas prices, general economic trends, availability of drivers (able to take advantage of business opportunities)
Rails	Limited capacity, general economic trends, global economic trends (export demands)
Automotive	Embedded labor cost, raw material costs, regulatory issues, economy (demand)
Retailers	Intense competition (fickle buying public), consumer confidence, economic trends (employment), credit trends
Drug companies	Expensive development of blockbuster drugs, keeping the pipeline filled with promise, generic competition, public opinion and scrutiny (lawsuits)
Entertainment (video games)	Competition, need for blockbuster game to generate broader enthusiasm
Media	Change in advertisers' preferences, changes in technology, difficulties in maintaining share (read: it's hard to come up with hit after hit)

again. The inability to execute isn't an anomaly. Companies that miss the market once will probably miss it again.

I'm not talking about a quarter where the company missed the consensus estimate by a penny but spent a lot of money of capital expenditures, research and development, and maybe took market share. It's the company that has missed the earnings estimates in the past by a wide margin, or a company that has a history of delaying projects, issuing product recalls, and losing market share, that is going to be considered extra vulnerable.

I don't think these kinds of stocks are worth holding during earnings season. In fact, the best time to own them is after a major sell-off, where the stock could rebound 30 percent or more and still be in a downtrend. Of course the best bet is to not be long such companies to begin with. Sure, there are mitigating factors, as I've pointed out numerous times in this book, but once a company misses the consensus earnings report, it has to be considered higher than normal risk until it has gone six quarters without missing again. That means you should only consider the stock as a trading vehicle at best.

Hot Stock Hits a Roadblock

One of my favorite companies is Whole Foods Market (stock symbol WFMI). I love the store. My wife loves it even more, and she is willing to drive out of the way and spend more money to bask in the ambiance of the pioneering organic supermarket. The company's stock has reflected its success, which went many years without any pure competition or competition from traditional grocers.

As the company began to expand its national presence, it caught the eye of Wall Street and share price went on automatic pilot. The share price simply matched the underlying fundamentals.

- In 2002 the company generated $2.27 billion in total revenue.

- In 2002 the company earned $0.60 a diluted share.

- In 2005 the company generated $4.7 billion in total revenue.

- In 2005 the company earned $0.99 a diluted share.

Each year *Fortune* ranks the best companies to work for in America. Whole Foods Market has made a solid showing in the list in each of the last 10 years, progressively coming in higher and higher:

- Ranking in 2004: 47

- Ranking in 2005: 30

- Ranking in 2006: 15

The company's stores are getting bigger and bigger, with new stores now averaging near 60,000 square feet. The company isn't an unknown to investors, even those who don't live near or have never set foot in one of the stores. The stock rallied to $72 from $7 in less than six years (what a way to begin the new millennium) and then began to struggle. (See Figure 11.7.)

When a company enjoys the kind of success that Whole Foods has over the years, it's easy to assume it'll hit a bump in the road. It is a mistake, however, to make adjustments in your portfolio until those bumps in the road actually appear. Just as a company that has poorly executed is highly likely to make such gaffes again, so too will good management deliver again and again, even if they hit the occasional speed bump.

The first time a company that could do no wrong finally falls short of expectations, the typical refrain from management is that they are happy with the results, the progress, and the bright future. It's the Street that isn't happy. Of course by the time this scenario plays out, it means the Street estimate had been too low for so long while the stock was moving higher that analysts began to expect too much.

That's the way the game is played. When a stock has rallied 1,000 percent in six years, the hurdles go from Olympian to

FIGURE 11.7 Emergence of New Star Stock
Chart courtesy of Prophet Financial Systems (www.prophet.net).

(Continued)

Hot Stock Hits a Roadblock *(Continued)*

Herculean. After all, the higher the stock has gone up, the larger the myth becomes. Whole Foods Market is a myth but it has also become a target. The company is now in the crosshairs of one of the most dangerous competitors ever known in the business world: Wal-Mart.

There are three companies that can get investors to jump off the bandwagon of would-be rivals simply by announcing they are entering the business:

■ Wal-Mart

■ Google

■ Microsoft

In the supermarket world there are already just a handful of players that dominate the landscape, and then there is Wal-Mart. It still remains to be seen whether Wal-Mart will be able to attract organic food buyers who have bought in to the lifestyle hook, line, and sinker. With an ever-changing competitive backdrop, the fix was in for the organic pioneer to face its first real challenge in years.

In the quarter that ended September 25, 2005, Whole Foods shares earned $0.25; the Street was looking for $0.27. The shares were already under pressure going into the earnings release on November 9. The stock, which closed the previous session at $72, spiked lower to $66 once the news was received. But this is a company that has a lot of investor goodwill, and there was no way the shares would languish or fall apart.

Instead the stock began to rebound almost immediately, even climbing to a new high just weeks later. (See Figure 11.8.) *But investors had a new set of risk to deal with!* The company made a miscue, and now shareholders who were up a ton or new shareholders considering making a new purchase had to take different action into the next earnings release.

On February 8, 2006, the company's financials for the quarter that ended on January 15 were released. The stock, not un-

FIGURE 11.8   A Star Falls

Chart courtesy of Prophet Financial Systems (www.prophet.net).

like the period leading up to the preceding earnings releases, experienced some selling pressure. Certainly the selling came from smart investors adjusting for the new realities of the company. Investors were making adjustments for greater risk of an earnings miscue.

The company earned $0.40 for the quarter, a great number when one figures the preceding quarter saw earnings of $0.25, but the Street was looking for $0.41. The stock, which had closed at $70 the day before, plunged to $63 as investors digested the news. The sellers were obviously those folks who hadn't adjusted their holdings for extra risk and had to do so now.

Those investors who sold at higher levels and still had a small position were in a position to see if the stock could snap back again, despite a dent in that armor of goodwill. The stock moved lower but was able to rebound back to $72, but it was downhill thereafter.

In fact, after missing the consensus earnings estimate two times in a row, the stock became as vulnerable as it's ever been. At this stage, due to the higher risk profile, investors should have had a smaller position in the stock than they would have had six months earlier. The stock spiraled lower into the next earnings report and was hovering around $57 a

(Continued)

Hot Stock Hits a Roadblock *(Continued)*

share by the time the earnings for the June quarter were released.

On August 1 the financials were released and the company posted diluted earnings per share of $0.35; the Street was looking for $0.34. The stock gets hammered! Why? Management, perhaps untested at dealing with the additional scrutiny and higher expectations, flubbed the earnings guidance, spooking an already shaky shareholder base. The stock was slammed to $48, a full $30, or 38 percent, from where the shares were changing hands when the year began.

Valuation Risk

How do you know when a stock is overvalued or undervalued? There is a tendency for investors to not want to buy stocks with high PE ratios. I believe this notion comes from a lot of television and those rigid financial publications that preach value. I recommend low PE stocks all the time, but there is nothing wrong with buying stocks with high PE ratios. On the contrary, try this experiment. Every day for one week take a look at the top 10 percentage gainers for the NYSE and NASDAQ Composite, and at the end of the week I bet you'll have 50 stocks or more with PE ratios over 25, a number commonly considered high by the experts.

The point is that valuation, like beauty, goes beyond surface valuation multiples such as price to earnings, price to sales, and price to book ratios. Sure, if all things were equal, I'd take the stock with the lower PE than the higher PE, but how often are all things equal? The most important thing to consider is that valuation risk is actually more prevalent in stocks with low valuation multiples than with high valuations. Moreover, while there is a sense among investors that the more expensive the share price the more vulnerable the stock is, the exact opposite is actually true.

The cheaper the share price, the more overvalued the stock. Yes, a $1 stock is an exponentially more expensive proposition than a

$100 stock. I've always said that cheap stocks are cheap for a reason and most stocks under $5 a share are overvalued. This really must be tattooed on the trigger finger of many investors. The value of a stock is not dictated by its share price!

Boxing Yourself into an Emotional Corner

Telling you to shed your emotions is unrealistic. Yet you must come to grips with how your emotions can get out of control. Labeling is a big mistake, too, whether you're labeling yourself or the stock market. Emotions get the better of investors—it's a fact of human life, and we are all human. However, when investors are uninformed and have unrealistic expectations, those emotions are magnified and the mistakes have deeper financial consequences. Let me outline some of the more common emotional mistakes that I want you to avoid.

Calling yourself bullish or bearish is a huge mistake and results in missed chances to make a lot of money, as this puts you into a frame of mind that will automatically dismiss opportunities.

"I'm Bearish"

If you are bearish, then screaming buying opportunities will not be recognized, even when they're right in front of you. Instead of acknowledging that companies are producing better earnings and that management is offering better guidance, you see numbers that were jerry-rigged in some form or fashion. Instead of hearing that guidance is better, you hear bravado that can't be achieved. Even more sadly, you actually begin to root against the stock market, and every move it makes higher only incenses your disdain. I know many dyed-in-the-wool bears, and they always miss the rallies because they're waiting for the other shoe to drop.

No matter how low the market or particular stock declines, bears are still looking for more downside. Talk about kicking someone when they're down, bears have targets for the major indexes and stocks that wouldn't be justified in a $1 trillion economy, let alone a $13 trillion economy. I've seen bears who are never happy about being right; they think every stock they don't like should fall to $1 a share.

"I'm a Raging Bull"

There isn't much confidence in the stock market these days, especially the U.S. stock market, for a variety of reasons including the super economic growth in other nations and a feeling that the decline in America's popularity around the world is going to harm it economically. (I don't subscribe to talk that America is so unpopular or will suffer economically.)

There are times when investors become too myopic about a certain stock. They're so busy being cheerleaders that they never see the stuff that's going on with the other side. Just as bears begin to root for good stuff and rationalize certain events in order to dismiss them as one-offs, dyed-in-the-wool bulls never see the glass as half empty.

Let the pundits be the bulls and bears, and you just focus on making money, reading the true messages of the markets, and block out all the other stuff.

When in Doubt

I've been accused of being too bullish, and there are times when I switch gears later than I should. However, there are numerous reasons for optimism with respect to the stock market.

Whenever you're not sure where the market will ultimately go, pull up a 50-year chart (see Figure 11.9). There are dips and disasters but at the end of the day the market goes higher.

I also feel the market will move higher in the end because of my faith in God. I know this sounds corny to some, but to me the stock

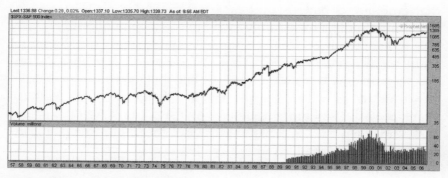

FIGURE 11.9   A 50-Year S&P Chart
Chart courtesy of Prophet Financial Systems (www.prophet.net).

market represents all the businesses and all the workers out there giving it their all every day. I think these people will be rewarded, and as such so, too, will the value of the company benefit. This doesn't mean that stocks can't get too far ahead and be overvalued. The fact of the matter is that because of emotions, the stock market often gets too far ahead or too far behind where it should be valued.

Swearing off the market is a drastic emotional state that harks back to the times we would take our basketball and leave the park because neither side picked us. The stock market doesn't owe you anything. The stock market isn't out to get you. Sure, there are people on the other side of the trade, and perhaps in the past they simply outthought you, but it happens to all of us. Swearing off the stock market is irrational.

You may be avoiding stocks because you lost money on them in the past. It might be smart to be more cautious with a stock because you lost money on it before, but that's because there was a flaw in the company, either management, product, or industry factors that could be repeated. On the other side of this same emotional coin, there is a time to throw in the towel. I know investors now who talk about buying stocks that were high flyers in the 1990s because they made money with them before.

I know I said that people are rewarded and therefore stocks benefit as well, but it also takes success if a stock is to increase in value. It takes a business model that makes sense.

Summary

At the end of the day, what really separates those investors who consistently make money in the stock market from investors who can't get out of the starters' gate? It boils down to a few things, including managing risk, via asset allocation but also via your own internal turmoil to stay even-keeled and open-minded. You won't be afraid of losing money, which is the first step to actually making money in the stock market.

Emotional mistakes are killers and hard to recover from, so keep the following in mind to minimize such mistakes:

- Understand and take into account the various types of risk: company-specific, industry-specific, and valuation.

- Understand that even great companies hit roadblocks, have growing pains, and need to regroup.

- Know when the bloom is off the rose and the hype is no longer enough to get a stock to go. Often when a company begins to live up to the hype, its shares pull back because that success was already built in to the share price, and the next challenge of sustaining sales and profits begins with a new set of skepticism. That puts pressure on the stock.

- Don't label yourself. Be an opportunist and let the pundits be bulls or bears.

- Don't hate stocks so much you miss chances to make money, and don't love stocks so much you go down with the ship. Ironically there is another emotional trap along these lines—people who are bearish when the market is down and bullish when the market is up, thereby never buying stocks when they're cheap and always buying stocks after they've already made a big move.

In the end, crossing the street involves a certain degree of risk. We do it because we want to get to the other side. We assess traffic and walk across even when we see a car on the horizon, and we know we'll make it across fine. Look at the stock market the same way. Sometimes stocks bend to oncoming traffic, but when you are in the right lane you'll make it to your destination.

The Care and Feeding of Your Portfolio

I t's now time to set up your portfolio. You need to be positioned in several niches of the stock market rather than buying one stock at a time to see how it works out before buying another stock. Trying to win big with one stock and an unrealistic holding period is the number one destroyer of wealth in the stock market.

Instead, you're going to approach investing with a level head and a complete game plan. I like to see investors begin with stocks of companies they are familiar with. It doesn't have to be the hottest thing around. You may want to go with companies that you feel are stable and that you have been able to ascertain through your own fundamental research are still undervalued.

So where do you begin?

Finding Ideas

The problem with just buying stuff you know or like is that you could be late to the party, or maybe you're the only person who likes that stuff. I remember the first time I went into a Costco with my wife in 2001. I felt like Spanish explorer Ferdinand Magellan; I knew other people had been there before me, and the store was packed when we got there, but I felt like I had discovered the place. Instantly it became a favorite stock of mine and one I toss out when folks stop me on the street for a hot tip.

Of course I was late to the party, but Costco continued to be a winner. There are millions of people who haven't yet had their Magellan moment, although as the company's successes get greater, so too will expectations. The stock is stable but could deliver solid gains for many years to come.

You could go out and buy stable stocks at any given time and hold them through cycles, the inevitable ups and downs, a natural part of life and business. So I want you to begin with a list of names of companies where you have a certain comfort level.

Compiling Your List by Looking at the World around You

It's easy to get this list started. My son began attending a new school when he entered fourth grade, and the route from the house was different and longer than the year before. On the second day of school, while driving home after dropping off my son, I noticed a solid portfolio blossoming before my eyes (on the first day I, like all parents, had been beaming with too much pride and joy to be cognizant of my surroundings). I got on Route 17 in New Jersey and I came upon the following sights:

- Stryker (stock symbol SYK). One of the nation's leading medical device products, a well-positioned innovator of replacement body parts like knees and hips, this is an industry that is guaranteed to enjoy great growth as baby boomers get older but abandon the notion of slowing down to rocking chairs. This generation of old folks will be more active than any before; consequently there will be a lot of broken bones and worn-out knees, hips, elbows, and other joints.

- Federal Express (stock symbol FDX). Federal Express has an office along this highway and thousands of other highways, too. But this is more than a domestic play: The company has planted seeds around the world, including a great stronghold in China. Federal Express is a great proxy for global commerce. The company also benefits from Internet commerce, which continues to enjoy incredible growth. Moreover, the company doesn't have a lot of competition, just UPS, DHL, and the U.S. Post Office.

- CSX Corp (stock symbol CSX). I saw a truck with "CSX Corp" on the side, going by on an overpass, which was interesting since CSX is the largest railroad on the eastern coast of the United States. I happen to be a fan of the rails. I think they make the perfect proxy for the American economy. With that said, you have to understand that the stock is cyclical and performs better when the economy is strong and solid. When the economy slips the stock typically stumbles. There are business factors, however, that favor this company no matter what the business cycle:

  - The roads are crowded—there simply isn't enough room on the highways for truckers to meet demand, and even if there were, there aren't enough people willing to drive trucks. These capacity and personnel problems will fuel the growth of rails.

  - As the rest of the world becomes richer, there is greater demand for U.S. goods, and those goods have to be carried to the shippers. The biggest example of this is the surge in demand for U.S. coal from China and other nations, a trend that will only increase over the years.

Then there was the usual array of restaurants that have become ubiquitous in the American landscape. (I love capitalism, but it is sort of sad that every stretch of road looks just like every other. Individuality is very important.) Of the restaurants McDonald's (stock symbol MCD) looms the largest, and not just because of the giant arches logo that towers above its locations. The stock peaked in 2000 at $44 and tumbled all the way to $12 by early 2003. Since then the stock has come back as the menu has changed to healthier fare and helped to shed the negative image of the company.

There were many other publicly traded companies in plain sight doing business and thriving. So part of getting started is to look at your immediate world. I would caution, however, that you don't get too enamored in loading up on stocks in industries that you know very well. Sure, if you know the best company in your industry and you look at the fundamentals and determine there is still value, then by all means buy some shares. The key word here is *fundamentals*; you can't let your feelings for the company and/or its products supersede the facts. If a stock is overvalued or if management isn't up to the task, Wall Street isn't going to have the emotional attachment that you have.

You don't want to become one of these people saying the rest of the world is wrong while you're losing your shirt. I see and hear this all the time. It is the most ridiculous rationale this side of "Sure your stocks are up, the market is up," from people who were afraid of their own shadow when stocks were cheap and then want to diminish the success of those who were buyers on weakness.

Choosing Companies through Screens and Screening

Another way to gather ideas for your portfolio is through scanning your screens, doing searches for stocks that look compelling (by price movement and volume shifts), and then digging further (fundamental research). When your monitor is set up the way I outlined in Chapter 10, it will tell different stories every day. Remember to use a top-down approach when doing your initial legwork. Understand what's moving the broad market and what the implications of those drivers would be on your holdings.

Make sure not to get too caught up in the rationale of the day. In other words, the stock market reacts to emotions on a day-to-day basis, so while it is true that consistent earnings growth triggered by top-line revenue growth and margin expansion will have the final say on share price, there are times when the broad market and individual stocks are reacting solely on emotions.

I really cringe when I'm battling someone on TV about the market and they say it's only about earnings. That is just plain old oversimplification. If emotions don't impact the stock market, then explain the NASDAQ trading above 5,000. It wasn't earnings or even realistic hopes of earnings; it was emotions and dreams of riches that created buckets and buckets of cash that had to find a home. The fact is there was too much money chasing too few ideas, but it happens every day. The shorter the time frame, the greater the impact of emotions. Companies will report earnings results and immediately a stock will roar higher or sink like a stone, only to settle down and move in an opposite direction days and weeks later.

So you will monitor the market for anomalies and clues. I check thousands of stocks each day, watching for the odd action of an individual stock or an industry group.

Using the Media to Your Advantage

When the pile-on effect has driven a stock too low, or excessive hype experts in the media have driven a stock too high, make sure you position or reposition yourself to take advantage.

Then there is the media—newspapers, magazines, television programs, and the Internet; surely you will find ideas there every day. Let's face it; you want and need to listen to other voices when you're investing in the stock market, but you also have to dig deeper. Remember the life cycle of an investment: Getting in is the easiest part; managing the bumps and exiting are infinitely harder. If you are going to use these cheap and free sources for ideas, then try to separate entrenched bias from facts and real observations.

Television regulars, newspaper and magazine columnists, and bloggers all have their own bias that often taints their opinions. I'm usually bullish, I'm usually an optimist, and I find the silver lining. But I also find the red flags through my fundamental checklist or by checking the options activity, insider activity, recent news, listening to conference calls, watching for macroeconomic trends, and so on.

The main thing I like to look for is when a staunch bull becomes a bear, or vice versa. When a bull becomes a bear, I see it as a form of capitulation. Typically when this happens the market is already going to be down a bunch and it will look extremely vulnerable, too. It's one thing when the crowd tosses in the towel, but when someone who watches the market professionally on a day-to-day basis calls it a day (after it's already come down hard), then you should begin to tighten your list of buy (long) candidates down as it will soon be time to buy.

When a bear tosses in the towel, which is even rarer than a bull turning sour, be prepared to take profits very soon thereafter. Just like the case with the tried-and-true bull losing an appetite for stocks, a bear will swallow his or her pride and capitulate only after a huge move to the upside has been made. I must say there are a lot of bears who just seem negative all the time. These curmudgeons wake up on the wrong side of the bed every day. It is not often that a bear will turn positive on the market; when they do I get real nervous.

Okay, you have a bunch of ideas—in fact, your list is very long and there is as much confusion now as there was at the beginning of the process. Now you are going to go through the following steps:

1. Check the fundamentals. Look for top-line growth, making sure it's organic; look for expanding margins; look for strong or improving cash flow. Then check on the same from at least three rival companies.

2. Once you have filled out this relative comparison sheet, you compare valuation metrics. You are checking for a range valuation—historic, current, and projected—to see where your idea should fit among its peers.

During this process you may find that you were on the right track with the idea you initially found intriguing but then discover there is an even better play in the group. (I often rank my favorites from top to bottom when I set up my screen.) When you are whittling your list down, make sure not to fall victim to the share prices. It is possible that the best stock in the group is the stock that has already moved up a bunch. So what if the stock is substantially higher over a given period of time? If the fundamentals say it's still undervalued, then consider buying that stock.

I've made the mistake, most recently in late 2005 and early 2006, of not buying the best name in a group because I didn't want to chase the stock. I mentioned Tweeter to our clients even though I liked Game Stop a lot more as an investment but I felt the latter's shares had gotten away from me. It was a huge mistake.

Once your list has been sharpened to the few best names in six or seven different industries, it's time to take a look at the charts.

Combining Fundamentals with Technical Evaluation

One of my favorite retail stocks is American Eagle (stock symbol AEOS). I've recommended it to my clients on numerous occasions over the last four years and I've also mentioned it on television. The company began to experience growing pains in calendar year 2005. During that year the top line grew slower than the previous year and the gross margin actually declined year over year. As a result the stock, which began the year at $24 and rocketed to $33, finished the year slightly lower. In the teen retail business it would have been easy to write off the company as a flash in the pan, but just as companies with a history of poor executing are prone to disappoint in the future, so too are companies with track records of great execution likely to get their act together after stumbling.

The Fundamental View

Take a look at Table 12.1. Although the gross margin was lower in fiscal year 2005, the American Eagle's operating margin from continuing operations edged higher to 12.7 percent from 11.9 percent. However, there were too many red flags to keep the momentum that the stock began with at the start of 2005. More alarming than the declining gross margin is that the comparable store sales decreased to 15.5 percent from 21.4 percent.

In March 2006 the company posted net earnings of $197.5 million, and the earnings came in ahead of the consensus estimate by $0.02 for the quarter (fourth quarter, fiscal year 2005) that ended on January 30, 2006. In addition to the solid results for the previous three months, the same-store sales figures for the most current month were released and came in above the consensus, too. Furthermore management made positive comments about the month of February that suggested the then-current quarter would be better than expected.

The fundamental picture looked better and the rationale to own the stock based on absolute performance and potential was in place. Moreover, the chart suggested the stock was a screaming buy, as well.

TABLE 12.1   American Eagle: Looking Beneath the Top Line for the True Health of the Company

Income Statement	FY 2005	FY 2004
Net sales	$2,309.4	$1,881.2
Comparable store sales	15.5%	21.4%
Gross profit	$1,073.8	$877.8
Gross margin	46.5%	46.7%
Income from continuing operations	$293.7	$224.2
Operating margin	12.7%	11.9%

The Technical View

After fine-tuning the ideas through fundamental research, we then take a look at the charts. We are looking for certain chart patterns that include:

- Breakouts

- Double bottoms

- Cup and handles

American Eagle's stock formed a *double bottom* in December 2005 and began to move higher. In the process it reached a key resistance point at $37 in January 2006. The move from the bottom where the stock had seen some sideways action and began to inch higher is called a *cup* formation. The subsequent pullback created a *handle* (usually a 3 to 6 percent pullback). Then the stock was able to break out with a *breakaway* gap (when a stock opens higher than the previous session close and also happens to open above a key resistance point). (See Figure 12.1.)

The American Eagle stock chart was perfect: It gave investors the three best buy signals possible in just three months. Not every chart is going to be a textbook example like this, but you should be on the prowl for one of these formations as a sign to begin building a position, provided the fundamental story is positive.

Note: Once you have your universe of stocks in place, you may actually want to look at the charts before drilling down into the in-

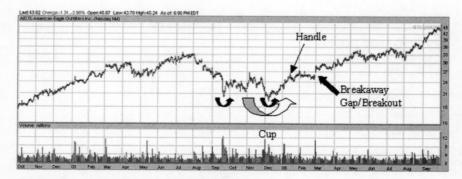

FIGURE 12.1   American Eagle: Multiple Buy Signals
Chart courtesy of Prophet Financial Systems (www.prophet.net).

come statement, balance sheet, and cash flow statement. The temptation will arise to skip the fundamental part of the process, but that would be a major mistake. If you are pressed for time, at the very least look at the income statement, see how the company is doing year over year, check for the direction of margins, and make sure the business doesn't have too much debt.

This will only take several minutes. If you can squeeze in a little more time, check the news stories on the day the company last posted its earnings results for extra tidbits, look at the short position, and glance at the insider activity.

Insider Activity

Insiders have been selling their stock for years and it never raised an eyebrow until the 1990s, when corporate insiders who never generated any profits for shareholders made outrageous fortunes. Making matters worse were the countless insiders whose share prices were higher based on accounting scams; these people were big-time sellers, making billions of dollars. Awarded as an incentive and reward for doing a great job, the corporate stock option was the centerpiece of the wave of corporate malfeasance in the 1990s.

Just like the golden ring in J.R.R. Tolkien's *Lord of the Rings*, the corporate stock option in the 1990s changed the minds and souls of people. I think it was part of a greater problem for a nation that had lost its moral compass in a sea of decadence not seen since the Roaring 1920s. Is it any coincidence both ended in disaster? The stock market crashed, a recession ensued, and enemies of America felt more emboldened.

In an article by Russell Coff and Peggy Lee in the *Strategic Management Journal*, in-depth research, published online September 2002, found that insider trading at research and development companies offered the most accurate prediction of future stock movement. Essentially, according to the report, insider selling means management knows its R&D efforts haven't amounted to a hill of beans. Conversely, when these insiders are buying, it suggests early R&D success.

This makes a lot of sense, but these days any large insider selling is viewed with suspicion and even contempt no matter what kind of company or industry. But when a company isn't making money and the insiders are getting rich beyond anyone's wildest imagination, you want to avoid the stock. The same research paper mentioned Gary Winnick of Global Crossing fame; he sold $734 million worth of stock in the company before it came completely unglued.

More and more of those outrageous situations are getting a second look, and there could be criminal charges and convictions. For instance, Gregory Reyes, CEO of Brocade Communications Systems from 1998 to 2005, was charged with manipulating paperwork to get the optimum price for his stock options as well as those of fellow executives. The government says a lot of the $500 million Reyes made from selling company stock came from this illegal maneuvering.

Once I was cohosting on CNN's financial news network and interviewing Scott Livengood, then CEO of Krispy Kreme Doughnuts (stock symbol KKD). This was in the winter of 2003, and I kidded about how he had the best name since he had to be living good with one of the hottest stocks in the market. The interview was going great when I zapped him: "If everything is going so well, then why are you selling so much stock?" The man was incensed. He later explained that he worked hard and didn't want all his eggs in one basket even if it was his company.

At the time the stock was the on fire and very popular with individual investors. Yet in a September filing it was revealed that management sold 535,710 shares for a total of $23.2 million between June and September of that year.

Scott Livengood sold 235,500 shares, a reduction of 73 percent of his total holdings. Other insiders sold large portions of their holdings, too: 29, 89, 49, and 17 percent. The insiders had additional shares held in trust that also were big sellers. In all the insiders sold over $100 million in stock in 2003. (See Figure 12.2.)

Interestingly, while the insiders were dumping, the stock was rising, and so too was the interest of large investors. When the September filing was made, institutions owned over 60 percent of the stock and, according to First Call, six brokerage firms had raised their earnings estimates for the company. The short position at the time was more than 21 percent of the shares floated.

I have a tremendous amount of respect for legitimate shorts, folks who aren't trying to drive a company out of business but simply be-

FIGURE 12.2   Krispy Kreme: Plenty of Time to Get Out While Insiders Were Dumping Their Shares
Chart courtesy of Prophet Financial Systems (www.prophet.net).

lieve a stock is overvalued. Yet these folks can often be too early or too myopic. I once asked one of the most famous investors in history what his target was for his short position on Fannie Mae (stock symbol FNM) and he said $5.00. I almost doubled over from laughter, but he was dead serious. At the time, the stock was changing hands at $48 a share, down from $72 just several months earlier.

When there is a short position north of 20 percent of the float but you are still attracted to the stock, make sure you only buy it as a trading idea—don't hold it if it pulls back more than 5 percent of your purchase price. I don't believe in steadfast stop-losses for fundamentally sound holdings, but the shorts are smart folks. Also, the shorts fight hard, and will continue to pass to their short positions even as the stock is taking off. Pat Russo, who owned a brokerage firm on Staten Island, New York, was the first to tell me that "the shorts go out on their shields." He was right.

The flip side of insider selling is insider buying, and I think this action has a greater ability to predict the future than selling does. Of course there are times when insider buying seems more disingenuous than an indication that management believes so much in the company they're willing to put their money where their mouth is. I worry about insider buys that are mentioned in press releases; I think it indicates management is trying too hard. Moreover, I'm not impressed when a multimillionaire buys a few shares. I once listened to a conference call (I forget the company) where the CEO, when asked if he would be buying more stock in the open market, remarked, "No, I bought and the share still went down. Why should I keep buying when I'm awarded shares for my work?"

That was candid stuff, but probably how the overwhelming majority of corporate insiders feel. That's why I like to see insider buys in small- to mid-cap companies where management isn't drumming up publicity. When Steve Case bought $1 million worth of AOL stock in February 2002, the stock was at a two-year low, having plummeted to $24 from a high of $87. Investors didn't take the bait as the stock continued to slide and hit $9 just a few months later.

Case Study

ICO, Inc. (stock symbol ICOC) is a global producer of custom polymer powders and plastic film concentrates, based Houston, Texas. In 2005 the company benefited from a rise in resin prices (a direct result of higher crude oil prices) and also strong foreign currencies. In the fiscal fourth quarter of 2005 that ended on September 30, the company saw its revenues increase by 4.9 percent year over year and its operating margin climb to 3.64 percent from 2.86 percent. The actual results were announced on December 7.

In December 2005 the company's insiders became aggressive buyers of the stock. From then through June 2006 the insiders purchased more than 156,000 shares of common stock at prices ranging from $3.10 to $4.95; the CEO bought more than 89,000 shares. The stock more than doubled from the time of the first purchases. (See Figure 12.3.)

FIGURE 12.3   ICO, Inc.: Insiders Were Buying like a Pack of Piranhas
Chart courtesy of Prophet Financial Systems (www.prophet.net).

Building Your Portfolio

You've narrowed your list and now it's time to build your portfolio. Once again you have to consider the big picture, or macro conditions.

Where is the economy going to be in the next six months to six years? This is important, as you must balance your portfolio, not necessarily to try to take advantage of each twist and turn in the economy but so that you are in a position to always have some niche of your portfolio working. Timing is important, as are anticipation of economic conditions and the direction of interest rates. Moreover, you need to know where energy prices are heading.

I'm not asking that you be an economist or some sort of pundit. Just pay attention to trends.

Business Cycle

Life is cyclical, and so too are the fortunes of business. With some businesses, the sweet spot of the year is well known; many retailers make their profits for the entire year in the time period from the day after Thanksgiving to New Year's Eve. The broader economy also moves in cycles where there is nonstop growth that is followed by a period of slower growth and adjustment to that slower growth. (See Table 12.2.)

One thing to remember is that the stock market is a harbinger of things to come; it actually knows and reflects many things that will come to fruition later (not just economic, but political, too). With that in mind you can't be reactionary with your stocks. If you wait for the official news, more often than not it will reflect what the market and individual stocks have already been telling you.

In 2002 the Morgan Stanley Cyclical Index (stock symbol CYC), peaked in May and proceeded to decline hard and fast (Figure 12.4). The third quarter saw the gross domestic product (GDP) come in at 2.4 percent, which was okay and actually gave the index a bounce when it was announced in October, but the market knew the economy was sliding before it became official—the fourth-quarter GDP growth was only 0.2 percent. When the CYC Index began to take off after declining to a low in March 2003, it

TABLE 12.2 Influence of Business Cycle

Cyclical	Noncyclical
These are companies with businesses that do better when the economy is healthy and gain strength as they sell stuff people don't necessarily need but truly covet. These companies are sensitive to the economy.	These are companies that sell stuff people need or are unlikely to go without. These companies are called defensive because not only do their share prices hold up during economic hardship, they often increase in value.
Examples of cyclical industries include: Durable goods like heavy equipment Air travel/leisure Raw material makers like steel, textiles, and chemicals Semiconductors Homebuilders	Examples of noncyclical industries include: Utilities Household nondurables (e.g., toothpaste) Tobacco Health care Pharmaceuticals
These stocks have wider share price gyrations, therefore greater risk/reward ratios. When they take off, the sky is the limit; when they falter, look out below.	These stocks have narrow share price movements but in many cases also pay solid dividends. The upside is limited but so, too, is the downside.

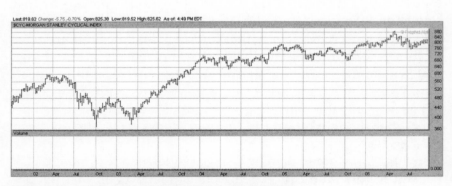

FIGURE 12.4   Morgan Stanley Cyclical Index, 2002 to 2006
Chart courtesy of Prophet Financial Systems (www.prophet.net).

shouldn't have been a surprise that the third quarter experienced 3.5 percent GDP growth and the fourth quarter was 7.5 percent.

Gross domestic product is the value of the economic output of a nation during a given period of time. The GDP tallies the prices of all final goods and services. Typically the measure is for a one-year period. (See Table 12.3.)

Fielding a Winning Team

Your portfolio is a team working for your financial prosperity. You've found a lot of great names, you have a good feeling about the broad economy, and you've looked at the possibilities based on the charts. Now that you've assessed the economic backdrop, let's put together the portfolio. Remember, we are not trying to load up on hot stocks. Think of your portfolio like the lineup of a baseball team. Have you ever wondered why no team has just fielded a team of home run hitters? Several reasons:

- They tend to strike out a lot.
- They're usually big guys who don't run the bases as well as other (smaller) players.
- They're expensive.
- They may be liabilities in the infield.

With $200,000 or less, I believe your portfolio should be broken into 10 boxes. These brackets will be populated based on the direction of the economy with an emphasis on generating income, but mostly seeking to be positioned in the hot stocks before they become the hot stocks.

TABLE 12.3   Quarterly Changes in U.S. Gross Domestic Product

2002		2003				2004				2005				2006
3Q	4Q	1Q	2Q	3Q	4Q	1Q	2Q	3Q	4Q	1Q	2Q	3Q	4Q	1Q
2.4	0.2	1.2	3.5	7.5	2.7	3.9	4.0	3.1	2.6	3.4	3.3	4.2	1.8	5.6

Creating a Balanced Portfolio

When doing media spots, I'm often asked about what stocks or sectors I like at that very moment. I think that question feeds into one of the worst habits of investors with respect to establishing a portfolio. The key to building a balanced portfolio is to be positioned in stocks *before* they become hot.

Think of a clock: Each number is an industry, and the second hand, minute hand, and hour hand represent times those industries are going to be hot. What too many investors are doing is following the second hand in hopes of instant gratification.

This method of chasing what is hot for the moment results in a portfolio loaded with stocks that have pulled back; it reduces future buying power and creates emotional baggage. You want to be positioned and let the hour hand come to you; don't chase the second hand. To do this you have to understand conditions of the economy, the stock market, the industry, and then the stock.

The Core Portfolio

The *economy is solid and turning higher* and you want to be ready. You need to establish your core portfolio. I've outlined a hypothetical portfolio in Table 12.4. Your portfolio doesn't have to look exactly like this; you're going to be looking for ideas all the time, but stick to the spirit of this format. The most important thing is to have equal dollar amounts allocated to each idea so one loss doesn't wipe out several winners.

Table 12.4 is ideal for someone with $200,000 or less to invest in the stock market. If you have more than $200,000, then you could expand the boxes to 15, but trading ideas should never exceed more than three, and there should be one more box allocated for cash as well.

TABLE 12.4   Your Core Portfolio

Core Portfolio							Trading Ideas		Cash
Semi Chips	Tech	Casinos/ Gambling	Metals	Retailers (Teen)	Rails/ Trucker	Oil Driller	Hot Stock	Hot Stock	Cash

My basic portfolio includes a cross section of the economy that should produce a couple of winners at any given time. Maybe higher oil will hurt retailers (although teenagers always seem to have money to spend and do so without regard to prices; in fact, they are *more* label conscious than their parents). I wouldn't always have metals in the portfolio, but in recent years the boom in the global economy has made this a great place to be. Moreover, owning metals can neatly offset the slowing growth in other companies in your portfolio, which see slower or even lower earnings because of higher commodity prices.

The most important thing is to make sure there is balance, that no more than three stocks in your portfolio react to the same news drivers. You don't want Intel to say it is spending less on capital expenditures and all the stocks you own dive into the red column. Even your hot stock positions should be in different industries.

Some other things I take into consideration:

- I prefer semiconductor companies that aren't overly dependent on personal computers. By the same token, make sure the company isn't overly dependent on one hot product, like powering the iPod. Chip stocks with the best growth usually get the highest valuations.

- Technology stocks are great when they have momentum; make sure you have exposure to this niche when the economy is doing well.

- Casino stocks have become extremely volatile but for the most part the bias remains to the upside. These stocks get ahead of themselves, so if your work is mixed don't feel bad about taking profits. To a lesser extent the hotel stocks share most of the same economic drivers.

- Metals could be either precious metals or base metals used in the building of residential and commercial real estate.

- I like teen retailers but they are fickle; luxury retailers are also a good bet in this environment. Also consider food retailers: When households gain more disposable income, they are more likely to have dinner away from home.

- I like oil drillers and service companies because you have to get the stuff before you can sell it. Refinery companies are a good investment when gasoline inventories begin to dwindle.

- Hot stocks are momentum plays, stocks that have broken out on huge volume. You must be very nimble with these ideas and prepared to take profits within a short period of time (30 days or less). For the most part these stocks will have huge followings, so they'll be liquid, but they are a game of musical chairs; never fret if you take profits in these too early.

- Once you have all the boxes filled, be on the lookout to make adjustments, and always have cash on hand.

What if the *economy is peaking and probably going to slide*? Under these conditions you want your portfolio to be more defensive. But don't dump good cyclical names where management is delivering when the economy slows—do so only when the economy appears to be on the verge of tumbling hard. (See Table 12.5.)

There are going to be times when you'll be tempted to get out and stay out of the stock market. The biggest problem with this notion is the assumption that you're going to pick the exact bottom and get back in. The reality is, once you're out of the market, you'll not pay attention and not really know when there are screaming values. Mostly you will miss out on other ways to make money in the stock market.

When the market gets sloppy and begins to slip, you have to consider having at least one short idea, based on knowing a stock is extremely overvalued. I'm still puzzled as to why so many people will not go short—that is, bet on a stock moving lower in value. Even the most miserable folks I know, those who always hate the stock market, don't ever go short. The idea when the market is slowing is to be in stocks that have strong core businesses that won't be negatively impacted in a slower economy.

TABLE 12.5   Defensive Portfolio

Core Portfolio							Trading Ideas		Cash
Drug Company	Cons. Staple	Beverage Stock	Growth Stock	Growth Stock	Retailers (Discount)	Short	Hot Stock	Cash	Cash

Things to consider in developing a defensive portfolio:

- Drug companies have been difficult investments in recent years as a combination of losing patent protection on blockbusters and legal actions have cast a dark shadow over the industry. At one time, drug companies dominated lists of most admired businesses; now they are seen as confused and mostly scorned by the general public. Try to go with the company with the best pipeline and the largest financial commitment to discovering new drugs (measured by R&D as a percentage of sales).

- Consumer staples are the things we use all the time, like toothpaste and toilet paper.

- With beverages you can knock down two birds with one stone, as you get the defensive protection to counteract the domestic economy but you get exposure to the global economy, too. In recent years I have favored Pepsi over Coke.

- Consumers still spend money when the economy slows but they spend it much more selectively. I like discounters under these conditions. Experts will push Wal-Mart or Kohl's but I like the deep discounters like Rent-A-Center or Fred's.

- You must go short when the market is under pressure. It is amazing that the market can be down as much as 70 percent of the time in any given year (even in up years) and investors refuse to go short or are intimidated by the process. There are times when the market is sinking enough to justify more than one short position.

- Hot stocks can buck the overall market trend and stay hot in down markets. Once again, the key is to be nimble. If you aren't in a position to check on such positions at least once during the session, then it would be smart to avoid them all together. This box is also for topical plays like bird flu or hurricanes, timely events that generate a lot of short-term buzz.

- Of course you want to have cash ready to take advantage of the market sell-off.

My goal is to get you not to trade too much and not to fall prey to the directional shifts of the stock market. The economy is cyclical, as is the stock market. You're going to have to ride out a few of these bumps to maximize your gains. I mention growth in two of the boxes in Table 12.5. These represent your best cyclical holdings, companies that are growing the top line by 20 percent or more year over year, are expanding their margins, carry little to no debt, and have the ability to keep it going for the next year or longer.

Allocation of Funds

Make sure you are using the same dollar amount in each allocation box—*no exceptions.* So many portfolios are harmed with poor distribution of funds. The two biggest mistakes:

1. *Buying the same number of shares.* Investors like to do this, although I'm not sure why.

2. *Buying a lot of shares of a cheap stock.* This is their version of the home run swing, plus it feels great to brag at the local pub, "I have 100,000 shares of XYZ."

I don't advocate options, but when the market takes off in a straight line on the upside or falls through a trapdoor on the down side and you are trying to gain leverage, monies set aside for trading ideas could be used for calls or puts. I must say I'm very reluctant to give the nod to any options at all—I believe they're ultimately a sucker's game. But if you pick your spots right, they can generate huge financial windfalls.

Nurturing Your Portfolio

Your portfolio is in place and now it's time to become a caretaker. Keep in mind that even if all your boxes are filled, you are always on the lookout for new ideas and always making sure the positions you own continue to make the grade. Once again you will use charts but mostly you will rely on fundamentals, how well the company is doing. Earnings announcements and other economic updates from the company will be important tools. Watching for shifts in the economy is a must as well. Remember, if there are signs that the economic backdrop that was beneficial for your holdings is changing, then you can take action.

Scaling Out and Scaling into Positions

Exiting is where most people make their stock market mistakes, and for the most part they make the mistake of selling too early and for too little money. I've had ideas that have been the number one percentage gainer of the day and I've looked into our database to see which clients were long. Lo and behold, there are always a number of clients who had been in the stock but had already sold it for a minuscule gain or even a loss.

Keep this in mind: You are going to be in the stock market for the rest of your life, so stop treating it otherwise. The stock market doesn't go up in a straight line and neither have the great stock investments of all time. You don't have to play the market like a scared rabbit. Of course, I say this in the aftermath of the stock market meltdown of 2000, when a lot of novices lost a lot of money. When you think back to the horror stories, ask yourself a few questions:

- Did you or your friends lose a lot of money in a company that was profitable and actually had an operating history older than two years?

- Where is the current share price of the quality stocks that you sold because you lumped them in with the nonquality names in your portfolio at the time?

- Take a look at the five-year stock chart of the top 10 places you spend your paycheck each month. I bet 8 or 9 of them are up nicely—and going to go even higher.

You must think fast, but that doesn't mean you should sell because of a case of the nerves. Instead you want to act smart, too.

It is best to build equity positions over time and not to buy the entire position in one trade. The exception to this is when you're buying high-flying stocks, positions that you think will be short-lived. If you hesitate your cost could be higher than you wanted, and then you will be more reluctant to sell even though the signals and underlying movement suggest exiting is the best course of action.

As the stock increases in value there will be higher hurdles to cross, and that increases the risk of pullbacks. In fact, as the stock moves higher, look out for brokerage downgrades based on valuation. These have an immediate impact on the underlying share price, but I've seen stocks rebound from this situation. Nonetheless this is a shot across the bow and highlights the increased risk going forward.

Once you're up more than 40 percent in a position and you've held the stock for less than a year, you want to play it close to the vest. You don't have to exit automatically, but you don't want to allow a big win to evaporate or even become a loss. I think it is better to exit profitable ideas in two parts when the stock is still moving higher. If there is something alarming, a real fundamental challenge and not just theory or rumor, then exiting the entire position is best.

Keep in mind that there is a psychological aspect to investing in the stock market that can hamper your efforts in the future. Leaving money on the table is infinitely less damaging to the psyche than letting a winner become a loser. By the same token, having the nerve to own a great stock for years and handling the bumps that come with the market is the way to big money. And always remember, you can take profits on a great company's stock and buy it back. Never sell the stock and totally discard it mentally. More than likely you'll be happier that you bought it back (most likely on weakness) than if you simply ignored it because you already made money in it before and the play is over in your mind.

Listening to the Conference Call

The conference call is open to the public, and I think there is no better way to learn about the health of note only the companies you're invested in but also the industries themselves. The analysts asking questions during the call have intimate relationships with the companies and will ask about things you never thought of.

There will be scuttlebutt and questions that really bring the company into focus beyond a numeric story of execution. Most conference calls are archived so you don't have to interrupt your daily schedule; listen to them in the evening after you've assessed the financial documents (this way you can be listening for specific questions that you may have).

- When a company defends missteps, I become worried.

- When a company doesn't provide guidance, I become worried. Even though I believe financials should only be released twice a year and there should only be quarterly updates, I'm leery when a company says it can't provide guidance.

- When management is combative during the call, it's a sign of frustration and a lack of confidence.

- When too many people speak on the call it bothers me, too. I like hearing from the CFO and CTO (when it's a tech company), but I want the CEO front and center taking all the hits. When other members of the executive team are doing too much talking, it is a red flag, especially when others besides the CEO are giving the Street disappointing news and developments.

Additional Tidbits

Challenges you must consider when actively managing your investments include when to add to a potential loser and whether to just buy exchange-traded funds or mutual funds.

Averaging down gets back to the Captain Ahab syndrome, and you want to be very careful. If you think the Street has gotten it wrong and your conviction isn't just a hunch or a prayer, then you can buy a stock you already own at a lower entry point. Here is the rule, however, and you must pay heed to it: Do not add the two entry prices into one entry price. This is very dangerous and will lead to disaster. I hear people say all the time, "My average cost is X." Big mistake.

Let's say you own a stock at $100 a share and it pulls back to $50 a share, and you decide to buy more. Most investors would now say they own the stock at an average cost of $75. Here's the danger to consider. Let's say this stock rebounds to $70 a share and in your mind this is still a losing position (after all, your average cost is $75, right?), so you don't sell. Let's face it, you at least want to break even, right?

The stock begins to pull back again. You will eventually take a loss on the position or hold it, tying up money on a stock that is moving in the wrong direction. In such a case, treat both positions as separate entities—imagine they have completely different stock symbols. With that in mind, would you take profits on a position that's up 40 percent? Of course you would. By treating these positions as separate investments, you cash in on a huge gain and have cash available for less challenging ideas.

What about exchange-traded funds (ETFs)? you may ask. I think they are a better route than mutual funds, which are overdiversified and expensive. However, I still think the only way to really make a lot of money in the stock market is to try to be in the best idea in an industry. While the same tide may lift all ships, you want to be in the stock that is the front runner, and that isn't always the biggest company in the group. With an ETF or mutual fund, you're going to have the best stock and the worst stock, too.

In Closing: My Dream for You

You must always be in the stock market. It's not something you can leave and come back to and expect to have great performance. Being in the market doesn't mean you're always fully vested, but it *does* mean you are investing time and looking for opportunities. Over the past 10 years investors have fallen into a pattern of chasing performance. First it was the stock market, then real estate, and recently commodities and the art market have also surged. Each of these booms leaves a lot of folks holding the bag. It is folly to assume you're going to jump in and out of different asset classes at the exact bottom and top.

I know people who study the market for a couple of hours every night and never once look at the income statement. Charts are important, but to become rich in the market you must be invested in great companies and ride out dips in the share price, especially if those dips are the result of the Street overreacting.

Trading for the sake of trading is nuts. It guarantees you'll never have a grand slam, and therefore the balance of risk and reward shifts out of your favor. A certain portion of your portfolio could be used to generate quick cash, but not the entire portfolio.

The opposite side of this is to just buy and hold out of fear of losing money or because of blind faith in the investment. Many investors point to Warren Buffett's success as a rationale for holding a stock too long. You must understand that those big-boy methods for investing apply to big boys. Could you afford to hold on to a large investment in a stock that moves sideways for six years before deciding it's not a good investment? There are strategies for protecting multimillions and there are strategies to create millions in the market—and these are distinctly different strategies.

Listen to the messages of volume, share price direction, and other anomalies. Information gets out there and could help or harm your portfolio.

Put the same dollar amount into each position; don't load up, which is the gambler's dilemma, where you are guessing that the next bet will be the big winner. Assuming things will be different simply because your change of luck is overdue leads to major losses and mistakes.

Great companies can have overvalued stocks and so-so companies can have cheap stocks. When top-line growth begins to slow, a stock with elevated valuation metrics could dip, but the keys are the margins, particularly the operating margins. When margins stall, it's time to consider taking profits.

Most stocks that are changing hands over $100 a share are undervalued and most stocks trading under $10 a share are overvalued.

Control your emotions. If you move with each knee-jerk movement of the crowd, you're going to be in a lot of trouble. The initial move in the market, whether it's the broad reaction to the Federal Reserve, geopolitical events, or blind selling of individual stocks on circumspect news, check the fundamentals to see if anything has really changed. Don't panic. I want you to be smart, act fast (which sometimes means not acting with the crowd), and get rich.

Industries for Relative Evaluations

TABLE A.1 Homebuilders

Homebuilders/Engineering		Homebuilders/Engineering	
ALS	Alstom	TOL	Toll Brothers Inc.
FLR	Fluor Corp.	RYL	Ryland
CTX	Centex Corp.	KBH	KB Home
LEN	Lennar Corp.	GVA	Granite Construction Inc.
CMH	Clayton Homes Inc.	INSUA	Insituform Technologies
DHI	D.R. Horton, Inc.	MDC	MDC Holdings Inc.
PWR	Quanta Services Inc.	MTZ	Mastec Inc.
JEC	Jacobs Engineering Group Inc.	NHL	Newhall Land & Farming Co.
PHM	Pulte Corp.	SPF	Standard-Pacific Corp.
NVR	NVR Inc.	DY	Dycom Industries Inc.

TABLE A.2 Telecommunications and Networking

Telecommunications Providers		Networking	
T	AT&T Corp.	CSCO	Cisco Systems Inc.
BLS	BellSouth Corp.	NTAP	Network Appliance Corp.
S	Sprint	BRCD	Brocade Communications
Q	Qwest	CVG	Convergys Corp.
LVLT	Level 3 Communications	DASTY	Dassault ADR
CDWC	CDW Corp.	COMS	3Com Corp.
DT	Deutsche Telekom AG	CS	Cabletron Systems Inc.
CHL	China Mobile (Hong Kong) Ltd.	JKHY	Jack Henry & Associates Inc.
FTE	France Telecom	NOVL	Novell Inc.
TEF	Telefonica SA	CERN	Cerner Corp.

TABLE A.3   Telecommunications Equipment

Telecommunications Equipment		Telecommunications Equipment	
NOK	Nokia Oyj	JNPR	Juniper Networks
ERICY	Ericsson Telefon AB	FDRY	Foundry
NT	Nortel Networks Corp.	TLAB	Tellabs Inc.
QCOM	Qualcomm Inc.	CMVT	Comverse Tech.
ALA	Alcatel SA	ANDR	Andrew
LU	Lucent Technologies Inc.	ADCT	ADC Telecommunications
JDSU	JDS Uniphase Corp.	FNSR	Finisar
MOT	Motorola Inc.	SONS	Sonus Networks Inc.
GLW	Corning Inc.		
CIEN	Ciena Corp.		

TABLE A.4   Automakers and Auto Parts

Automakers		Auto Parts	
TM	Toyota Motor Corp.	DPH	Delphi Automotive Systems Corp.
F	Ford Motor Co.	GPC	Genuine Parts Co.
DCX	DaimlerChrysler AG	MGA	Magna International Inc.
HMC	Honda Motor Co. Ltd.	JCI	Johnson Controls
GM	General Motors Corp.	LEA	Lear Corporation
NSANY	Nissan Motor Co. Ltd.	ALV	Autoliv Inc.
FIA	Fiat SpA	BWA	Borg Warner Inc.
VOLVY	Volvo AB	CTB	Cooper Tire
SCVA	Scania AB	GT	Goodyear
PCAR	Paccar Inc.	VC	Visteon

TABLE A.5 Tools and Appliances and Machinery

Tools and Appliances		Machinery	
DHR	Danaher Corp.	CAT	Caterpillar Inc.
ELUX	Electrolux AB	DE	Deere and Co.
BDK	Black & Decker Corp.	FMC	FMC Corp.
SWK	Stanley Works	CNH	CNH Global NV
MYG	Maytag Corp.	KMT	Kennametal Inc.
SNA	Snap-On Inc.	AG	AGCO Corp.
MKTAY	Makita	MTW	Manitowoc Company Inc.
		JLG	JLG Industries Inc.
		CAT	Caterpillar Inc.

TABLE A.6 Retailers and Apparel

Retailers		Apparel	
GPS	Gap Stores	GUC	Gucci Group NV
DDS	Dillard's	JNY	Jones Apparel Group Inc.
FD	Federated	VFC	VF Corp.
JCP	JC Penney	BNG	Benetton Group SpA
KSS	Kohl's	RL	Polo Ralph Lauren Corp.
WMT	Wal-Mart	LIZ	Liz Claiborne Inc.
TGT	Target	COLM	Columbia Sportswear Co.
TIF	Tiffany	TOM	Tommy Hilfiger Corp.
JWN	Nordstrom's	WACLY	Wacoal Corp.
SKS	Saks	COH	Coach Inc.

TABLE A.7   Airlines and Aerospace/Defense

Airlines		Aerospace/Defense	
LUV	Southwest Airlines Inc.	BA	The Boeing Co.
JBLU	JetBlue	LMT	Lockheed Martin Corp.
ALK	Alaskan Airlines	GD	General Dynamics Corp.
DAL	Delta Air Lines Inc.	NOC	Northrop Grumman Corp.
AMR	AMR Corp.	LLL	L-3
RYAAY	Ryanair Holdings PLC	GR	Goodrich Corp.
CAL	Continental Airlines Inc.	UTX	United Technologies
U	US Airways Group Inc.	TXT	Textron
UAUA	UAL Corp.	ATK	Alliant Techsystems Inc.
NWAC	Northwest Airlines Corp.	BEAV	BE Aerospace Inc.

TABLE A.8   Advertising and Containers/Paper

Advertising		Containers/Paper	
OMC	Omnicom Group Inc.	AVY	Avery Dennison Corp.
WPPGY	WPP Group PLC	SEE	Sealed Air Corp.
IPG	Interpublic Group of Companies	MMM	3M Company
LAMR	Lamar Advertising Co.	TIN	Temple-Inland Inc.
HADV	Havas Advertising SA	SSCC	Smurfit-Stone
POS	Catalina Marketing Corp.	BMS	Bemis Co. Inc.
TNO	True North Communications Inc.	CCK	Crown Cork and Seal
DCLK	DoubleClick Inc.	PKG	Packaging Corp. of America
		IP	International Paper
		KMB	Kimberly Clark

TABLE A.9   Beverages and Food Processors

Beverages		Food Processors	
KO	Coca-Cola Co. (Coke)	UN	Unilever NV
PEP	Pepsico Inc.	UL	Unilever PLC
COT	Cott Beverages	DA	Groupe Danone
CSG	Cadbury Schweppes PLC	SYY	Sysco Corp.
CCE	Coca-Cola Enterprises Inc.	SLE	Sara Lee Corp.
PBG	The Pepsi Bottling Group Inc.	HNZ	HJ Heinz Co.
KOF	Coca-Cola Femsa SA de CV	CPB	Campbell Soup Co.
PB	Panamerican Beverages Inc.	TSN	Tyson Foods
BUD	Anheuser Busch	GIS	General Mills Inc.
BFB	Brown-Forman Corp.	K	Kellogg Co.

TABLE A.10   Biotechnology

Biotech		Biotech	
BGEN	Biogen Inc.	GILD	Gilead Sciences Inc.
MEDI	Medimmune Inc.	AFFX	Affymetrix Inc.
AZA	ALZA Corp.	DNA	Genetech
CHIR	Chiron Corp.	VRTX	Vertex Pharmaceuticals Inc.
SEPR	Sepracor Inc.	ICOS	ICOS Corp.
GENZ	Genzyme Corp.	ABGX	Abgenix, Inc.
MLNM	Millennium Pharmaceuticals Inc.	ENZN	Enzon Inc.
HGSI	Human Genome Sciences Inc.	PDLI	Protein Design Labs Inc.
CELG	Celgene Corp.	CEPH	Cephalon Inc.
MEDX	Medarex Inc.	IMCL	ImClone Systems Inc.

TABLE A.11 Generic and Brand Name Drug Makers

Generic Drugs		Brand Name Drug Makers	
BRL	Barr Laboratories Inc.	ABT	Abbott Labs
MYL	Mylan Laboratories Inc.	AGN	Allergan Inc.
BVF	Biovail Corp.	ABI	Applera Corp.
WPI	Watson Pharmaceuticals Inc.	BMY	Bristol-Myers
KG	King Pharmaceuticals, Inc.	LLY	Eli Lilly
TEVA	Teva Pharmaceutical Industries	MRK	Merck & Co.
		PFE	Pfizer
		SGP	Schering Plough
		WYE	Wyeth

TABLE A.12 Casinos and Hotels

Casinos		Hotels	
IGT	International Game Technology	MAR	Marriott
HET	Harrah's Entertainment Inc.	HOT	Starwood Hotel & Resorts
PPE	Park Place Entertainment Corp.	HLT	Hilton
MBG	Mandalay Resort Group	CHH	Choice Hotels International
STN	Station Casinos Inc.	IHG	Intercontinental
SLOT	Anchor Gaming Inc.	WYN	Wyndham
LVS	Las Vegas Sands		
BYD	Boyd Gaming		
WMS	WMS Industries Inc.		
WYNN	Wynn Casino		

TABLE A.13   Energy Exploration

Energy Exploration		Energy Exploration	
APC	Anadarko	NBR	Nabors Industries
APA	Apache	NE	Noble Corp.
ASH	Ashland	OXY	Occidental Petroleum
BHI	Baker Hughes	TOT	Total
CVX	Chevron	NBL	Noble Energy
DVN	Devon	WMB	Williams
EOG	EOG Resources	PPP	Pogo Producing Co.
XOM	Exxon Mobil	PNY	Piedmont Natural Gas
HAL	Halliburton	FST	Forest Oil
MRO	Marathon	RDC	Rowan Companies

TABLE A.14   Chemicals and Energy Exploration

Chemicals		Energy Exploration	
DD	E.I. Du Pont De Nemours & Co.	SLB	Schlumberger
DOW	Dow Chemical Co.	Sun	Sunoco
AKZOY	Akzo Nobel NV	RIG	Transocean
BF	BASF AG	HAL	Halliburton
PPG	PPG Industries Inc.	WFT	Weatherford
APD	Air Products and Chemicals Inc.	SII	Smith International
MON	Monsanto Co.	FST	Forest Oil
BOX	BOC Group PLC	COP	Conoco Phillips
PX	Praxair Inc.		

TABLE A.15   Health Care

Health Care		Health Care	
HCA	HCA—The Healthcare Co.	HCR	Manor Care Inc.
THC	Tenet Healthcare Corp.	CYH	Community Health Systems
HRC	HealthSouth Corp.	DGX	Quest Diagnostics
FMS	Fresenius Medical Care AG	ADVP	AdvancePCS
LH	Laboratory Corporation of America	LPNT	LifePoint Hospitals Inc.
HMA	Health Management Associates	AHG	Apria Healthcare Group Inc.
ESRX	Express Scripts Inc.	RCGI	Renal Care Group Inc.
LNCR	Lincare Holdings Inc.	QHGI	Quorum Health
CMX	Caremark Rx Inc.	TRIH	Triad Hospitals Inc.
UHS	Universal Health Services Inc.	CVTY	Coventry Health Care Inc.

TABLE A.16   Food Processors and Supermarkets

Food Processors		Supermarkets/Grocers	
WWY	WM Wrigley Jr. Co.	COST	Costco
CAG	ConAgra Foods Inc.	SWY	Safeway
ADM	Archer-Daniels-Midland Inc.	SVU	Supervalu
HSY	Hershey Foods Corp.	SYY	Sysco
DF	Dean Foods	KR	Kroger
KFT	Kraft Foods	OATS	Wild Oats
HAIN	Hain Celestial Group Inc.	WFII	Whole Foods
TR	Tootsie Roll Industries Inc.	WMT	Wal-Mart
FLO	Flowers Industries Inc.	GAP	Great Atlantic and Pacific
SFD	Smithfield Foods Inc.		

TABLE A.17   Computer Services and Computers

Computer Services		Computers	
EMC	EMC Corp.	IBM	Int'l Business Machines
DSS	Quantum Corp.	SUNW	Sun Microsystems Inc.
SNDK	Sandisk Corp.	HWQ	Hewlett-Packard Co.
STK	Storage Technology Corp.	DELL	Dell Computer
IOM	Iomega Corp.	RIMM	Research in Motion
RDRT	Read-Rite Corp.	HIT	Hitachi Ltd.
HDD	Quantum Corp.	AAPL	Apple
MXTR	Maxtor Corp.	GTW	Gateway Inc.
WDC	Western Digital Corp.	IM	Ingram Micro Inc.
		TECD	Tech Data Corp.

TABLE A.18   Financial Services and Brokerage Firms

Financial Services		Brokerage Firms	
FNM	Fannie Mae	BSC	Bear Stearns Companies
AXP	American Express Co.	GS	Goldman Sachs
FRE	Freddie Mac	JPM	JPMorgan Chase
COF	Capital One	LEH	Lehman Brothers Holdings
SLM	USA Education Inc.	MER	Merrill Lynch & Co.
FDC	First Data	PRU	Prudential
CIT	The CIT Group Inc.	RJF	Raymond James
TSS	Total Systems	LM	Legg Mason
ACF	AmeriCredit Corp.	AGE	AG Edwards
CACC	Credit Acceptance	SCHW	Schwab

TABLE A.19   Footwear

Footwear	
NKE	Nike Inc.
TBL	Timberland Co.
SKX	Skechers USA Inc.
WWW	Wolverine World Wide Inc.
KCP	Kenneth Cole Productions Inc.
DECK	Deckers
CROX	Crocs
PSS	Payless Shoesource
FL	Foot Locker Inc.

TABLE A.20   Medical Equipment and Pharmacy Benefits Management

Medical Equipment		Pharmacy Benefits Management	
BCR	C.R. Bard, Inc.	ABC	Amerisource Bergen
BOL	Bausch & Lomb	CAH	Cardinal Health
BAX	Baxter International	ESRX	Express Scripts
BMET	Biomet Inc.	MCK	McKesson Corp.
BSX	Boston Scientific Corp.	MHS	Medco Health Solutions
JNJ	Johnson & Johnson		
MDT	Medtronic Inc.		
STJ	St. Jude Medical, Inc.		
SYK	Stryker Corp.		
ZOLL	Zoll Medical Corp.		

TABLE A.21 Retail Household Products and Discounter Stores

Retail Household		Retail (discount)	
BBBY	Bed Bath & Beyond	ANN	Ann Taylor
BBA	Bombay	TLB	Talbots
PIR	Pier 1 Imports	LTD	Limited Brands Inc.
WSM	Williams-Sonoma	LIZ	Liz Claiborne
MIK	Michaels Stores	HOTT	Hot Topic
LOW	Lowe's	PSUN	Pacific Sunwear
HD	Home Depot	WTSLA	Wet Seal
		TWB	Tween Brands
		CLE	Claire's

TABLE A.22 Restaurants

Restaurants		Restaurants	
MCD	McDonald's	DRI	Darden
WEN	Wendy's	LNY	Landry's
YUM	Yum! Brands	EAT	Brinker
SBUX	Starbucks	OSI	OSI Restaurant Partners
APPB	Applebee's	PFCB	P.F. Chang's
CBRL	CBRL Group	PNRA	Panera Bread
CEC	CEC Entertainment		

TABLE A.23 Staffing and Conglomerates

Staffing		Conglomerates	
RHI	Robert Half International	HON	Honeywell
MAN	Manpower	GE	General Electric
MPS	MPS Group	FLR	Fluor
KELYA	Kelly Services	TNB	Thomas & Betts
ADO	Adecco	ETN	Eaton
KFRC	Kforce Inc.	IR	Ingersoll Rand
MNST	Monster	GWW	Grainger
		TYC	Tyco
		PH	Parker Hannifin
		DOV	Dover

TABLE A.24 Semiconductors

Semiconductors		Semiconductors	
AMD	Advanced Micro	NSM	National Semiconductor
ADI	Analog Devices	NVDA	Nvidia
AMAT	Applied Materials	QCOM	Qualcomm
JBL	Jabil Circuits	TER	Teradyne
KLAC	KLA-Tencor	TXN	Texas Instruments
LLTC	Linear Technology Corp.	MRVL	Marvell
LSI	LSI Logic	ALTR	Altera
MXIM	Maxim Integrated	QLGC	Q Logic
MU	Micron Technology	XLNX	Xilinx
MOT	Motorola	CREE	Cree Inc.

TABLE A.25   Computer Software and Electronic Commerce

Software/Programming		Electronic Commerce	
ORCL	Oracle	CKFR	CheckFree
BIBJ	Business Objects	CSC	Computer Networks
PMTC	Parametric	DST	DST Systems
UIS	Unisys	EDS	Electronic Data Services
BMC	BMC software	FDS	FactSet Research
EMC	EMC Corp.	FISV	Fiserv
MSFT	Microsoft	PER	Perot Systems
IBM	International Business Machines	UIS	Unisys
SAP	SAP Corp.	MA	MasterCard
CA	Computer Associates	NCR	NCR Corp.
COGN	Cognos		

TABLE A.26   Web Sites and Internet Security and Services/Products

Web Sites		Internet Security and Services/Products	
YHOO	Yahoo!	ISSX	Internet Self-Service and Security
EBAY	eBay	SYMC	Symantec
GOOG	Google	CHKP	Check Point Technologies
AMZN	Amazon	JNPR	Juniper
CNET	CNET	CSCO	Cisco
NTES	NetEase	NT	Nortel
NILE	Blue Nile	AKAM	Akamai
DLIA	Delia's	SVVS	Savvis
ELNK	EarthLink		
CKCM	Click Commerce		

TABLE A.27 Utilities

Utilities		Utilities	
AES	AES Corp.	DYN	Dynergy
AYE	Allegheny	EIX	Edison International
AEE	Ameren	EP	El Paso
AEP	American Electric Power	EXC	Exelon
CNP	CenterPoint Energy	FPL	FPL Group
CMS	CMS Energy	KSE	Keysapan
ED	Consolidated Edison	NI	NiSource
CEG	Constellation Energy	PPL	PPL Corp.
D	Dominion	PGN	Progress Energy
DTE	DTE Energy	PEG	Public Service
DUK	Duke Energy	TXU	TXU Corp.

TABLE A.28 Video Games/Retailers and Media

Video Games/Video Game Retailers		Media	
ERTS	Electronic Arts	DJ	Dow Jones
ATVI	Activision	TRB	Tribune
THQI	THQ Inc	TWX	Time Warner
TTWO	Take-Two	NYT	New York Times
MWY	Midway Games Inc.	GCI	Gannett
BBY	Best Buy	MDP	Meredith
CC	Circuit City	DIS	Disney
RSH	Radio Shack	PIXR	Pixar
TWTR	Tweeter Home Entertainment	CCU	Clear Channel
GME	GameStop	SIRI	Sirius Satellite
		XMSR	XM Radio

TABLE A.29   Money Center Banks and Super Regional Banks

Money Center and Super Regional Banks		Money Center and Super Regional Banks	
BAC	Bank of America	MEL	Mellon Financial
BK	Bank of New York	NCC	National City Corp.
BBT	BB&T Corp	NFB	North Fork Bancorporation
CINF	Cincinnati Financial	NTRS	Northern Trust Corp.
CMA	Comerica	PCL	Plum Creek Timber
CFC	Countrywide Financial	PNC	PNC Financial
FII	Federated Bancorp	PLD	Prologics
FITB	Fifth Third Bancorp	STI	Suntrust
GDW	Golden West Financial	WB	Wachovia
KEY	Keycorp	WM	Washington Mutual
LNC	Lincoln National	WFC	Wells Fargo

TABLE A.30   Truckers and Railroads

Trucks		Rails	
YRCW	Yellow Roadway	UNP	Union Pacific
ABFS	Arkansas Best	NSC	Norfolk Southern
UTIW	UTI Worldwide	CSX	CSX Corp.
EAGL	EGL Inc.	BNI	Burlington Northern
EXPD	Expeditors	CNI	Canadian National
R	Ryder	CP	Canadian Pacific
CNW	Con-Way	KSU	Kansas City Southern
UPS	United Parcel		
FDX	Federal Express		

TABLE A.31   Insurance and Reinsurance

Insurance		Reinsurance	
PGR	Progressive	WSH	Willis Group Holdings
ALL	Allstate	RE	Everest Re Group Ltd.
BRKA	Geico (part of Berkshire Hathaway)	TRH	Transatlantic Holdings
HIG	Hartford Financial Services	PRE	PartnerRe Ltd.
ING	ING Group	AOC	AON Corp.
AFL	American Family Life (the company with the duck)		
UNM	Unum		
CAN	CAN Insurance		

TABLE A.32   Gold

Gold	
AAUK	Anglo American PLC
ABX	Barrick Gold Corp.
AU	AngloGold Ashanti Ltd.
NEM	Newmont Mining Corp.
PDG	Placer Dome Inc.
GOLD	Randgold Resources Ltd.
HM	Homestake Mining Co.
BVN	Compania de Minas
GG	Goldcorp Inc.